JOSEPH
BATES

JOSEPH
BATES

The Real Founder
of Seventh-day Adventism

GEORGE R. KNIGHT

REVIEW AND HERALD® PUBLISHING ASSOCIATION
HAGERSTOWN, MD 21740

The author assumes full responsibility for the accuracy of all facts
and quotations as cited in this book.

This book was
Edited by Gerald Wheeler
Designed by Trent Truman
Electronic makeup by Shirley M. Bolivar
Type: 11/14 Berkeley Book

PRINTED IN U.S.A.

08 07 06 05 04   5 4 3 2 1

R&H Cataloging Service
Knight, George R.
    Joseph Bates: the real founder of Seventh-day Adventism.

    1. Bates, Joseph, 1792-1872. 2. Seventh-day Adventists-History. I. Title.

[B]

ISBN 0-8280-1815-4

DEDICATED

to

MERLIN BURT and **ALBERTO TIMM,**

doctoral students who helped me obtain a fuller

understanding of Joseph Bates' contribution

to the development of

SEVENTH-DAY ADVENTISM.

CONTENTS

CONTENTS

PREFACE

EVERETT Dick characterized Joseph Bates as "probably the most interesting character among the founders of the Seventh-day Adventist denomination" and as a "pioneer of the pioneers" among the shapers of Sabbatarian Adventism.[1] Dick is correct on both counts. Bates was indeed the pioneer of the Adventist pioneers. In fact, he not only brought the other two founding pioneers (James and Ellen White) into the Sabbatarian message, but he had to develop its outlines before there was anything for them to join.

And as far as being an interesting person, the story of his life is hard to beat in terms of just sheer adventure. Whether it is a colorful story about being captured by South American pirates, his years as a British prisoner of war, or cutting a hole in three feet of ice to baptize people, it is difficult to see Bates as anything but an exciting (and at times a bit eccentric) personality. On a personal note, I found Bates' early life to be especially interesting since I also left home as a teenager (age 17) to serve as a midshipman in training in the merchant marine and only later became a Christian.

Joseph Bates: The Real Founder of Seventh-day Adventism is the second volume in a series of biographies on the founders and shapers of the Seventh-day Adventist Church. The first volume was Gerald Wheeler's *James White: Innovator and Overcomer*. Projected volumes include Ellen White as a woman in a man's world and Adventism's prophetic voice; J. N. Andrews as Adventism's earliest scholar and missionary; W. C. White as his mother's assistant and a person at the center of action; and Ellet J. Waggoner as a leader in the revival of righteousness by faith. Each biography will focus on the individual's major contribution to Adventism.

In the "Foreword" to the first volume in the series, I wrote that James White "was the driving force behind the formation of Seventh-day Adventism as a denomination."[2] That is true. But undergirding White's contribution was one even more basic. The current volume argues that the *real founder* of the denomination was Joseph Bates. After all, it was Bates who in the 1840s developed the Sabbatarian Adventism that James White built upon in the 1850s and early 1860s to form the Seventh-day Adventist denomination. Without Bates' accomplishments White would have had no platform to construct the Seventh-day Adventist Church upon.

It was Bates who was Adventism's first theologian and first historian. Integrating those two fields into the flow of prophecy, he had by January 1847 developed what we today think of as great controversy theology. Bates was also Sabbatarian Adventism's first mission theorist and first missionary, in that latter role not only spreading the message of the Sabbath and the third angel to Canada, northern New England, and the Midwestern region of the United States, but bringing into Sabbatarian Adventism a who's who of the early movement. His converts included such prominent individuals as James and Ellen White, S. N. Haskell, M. E. Cornell, Annie Smith, R. F. Cottrell, John Byington, George I. Butler (indirectly), and many more. Also Bates would be the denomination's first health reformer, although he did not take the major role in making that topic an important aspect of Seventh-day Adventism.

Bates and the Whites had an especially close relationship in the development of the denomination. And they, despite being three strong-minded people, generally worked well as a team. The major exception to that generalization occurred at the crisis point of 1849 and 1850 when the founder of Sabbatarian Adventism reluctantly gave up leadership to the younger James White who would in essence build upon Bates' work to establish Seventh-day Adventism as a denomination. By that time the older man was nearly 60 years old and had reached the limits of his originality and creativity. It was time for the younger White, and eventually his protégés, to assume the leadership of the movement. It took a while for Bates to come to grips with that reality, but once he did he helped White in the role of senior statesman to form a church out of what had been a rather shapeless religious body.

From the above we can see that any account of Bates' life is much more than the biography of an individual. Rather, it is in part the story of a developing religious movement that by 1860-1863 came to be identified as the Seventh-day Adventist Church.

There has been one previously published scholarly biography of

Bates—Godfrey T. Anderson's *Outrider of the Apocalypse: Life and Times of Joseph Bates* (1972).[3] The current book is best seen as a complement to Anderson's work. It does not seek to redo what Anderson accomplished so well. Anderson did much to establish the chronology of Bates' life and work, and he went to great lengths to dig up historical details related to his topic. His spadework did not need to be repeated, even though it could be built upon and extended.

While my treatment of Bates is generally chronological, it is not slavishly so. Although it provides a description of his life, it also emphasizes the contribution of that life. In particular, the current work gives much more attention to Bates' theological and historical contributions than did Anderson.

Besides Anderson's biography, other treatments of Bates' life and work include Clarence Edwin Stenberg's M.A. thesis, "A Study of the Influence of Joseph Bates on the Denomination of Seventh-day Adventists," Jerry E. Daly's M.A. thesis, "Joseph Bates' Logbook of the Brig *Empress:* An Analysis and Appraisal"; and Virgil Robinson's *Cabin Boy to Advent Crusader,* a popular treatment for young people.[4] All future students of Bates will be especially indebted to Daly's transcription and contextualization of the Logbook. He has rendered what is at times almost illegible handwriting into an accurate and readable document.

Joseph Bates utilizes several sources either not previously available or underutilized by previous researchers. Included in that category are Bates' important *Vindication of the Seventh-day Sabbath,*[5] a copy having been discovered by Anderson in the Boston City Library in 1976; a collection of Bates' letters dating from 1824 to 1833, found by Alberto Timm in the Old Dartmouth Historical Society Whaling Museum Library in New Bedford, Massachusetts; the underutilized 1827-1828 logbook of the Empress; and the all but totally neglected periodicals of the other post-disappointment Adventist movements as well as those of other groups.

Of course, I have also utilized Bates' *Autobiography* (1868),[6] the many articles by him or related to his work in Sabbatarian periodicals, and the few extant unpublished letters from or about him and his wife. Andrews University Press has released a new edition of Bates' *Autobiography* as a part of the Adventist Classic Library to accompany this biography. It is unfortunate that more letters of the Bateses did not survive, since the few we have are quite informative in terms of personal information. In general I have maintained Bates' original spelling and punctuation, but at times I have corrected them where I deemed it necessary for the best flow of his ideas.

Mention also should be made of several of my doctoral students whose research aided my own understanding of Joseph Bates' contribution to Adventism and the development of Adventist theology during its earliest period. Merlin Burt's insightful dissertation on the historical development of Sabbatarian Adventist theology between 1844 and 1849 was especially helpful. Burt's work has provided a major breakthrough in our understanding of the sequential steps that took place between the demise of Millerite Adventism and the rise of the Sabbatarian movement. As a result, his research greatly enriched my understanding of Bates during the crucial period between 1845 and 1848. Also significant was Alberto Timm's dissertation on the sanctuary and the three angels' messages as integrating factors in the development of Seventh-day Adventist doctrine between 1844 and 1863.[7] The contextual work of Joseph Karanja, who at one time intended to write his dissertation on Joseph Bates, also enlightened me on several important points.

I would like to express my appreciation to those individuals who have provided me with necessary documents. In particular, I would like to thank Sandra White of the interlibrary loan department of the James White Library at Andrews University; Jim Ford and his staff at the Adventist Heritage Center at Andrews University; Tim Poirier and Jim Nix of the Ellen G. White Estate in Silver Spring, Maryland; and Merlin Burt, Janice Little, and Patricia Chapman of Loma Linda University Library and White Estate Branch Office.

Additional appreciation goes to Bonnie Beres, who typed the manuscript; to Michael Campbell, who spent many hours searching out and copying documents; to Merlin Burt, for reading the manuscript and offering constructive suggestions; to Jeannette Johnson and Gerald Wheeler, who guided the manuscript through the editorial process; and to the administration of Andrews University for providing financial support and time for research and writing.

My hope is that *Joseph Bates: The Real Founder of Seventh-day Adventism* will be helpful to its readers in understanding both the man himself and how Sabbatarian Adventism originated and developed.

George R. Knight
Andrews University
Berrien Springs, Michigan

---

[1] Everett Dick, *Founders of the Message* (Washington, D.C.: Review and Herald Pub. Assn., 1938), p. 105.

[2] George R. Knight, "Foreword," in Gerald Wheeler, *James White: Innovator and Overcomer* (Hagerstown, Md.: Review and Herald Pub. Assn., 2003), p. xi.

[3] Godfrey T. Anderson, *Outrider of the Apocalypse: Life and Times of Joseph Bates* (Mountain View, Calif.: Pacific Press Pub. Assn., 1972).

[4] Clarence Edwin Stenberg, "A Study of the Influence of Joseph Bates on the Denomination of Seventh-day Adventists," M.A. thesis, Seventh-day Adventist Theological Seminary, 1950; Jerry E. Daly, "Joseph Bates' Logbook of the Brig *Empress:* An Analysis and Appraisal," M.A. thesis, Loma Linda University, 1981; Virgil Robinson, *Cabin Boy to Advent Crusader* (Nashville, Tenn.: Southern Pub. Assn., 1960).

[5] Joseph Bates, *A Vindication of the Seventh-day Sabbath, and the Commandments of God: With a Further History of God's Peculiar People, From 1847 to 1848* (New Bedford, Mass.: Benjamin Lindsey, 1848).

[6] J. Bates, *The Autobiography of Elder Joseph Bates; Embracing a Long Life on Shipboard, With Sketches of Voyages on the Atlantic and Pacific Oceans, the Baltic and Mediterranean Seas; Also Impressment and Service on Board British War Ships, Long Confinement in Dartmoor Prison, Early Experience in Reformatory Movements; Travels in Various Parts of the World; and a Brief Account of the Great Advent Movement of 1840-44* (Battle Creek, Mich.: Seventh-day Adventist Pub. Assn., 1868). Bates' *Autobiography* was later republished along with some helpful biographical data. See James White, ed., *The Early Life and Later Experience and Labors of Elder Joseph Bates* (Battle Creek, Mich.: Seventh-day Adventist Pub. Assn., 1878). Later still, C. C. Crisler produced an abridged and edited version as *Life of Joseph Bates: An Autobiography* (Washington, D.C.: Review and Herald Pub. Assn., 1927).

[7] Merlin D. Burt, "The Historical Background, Interconnected Development, and Integration of the Doctrines of the Sanctuary, the Sabbath, and Ellen G. White's Role in Sabbatarian Adventism From 1844 to 1849," Ph.D. dissertation, Andrews University, 2002; Alberto R. Timm, "The Sanctuary and the Three Angels' Messages, 1844-1863: Integrating Factors in the Development of Seventh-day Adventist Doctrines," Ph.D. dissertation, Andrews University, 1995.

Joseph Bates

CHAPTER I

A TRAVELIN' MAN

WHAT'S the news, Captain Bates?"
"The news," he replied, is that "the seventh-day is the Sabbath, and we ought to keep it."

Bates had just accepted the seventh-day Sabbath himself, but the certainty of his conviction and the power of his enthusiasm so affected his neighbor James Madison Monroe Hall that he went home, studied his Bible on the topic, and observed the next Sabbath. His wife followed him a week later. Hall was Bates' first convert to an understanding that would shape both men's lives from the day of that fateful meeting. For his part, Hall thereafter held Bates in such high regard that he named his only son Joseph Bates Hall.[1]

Nine years later, in 1854, young Stephen N. Haskell met that whirlwind of energy, conviction, and enthusiasm named Joseph Bates. The 21-year-old Haskell had been introduced to the seventh-day Sabbath, but was not totally convicted on the topic. At that point, someone directed Bates to Haskell's house. Haskell reports that Joseph spent 10 days with them, preaching every night as well as on Sabbath and Sunday. But beyond that, the irrepressible Bates held a Bible study for Haskell and a few others "from morning until noon, and from noon until night, and then in the evening until the time we went to bed. He did that for ten successive days," Haskell later reported, "and I have been a Seventh-day Adventist ever since." He never once doubted the importance of the Sabbath thereafter.[2]

In the early 1850s Bates reports a five week missionary tour in Canada during which for more than 20 days he struggled with heavy snow and extreme cold, on one occasion "wading" through deep snow for 40 miles to take his message to an interested family. Another time Bates cut through three feet of ice so that he could find enough water to baptize seven people in 30° below zero weather.[3]

And who, you may be thinking, is this Joseph Bates? What drove the man? Where does he fit into Adventist history?

Joseph Bates, born in Rochester, Massachusetts, on July 8, 1792, was the fifth of the seven children of Joseph Bates, Sr., and Deborah Nye Bates. The next year the family moved the seven miles to New Bedford, just across the Acushnet River from the town that became Fairhaven in 1812. Bates' father had served as a captain during the Revolutionary War and was active in civic affairs, being one of the founders of New Bedford/Fairhaven Academy. The community's official records not only name the elder Joseph Bates as one of the 14 initial subscribers of the academy, but as one of the two men appointed to superintend its construction.[4] Like his father, the younger Joseph would be a leader and an initiator throughout his long life.

During his growing up years, New Bedford was becoming the whaling capital of the United States. Sailing ships were ever present not only in the town's harbor, but in the mind of young Joseph. He reports that his "most ardent desire was to become a sailor." Although he dreamed day and night of an adventurous life at sea, he was afraid to ask permission of his father, who had larger plans for the boy. Finally, in the hopes that a voyage would cure his son of his dreams, he allowed him a short journey by ship to Boston with his uncle. That concession, Bates later penned, was "to cure me," but it had "the opposite effect."[5]

A LIFE AT SEA

In June 1807, just before Joseph's fifteenth birthday, the disappointed father permitted him to sail as a cabin boy on the *Fanny* on its maiden voyage to Europe. That fateful decision would shape Joseph's life for the next 21 years.[6]

His early seagoing experiences might have led a more timid boy to give up his dreams and return home. For example, on the *Fanny's* return voyage from England the young seaman managed to fall off of one of the mastheads into the ocean near a large shark some of his mates had been baiting. If the shark hadn't shifted its position at that precise time, Bates would have had a very short career at sea.[7]

In the spring of 1809 Bates had another near-fatal experience when his ship struck an iceberg off Newfoundland. Trapped in the ship's hold, he and another sailor held each other tightly in the dark and prepared to die as they heard from time to time "the screams and cries of some of our wretched companions, on the deck above us, begging God for mercy." Later he made it out to the deck where he found the captain and second mate "on their knees begging God for mercy." The heavy pounding of the sea made even the lifeboat useless. Only a last minute act of God's "providence" saved both ship and crew, including the inept captain whom some had wanted to throw overboard at the height of the crisis.[8]

Years later Bates wrote of his spiritual stirrings at the time: "Oh, the dreadful thought! Here to yield up my account and die, and sink with the wrecked ship to the bottom of the ocean, so far from home and friends, without the least preparation, or hope of Heaven and eternal life, only to be numbered with the damned and forever banished from the presence of the Lord. It seemed that something must give way to vent my feelings of unutterable anguish!"[9]

After escaping from the ice pack he and his fellow crew members refitted their ship in Ireland, from which they resumed their voyage to Russia. But on the way Danish privateers captured and took them to Copenhagen. Several days after his capture the authorities interrogated Bates and his shipmates. Prior to that time the shipowner had attempted to bribe them not to tell the truth about the vessel's business dealings in Great Britain, in the hope that he could extricate both his ship and cargo. Their captors called Bates, the youngest of the crew, in first. Before they began the questioning they showed him a box crafted to lop off the two forefingers and thumb (kind of a mini-guillotine) of everyone swearing falsely. As James White would later write, rejecting the bribe and "testifying to the truth saved the forefingers and thumb of his right hand, with which he" would later write "in advocacy and defense of the noblest reforms of the age." Bates' crewmates later met several from another ship who had lost their thumbs and fingers.[10] It is impossible to judge at this distance whether Bates needed the mini-guillotine to encourage him to tell the truth in 1809. But we do know that meticulous honesty in even the smallest matters would characterize his later life.

SHANGHAIED BY THE BRITISH

His adventures between 1807 and 1809 were but a small foretaste of the difficulties Bates was yet to face. A major turning point in his life took place on April 27, 1810. That evening a press-gang consisting of an officer and 12 men entered his boarding house in Liverpool, England, and seized him and several other Americans and "dragged" them at sword-point as "recruits" for the British navy in spite of their documents declaring that they were United States citizens.[11]

To us such treatment may border at the edges of our imagination. But those were different times. Britain was in the midst of its death struggle with Napoleon, and its navy had a constant need for men to staff its ships. Because of the low pay, filthy living conditions, poor rations, and customary floggings, it was almost impossible to gain enough recruits. Beyond that, desertions were frequent, with many deserters joining the American merchant service.

The Royal Navy's answer to such problems was impressment. Britain not only claimed the right to stop and search American merchant ships on the open sea in quest of deserters, but navy press-gangs scoured the British waterfront periodically, recruiting in the process both English and American sailors for enforced duty upon his majesty's ships. Historians estimate that England compelled some 6,000 Americans into the British navy. The practice would eventually be one of the causes of the War of 1812 between the United States and England.[12]

Bates would spend the next five years (1810-1815) as a "guest" of the British government, serving about half of his time as a sailor in the Royal Navy and the other half as a prisoner of war. His Autobiography records his many adventures during those years. Here we will only deal with certain incidents that illustrate traits that would characterize him for the rest of his life.

One was a persistent and bold reaction to injustice. Bates, of course, was limited in what he could do in his state of enforced servitude. He did, however, make several abortive attempts at escape.[13] More significantly was his reaction to certain unjust officers. That latter course went hard against him when, after three years in the Mediterranean serving against the French, his ship was scheduled to rotate back to England for repairs and a one-day shore leave for the crew. The thought of that one day's leave and the chance it offered for escape had kept him going. But there was to be no leave for troublemakers like Bates. As his ship departed for England the British navy immediately transferred him to another vessel that had just arrived to commence its three years of line duty. "I began," writes Bates, "to learn that I was doomed to drag out a miserable existence in the British navy."[14]

But all was not lost. Bates' father was a man of some influence and patriotism, and in early 1812 he had prevailed upon United States President James Madison to expedite his son's release. As a result, the father had documents sent through a family friend proving Bates' American citizenship and demanding his freedom. But before he could gain it, the United States on June 18, 1812, declared war against Britain and Bates was counseled to become a prisoner of war.[15]

Becoming a prisoner, however, was not as easy as one might expect. The British urged the 200 Americans in Bates' squadron to fight for them against the French. Only six, including Bates, refused. The result was drastically reduced rations and "no strong drink." Bates and his colleagues endured that treatment for the next eight months, with progressively more of the Americans following their lead.[16]

On one occasion, in a conflict with the French fleet, all of the Americans except himself, Bates claims, assisted the British. For his intransigence a British officer knocked Bates to the floor and ordered him put in leg irons. Bates told the officer he was free to do so, but that he would not work for the British because he was a prisoner of war. At that point the officer notified Bates that when the action began he would have him "'lashed up in the main rigging for a *target,* for the Frenchmen to fire at!'" Once again Bates informed the officer that he was free to do so, but that he hoped he would remember that he was a prisoner of war.[17] That spirit of independence and determination would characterize Joseph Bates for the rest of his life.

After eight months the British authorities shipped the prisoners back to England, where 700 of them were locked up on an old ship. But after several escapes and attempted escapes they were eventually sent to Dartmoor prison, a maximum security unit from which they had no hope of escape.[18]

It is in the records of Dartmoor that we find the most precise physical description of Bates available to us. The documents describe the 21-year-old as five feet nine inches, stout, with a round and sallow visage. His hair was brown, eyes gray, and he had a mole on his right cheek.[19]

Bates was still incarcerated in Dartmoor when news came of the signing of the Treaty of Ghent on December 24, 1814. But peace or no peace, it would be another four difficult months before the American prisoners would be released from Dartmoor prison. Bates received his freedom on April 27, 1815, "just five years to a day from the time I was impressed in Liverpool," and three weeks after he had witnessed the "Dartmoor massacre," in which the guards killed or wounded more than 60 of his fellow Americans for protesting their continuing imprisonment four months after the end of the war.[20]

Bates arrived home in mid-June 1815 after an absence of six years and three months with nothing but the clothes he wore and the little bag in which he had hoped to store his possessions in an escape. But the trip home had its own adventures. The rowdy prisoner crew, in their anxiety to get home, mutinied when the captain said he would be landing in New York rather than New England. Despite threats that they would be tried for mutiny on the high seas, Bates and the others took over the ship and scattered when they made landfall. Apparently none of them was ever brought to justice.[21]

After borrowing some money from a friend of his father in Boston, Bates bought some decent clothes and sped home, arriving on the evening of June 14 or 15, 1815, to be met by his parents, siblings, and friends. And then Bates renewed his acquaintance with Prudence Nye, who would eventually become his wife.[22]

BACK ON THE HIGH SEAS

But dallying around home wasn't for Bates. He was a travelin' man. "In a few weeks after my return," he penned, "an old schoolmate of mine arrived at New Bedford in a new ship, and engaged me for his second mate to perform with him a voyage to Europe."[23] Here we find another central trait in Bates' makeup. For most of the rest of his life home would be a place to return to for short periods of time before setting out for another voyage, or, in his later years, another evangelistic tour. He was a travelin' man in his early years, and he would remain so practically to the day of his death at the age of 79.

But just because he was a travelin' man didn't mean that he didn't desire a family. On his next trip home, after an absence of two and one-half years, he married Prudence Nye on February 15, 1818. Perhaps she might better have been named "Patience," marrying a man who had only been home three times in 10 years. The fact that her father had been a ship's captain had undoubtedly prepared "Prudy" (as Bates called her) for life as the spouse of a travelin' man. Their quite successful marriage would extend to her death 52 years later on August 27, 1870.[24]

Six weeks after his marriage Bates again set sail as chief mate on the ship *Francis F. Johnson* out of New Bedford. In spite of Bates' many absences, he and Prudy managed to have five children. The first, Anson Augustus, born November 15, 1819, died within two years. He was followed by Helen, whom Bates would first see in 1824 when she was 16 months old. Eliza followed in 1824 and Joseph in 1830. Joseph, who must have been a disappointment to his father, left for a life as a seaman on October 21, 1844, at the age of 14. We hear little of him throughout his life. One exception is that in 1857 he returned home to recuperate after a whale had thrown him from his boat. Then in 1865 we read that he died at sea of dysentery on September 11 at the age of 35. Bates' last child, Mary, was born in 1834. She would care for her parents during their last few years. While the Bateses' sons died before their parents, according to Joseph Bates' 1872 will all three daughters survived him and Prudence.[25]

Although Bates had served as the captain of the *Francis F. Johnson* for part of its return voyage in late 1817 and January 1818, his first commissioned captaincy was in the spring of 1821 when he took charge of the *Talbot,* with his brother Franklin as his chief mate.[26] From that point on Bates generally served as both captain and supercargo (i.e., he was in charge not only of the ship but also of the cargo and the business dealings of the voyage). As such, his responsibilities were sizeable.

His 1827 commissioning letter for the *Empress* enables us to see the trust that others placed in him. "We shall hereby appoint you," the commission reads, "Master of the Brig *Empress* now in New Bedford bound for the coast of Brazil.

"As respects the voyage, we cannot give any definite direction or instruction, but leave it altogether with your judgment, as we have an understanding she is to proceed to a port or ports in South America on the coast of Brazil to make sale of your cargo and to obtain business if any presents [itself] or [to] make sale of the Brig if an opportunity presents to any advantage. . . .

"As for the sale of the Brig, we shall depend on your judgment to do with her the best you can if an opportunity presents to sell."[27]

Those instructions help us glimpse the responsibility placed on the young sea captain. Independent judgment was repeatedly emphasized since Bates' voyages took place before the age of rapid communication. A ship's captain would be on his own for months or even years at a time.

The brig *Empress,* a ship of a type used frequently by American merchants, was registered with the port authorities at 125 tons, being 72 feet 9½ inches long, 20 feet 6 inches wide, and 9 feet 7 inches deep. The vessel carried a crew of seven besides the captain, although such ships often had a crew of 12 or 13 sailors.[28]

According to his *Autobiography,* Bates had many adventures and close calls during his years as a ship's captain in the 1820s. They illustrate certain characteristics that would constantly shape his life.

The first trait was courage. On December 4, 1827, Bates recorded in his ship's logbook that Argentine privateers had used large sweeping oars to overtake him during a somewhat windless day. The incident was significant since "it was not uncommon" in the wartorn waters of South America during the late 1820s "for the entire ship to be pillaged and the crews to be impressed into service" by the privateers.[29] Although Bates tried to outrun the pirates after they had fired on him, he soon saw the futility of it. But the attempted escape had infuriated the pirate captain, who told Bates that he had "'a good mind to blow your brains out here!'" Bates replied that he was in the captain's hands and he could obviously do as he pleased, but he did appeal to the fact that he was sailing under the American flag and hoped he would respect it.[30]

Even though the privateers "looked more like human butchers and desparados than the human species," Bates wasn't as much concerned for his cargo as he was for his six Brazilian passengers, whose nation was in armed conflict with that of the Buenos Airean privateers. After seven or eight hours, during which their captors ransacked Bates' ship, the pirate captain gave him permission to return to the *Empress.* "I will let you go,"

he said, "but I shall keep your passengers because they are my enemies."
"Sir," replied Bates, "you will not keep these poor fellows will you[?]"
They have "done you no harm." But that was exactly the man's intention.
"I told him," Bates noted in his daily log, "that I did not feel concerned respecting my vessel and cargo," which was American property, "but I felt
under an obligation to take these men to Rio [de] Janeiro as they had paid
me [for] their passages. . . . Finally after much persuasion he granted my
request." The incident ended with the pirates having taken clothing and
other incidentals, but they got none of the vessel's extensive gold dou-
bloons that the passengers and crew had thrown into the cook's large pot
of boiling beef and pork, even though the pirates had eaten a great deal of
the meat.[31] Bates' courage had saved six lives, even though he had to place
his own at risk.

Not only was Bates courageous, he was also honest when he could
have benefitted from the mistakes of others. In dealing with a Brazilian
merchant in early 1828, for example, Bates came up with more money
than he expected after having set sail. He rapidly went over the records of
the transaction without discovering any error, but still felt he had more
cash than he should have had. On a second count, some days later, he discovered the error. It wasn't his fault and he would put the ship in danger
because of sandbars and rough seas if he sought to return the money.
"But," he later penned, "the money was not mine, and I felt that I should
not be blessed of the Lord if I attempted to proceed on my voyage without an exertion on my part to pay it over."[32]

On March 8 Bates sent the merchant, who had claimed "that there was
no harm in lying once in a while," two letters. One was a spiritual appeal,
while the other explained the accounting error. "Since I parted with you,"
he penned, "I have been wondering how I came by so much cash. Once I
overhauled the accounts and concluded they were right. This evening
being more collected and free from care (and not satisfied) I had again
spread them before me and made a memorandum of sales and purchases
which soon led me to discover the error. . . . I have been devising the best
way to get this money safe to you [and] as it is now late and [as there is]
a prospect of a wind early in the morning, [I] have finally concluded to
send my boat. To double the diligence of my men [I] have promised them
960 reis each. I do not know of any other way."[33]

The error was no small amount—$500.34. That may not sound like a lot in our day, but it was roughly equivalent to Bates' annual salary (without commission). We should note that he was able to retire at the age of 36 after he had amassed $10,000.[34] Thus $500 was a princely sum, and certainly a temptation, especially since it wasn't his fault and since he had to put his ship at risk as well as his men who had to row through a heavy sea to return it. A sense of integrity would be central to his character for the rest of his life.

A major change took place in Bates' life in the spring of 1827 when he was baptized and joined the Christian Church (also known as the Christian Connexion). Afterward he claimed that he "found it much more trying to part with my family and friends." As a result, he captained only one more voyage. On June 20, 1828, having saved as both captain and part owner of the *Empress* enough money to retire on, he left the sea 21 years after he first sailed as a cabin boy.[35] By that time he had lived through more adventures than most people see in a lifetime.

AN EARLY "RETIREMENT"

But Bates was hardly the type of person to fully retire at age 36. Beyond civic activities, his first post-retirement project was to run the family farm left to him by his father, who had died at the age of 79 six weeks before Bates arrived home from his final voyage. His mother followed her husband a few months later. Bates, however, did more than farming. Godfrey T. Anderson's research has revealed scores of real estate transactions in Bates' name in the Register of Deeds in New Bedford. Most of them involved small parcels of land that he sold.[36]

One of Bates' more interesting occupations during this period was his work on the New Bedford toll bridge, for which he was both one of the owners and superintendent of repairs. One part of his work involved sending a diving bell some 25 to 30 feet down in the water to clear rocks out of the channel so that ships could pass by the drawbridge. The primitive diving bell was merely an inverted cone with two seats, an artificial light, and a large basket for collecting the stones. Since the cone was open on the bottom it filled partially with water. The unflooded part was the total air supply. The men worked from the seats to lift the obstructing stones into the basket. As superintendent, Bates went down in the bell a few times "for the purpose of ascertaining more correctly how the work could be accomplished." The main problem with the operation was that those in the bell developed "a shuddering sensation" in their heads and ears, "causing an involuntary working of the fingers there to let more air in, and relieve us of the painful sensation." They were apparently unaware of the rather simple process of holding the nose and blowing through it that modern divers use to equalize air pressure. Another problem, as we might expect, was the extremely limited supply of air. As it grew scarce inside the bell the diver would yank the "telegraphic cord, and be hoisted up for a fresh supply of God's free air."[37]

Our survey of Bates' early life shows him to be a person of quality. Such characteristics as honesty, courage, independence, determination, and hard work shaped the man who would become the primary founder of the Sabbatarian Adventist movement in the mid-1840s. Other characteristics that would follow him throughout his life were his ability to endure almost perpetual travel and his constant devotion to his family. Those last two characteristics may appear to be in tension with each other, and they were in Bates' life. In fact, it was his affection for his family that led him to leave the sea. And it would keep him near home for about 10 years. But by the 1840s his dedication to the mission of preaching Christ's Advent and the apocalyptic message of Revelation would challenge his desire to be with his family. His last three decades would once again find him to be a travelin' man. Then, however, he would not be journeying as a merchant but as a preacher of the Adventist message.

---

[1] J[oseph] B[ates] Hall to Melvin O. Bradford, Dec. 16, 1926; H. H. Gurney, "Early Day Experiences Recounted by H. S. Gurney," unpub. ms, Apr. 12, 1896.

[2] S. N. Haskell, "How I Accepted the Sabbath," *Review and Herald,* Apr. 7, 1896, p. 217; S. N. Haskell, 1909 *General Conference Bulletin,* p. 92.

[3] J. Bates, "From Bro. Bates," *Review and Herald,* Jan. 13, 1852, p. 80; J. Bates, "Letter From Bro. Bates," *Review and Herald,* Feb. 19, 1857, p. 125.

[4] J. Bates, *Autobiography,* pp. 18, 50; Anderson, *Outrider of the Apocalypse,* pp. 13, 14; the legal records appear in Charles A. Harris, *Old-Time Fairhaven: Erstwhile Eastern New Bedford* (New Bedford, Mass.: Reynolds Printing, 1947), p. 144.

[5] J. Bates, *Autobiography,* p. 18.

[6] *Ibid.*

[7] *Ibid.,* pp. 24-26.

[8] *Ibid.*, pp. 28-31.

[9] *Ibid.*, p. 29.

[10] *Ibid.*, pp. 33, 34; James White, "Elder Joseph Bates," *Health Reformer,* Jan. 1877, p. 3.

[11] J. Bates, *Autobiography,* p. 35.

[12] John Whiteclay Chambers II, ed. *The Oxford Companion to American Military History* (New York: Oxford University Press, 1999), p. 783.

[13] J. Bates, *Autobiography,* pp. 37-40, 86; J. Bates, *The Opening Heavens* (New Bedford, Mass.: Benjamin Lindsey, 1846), p. 24.

[14] J. Bates, *Autobiography,* pp. 48, 49.

[15] *Ibid.*, pp. 49-52.

[16] *Ibid.*, pp. 52, 53.

[17] *Ibid.*, pp. 53, 54.

[18] *Ibid.*, pp. 56, 57, 71.

[19] General entry book of American prisoners of war at Dartmoor Prison. Cited in Anderson, *Outrider of the Apocalypse,* p. 23.

[20] J. Bates, *Autobiography,* p. 84; Bates's recollection of his release date agrees with the official records of Dartmoor (see Anderson, *Outrider of the Apocalypse,* p. 23); J. Bates, Logbook of the *Empress,* April 10, 1828.

[21] J. Bates, *Autobiography,* pp. 89-96.

[22] *Ibid.*, pp. 96, 97.

[23] *Ibid.*, p. 97.

[24] J. Bates, [Obituary], *Review and Herald,* Sept. 6, 1870, p. 95; J. Bates, *Autobiography,* p. 108.

[25] J. Bates, *Autobiography,* pp. 108, 178; Anderson, *Outrider of the Apocalypse,* pp. 31, 32, 59, 41; J. Bates, "Note From Bro. Bates," *Review and Herald,* Oct. 29, 1857, p. 205; J. Bates, [Obituary], *Review and Herald,* Dec. 5, 1865, p. 7; J. Bates, "Last Will and Testament," Allegan, Mich., April 22, 1872.

[26] J. Bates, *Autobiography,* pp. 108, 139.

[27] A. and J. Bourne to Capt. Joseph Bates, Aug. 8, 1827.

[28] *Ship Registers of New Bedford, Massachusetts, 1796-1850,* 6 vols. (Boston: National Archives, 1940), vol. 1, p. 91, cited in Jerry E. Daly, "Joseph Bates' Logbook," pp. 10, 11; J. Bates, Logbook, May 10, 1828.

[29] Daly, "Joseph Bates' Logbook," p. 27; see also the discussion of the political situation between Brazil and Buenos Aires in pp. 25-32.

[30] J. Bates, *Autobiography,* pp. 213-219.

[31] J. Bates, Logbook, Dec. 4, 1827; see also J. Bates, *Autobiography,* pp. 213-219.

[32] J. Bates, *Autobiography,* p. 223.

[33] J. Bates, Logbook, Jan. 1, 1828; J. Bates to John Carroll, Mar. 8, 1828; J. Bates to John Carroll, Feb. 10, 1828, with an extended postscript dated Mar. 8, 1828; J. Bates, *Autobiography,* pp. 223, 224. The copy of the Mar. 8 letter found on page 224 has been edited somewhat.

[34] J. Bates to John Carroll, Mar. 8, 1827; A. and J. Bourne to J. Bates, Aug. 8, 1827;

J. Bates, *Autobiography*, p. 231.

[35] J. Bates, *Autobiography*, pp. 208, 209, 228.

[36] *Ibid.*, pp. 227, 231; J. Bates, Logbook, June 6, 1828; Anderson, *Outrider of the Apocalypse*, p. 43.

[37] J. Bates, *Autobiography*, pp. 251, 252; Harris, *Old-Time Fairhaven*, pp. 215, 216.

CHAPTER II

THE CAPTAIN GETS RELIGION

YOUNG Joseph Bates wasn't particularly religious, even though he reports that his "father had been a praying man from the time I had any knowledge of him." In fact, Bates notes, his father was one of the most devout individuals in New Bedford, a man who maintained a family altar and instructed his family "to fear God and keep his commandments." His mother, by way of contrast, did not embrace religion until about 1804. Three years later one of the revivalistic waves of the Second Great Awakening hit New Bedford and Bates felt "deeply interested in that work, and loved to attend their prayer-meetings," but before the revival was even over his mind had moved on to other things and his religious feelings subsided. Those other interests were his upcoming first voyage to Europe in 1807, which began soon after the revival had ended.[1]

Thus the sailors' life diverted him from religion. But in its own way it would help lead him to spiritual matters. Before that turnabout, however, Bates would develop in the areas of health and moral reform. For him, morality preceded religion.

MORALITY PRECEDES RELIGION

Alcohol has always been the temptation of seagoing men. Bates' father feared that after his long voyage as a teenager he would return home "like other drunken man-o'-war sailors." But while the young Bates imbibed his portion, he seems fairly early on to have seen the dangers. He reports that his five years on British warships and in British prisons, "schools of vice and debasement of moral character," convinced him of the necessity of reform, particularly in the area of "spirituous liquors."[2]

Bates and a Mr. Davis, who was one of his most intimate friends during his imprisonment, had spent hours discussing the "ruinous habits" of their fellow prisoners and agreed that after they were liberated they would "labor to avoid the dreadful habits of intemperance, and seek for a standing among sober, reflecting men."[3]

After his release, Bates sought to follow his decision but "soon learned that it was indeed a warfare to attempt to stem so strong a current of vice single-handed." In a short time he yielded to imbibing moderately and eventually confined himself to one glass of ardent spirits per day.[4]

Yet when he realized that he desired his daily glass more than he did his food he became alarmed, resolving in 1821 to "never drink another glass of grog or strong drink while I live." That time the victory was lasting. It gave him, he reported, "a new spring to my whole being, and made me feel like a free man."[5]

But the giving up of strong drink wasn't the end of alcohol for Bates, since at that time the general public did not consider wine, beer, and cider to be spiritus liquors. In 1822 he resolved to drink no more wine, but still occasionally imbibed beer and fermented cider. By 1824 he abandoned alcohol altogether. His decision, especially regarding wine, which most then saw as a polite beverage, brought him a great deal of misunderstanding and some jeering, but he was by that time beyond the point of turning his back on his convictions. From 1824 he never again used alcohol in any form except medicinally.[6]

About that same time he gave up tobacco in all its forms. In 1823 he and another captain agreed that they would discard chewing tobacco. "My chew of tobacco," he later reported, "I tossed into the ocean, never, no never to touch, taste or handle any more." His victory over cigars and chewing, he noted, "raised my feelings and elevated my mind above the fog of tobacco-smoke, which had to a considerable extent beclouded my mind, and freed me from an idol which I had learned to worship among sailors."[7]

The young reformer was quite proud of himself. "I was," he claimed, "now free from all distilled spirits, wine and tobacco. Step by step I had gained this victory—nature never required either."[8]

But alcohol and tobacco weren't the only sailor vices. His next campaign was to break himself of the "evil habit of swearing." Also he began to read the Bible more, especially on Sundays. In all of these things, Bates wrote, "I concluded that I was *making myself* a tolerably good Christian."[9] For him morality had definitely preceded religion. He desperately wanted to be a good person.

MOVING TOWARD CONVERSION

For all of their weaknesses and vices, the seamen of the age had a natural inclination toward religion. After all, as Bates pointed out, there was nothing in the stormy seas but "the thickness of a plank separating us from Eternity."[10]

It was in the face of losing such a plank that Bates dates his earliest religious stirrings. In chapter 1 we saw Bates' crewmates "begging God for mercy" as their ship verged on destruction in a Newfoundland ice field. That crisis brought Bates personally face to face with plunging to the bottom of the ocean "only to be numbered with the damned."[11]

But that ordeal was only one of several. An especially vivid experience took place in 1818-1819 when Bates' ship struggled for four days in a "furious hurricane." By "the third day at midnight, the gale had increased to a dreadful height. The raging elements seemed to set at defiance every living creature that moved above the surface of the sea. In all my experience I had never witnessed such portentous signs of a dreadful, devastating storm in the heavens. The sea had risen to such an awful height, it seemed sometimes that it would rush over our mast-heads before our heavy-laden ship would rise to receive its towering, foaming top, and the howling, raging wind above it, straining every stitch of sail we dared to show, and then dash us headlong again into the awful gulf below. . . . [We] were in great fear that the heavy gusts of wind would . . . leave us in the power of the next sea to be overwhelmed, and sink with our iron cargo to the bottom of the sea."[12]

The desperate crew did two things to save the ship. First, they cast 40 tons of iron cargo into the sea. Second, the captain asked the Colored cook (the only other Christian on the ship beside the captain himself) to pray. "Sinners as we were," reported Bates, "I believe it was remembered by Him whose ear is not closed to the distressed mariner's cry." He later found out that his wife also had been impressed to pray for him at that exact time.[13] Such events stood at the foundation of Bates' spiritual awakening.

The activities of his wife Prudy formed another foundation pillar undergirding Captain Bates' movement toward Christianity. When he sailed in August 1824 on the newly constructed *Empress* (of which he would become part owner), Bates provided himself with a number of "interesting books" to read during his leisure hours. But Prudence was quite convinced that he had taken more novels and romances than was necessary. As a result, she hid a pocket New Testament in his luggage, in which she had inserted a poem that had several lines on the fact that every person has their season for death.[14]

Impressed with the poem, Bates read it repeatedly. From that point, he reported, "my interest for reading novels and romances ceased." Such books as Philip Doddridge's *Rise and Progress of Religion in the Soul* and the Bible became the focal point of his reading.[15]

By now he could admit to himself that he desired to be a Christian, but he felt torn by the allurements of his old ways. He also feared that his officers and men might discover his growing interest in religion and taunt him. Caught in the tension, he decided to pray. "I determined to persevere until I found pardon and peace for my troubled soul." But, he reports, "I had no Christian friend at hand to tell me how, or how long I must be convicted before conversion." When he saw no clear light after two weeks of spiritual struggle he came to the place where he was "strongly tempted to jump overboard and put an end to myself."[16]

A major turning point came with the death of a sailor by the name of Christopher. As captain, it was Bates' duty to see to the burial, yet extremely conscious of his condition as a sinner in the sight of God, he did not see how he could pray in public or perform a religious service. The service itself was a spiritual crisis for the 32-year-old captain. From that point, Bates claims, "I felt a sinking into the will of God, resolving henceforward to renounce the unfruitful works of the enemy, and seek carefully for eternal life." On October 4, 1824, four days after the burial, he wrote and signed "a solemn covenant with God."[17]

Bates continued to look back on Christopher's death and funeral as a momentous occasion. In September 1827 as he passed the latitude of the burial he wrote that he would never forget the event, which was one of the "most conspicuous in my life. It's now 2 years & 11 months since I then promised the Lord that I would serve him the remainder of my life. Oh how far short I have come of this and how little has [been] done in the cause I then espoused. It is with shame that I acknowledge it, but hope it may be the means of stirring me up to more watchfulness to keep my promise with God."[18]

The memory of Christopher's burial not only affected Bates, but he used the event to stir up his crew, the next Sunday preaching a sermon on everlasting life.[19]

Late 1824 and early 1825 found him reading his Bible more and more. One of his great blessings while in port was going into the Brazilian forests to read. "I used to spend," he recalled, "the afternoon away somewhere in these forests; and sometimes for fear of reptiles, used to ascend a large tree, and fix myself securely in the branches, where I enjoyed most precious seasons in reading the Scriptures, singing, praying, and praising the Lord."[20]

Yet all was not right. Bates didn't believe that his sins were forgiven. On the other hand, he rejoiced that God had not forsaken him, that he was still under conviction.

One of his greatest lacks during this period was another Christian who could instruct him in what he should look for in the matter of conversion. He kept expecting some undeniable experience from God so that he would never thereafter doubt his conversion. But it alluded him. "I had not then learned," he later recalled, "the simplicity of God's gracious work on the sinner's heart." But experience or not, he had "fully resolved to persevere for a full and free salvation."[21]

The next major turning point came in March 1826, when Bates' ship arrived back in the States after an absence of 20 months. That return provided him with the first opportunity to attend church with other believers since he had made his covenant with God in October 1824.

Soon afterward an acquaintance asked him about his conversion, undoubtedly on the basis that his wife had become convinced that he had undergone one, because of the changed tone of his letters. Bates responded that he had as yet no assurance of its reality.[22]

Despite his uncertainty, he had decided to set up a family altar, which he did immediately. But he encountered a problem. One of his skeptical friends showed up at prayer time, and Bates was tempted not to go through with it. But "conscience and duty prevailed." He conducted the Bible reading and prayed for his family and friend. The friend, he reported, "looked very sober and soon withdrew." That episode was crucial in Bates' spiritual development. Up to that point he had sought to hide his religion. After it he would be a fearless advocate of religion for the rest of his life.[23]

Soon thereafter he attended a revival meeting. Bates found the experience of the converts to be so similar to his own that he concluded that he had indeed gone through a conversion. "For something like eighteen months," he wrote, "I had been unwilling to believe that the Lord had forgiven me my sins, because I had been looking for some evidence, or manifestation of his power . . . which would convince me beyond a doubt. My limited views of conversion, and strong desire not to be deceived in this important matter, caused me to overlook the simple manner in which God graciously condescends to pardon the guilty, pleading sinner.

"After meeting, my tongue was loosed to praise God for what he had done for me so many months before. From this time, all doubts and darkness respecting my conversion and acceptance with God, passed away like the morning dew, and peace like a river, for weeks and months occupied my heart and mind."[24]

Bates looked back on his conversion as finding "the Pearl of great price which was more riches than my vessel could contain," a "Pearl . . . worth more than all the vessels & cargoes that I have ever commanded." Again he wrote that through God's "rich mercy, in Jesus Christ, I have . . . found forgiveness of my sins; . . . and my only wish is, that I could teach [others] the way of life and salvation."[25] And teach he would. That mission dominated the rest of his life.

A NEW MAN AT THE HELM

A pastor of the Christian Church, also known as the Christian Connexion, baptized Bates by immersion in the spring of 1827. That same day, as he and the pastor were putting on dry clothes, he sought to enlist the pastor's aid in establishing a temperance society—something that was still quite rare at that early date. Failing in getting the pastor's cooperation, Bates set out on his own in enlisting others to found the Fairhaven Temperance Society.[26]

Bates would become a crusader for religious and reform causes to the day of his death. Now a new man, he ardently acted the part, as we see vividly illustrated during his next voyage as captain of the *Empress*.

The *Empress* cleared the New Bedford port for South America on

August 9, 1827, Bates having been home for about 16 months. That very evening he called his crew together, letting them know that his ship would be a temperance ship and that he expected them to behave as Christians on the voyage. His announcement greatly shocked the men, but having already set sail they couldn't do much about it.[27]

We will examine his radical reform package for his temperance voyage in the next chapter. The rest of the current chapter will discuss Bates' persistent evangelistic attempts to convert his crew and almost everybody else he came in contact with, his personal religious experience, his ever more intense appreciation of his family, and the beliefs that he held as a member of the Christian Connexion.

The logbook of Bates' final voyage deeply impressed with its piety the two scholars who studied it. Michael Ooley writes that "God was literally his constant companion. Day after day journal entries began in praise and ended in thanksgiving." And Jerry Daly informs us that "the entire record reads like a long prayer. Bates' preoccupation with religion overshadowed everything else."[28]

From the time of his conversion onward no infidel escaped Bates' attention if they ventured into his range. Out to convert everybody to his new-found faith, he even made an appeal to the Buenos Airean privateer who had captured his ship in 1827, a captain who claimed that he "expected to go to Hell, and that we should all meet there and that he had a good berth picked out." Bates preached to him of that "better place."[29]

His logbook for 1827-1828 indicates that he sought to convert an American counsel in Brazil, a Captain Peas, various passengers on his ship, prisoners being held in Brazilian jails, and a variety of unnamed sea captains and their officers. "One captain told me today," he wrote on January 28, 1828, "that he would give his vessel and cargo to any one that would teach him how to be saved. [I] told him to believe on the Lord Jesus Christ, that salvation was not to be bought but always free—without money & without price."[30]

On another occasion, Bates sent a letter to Lewis Carpentier, captain of the brig *Herminia,* urging him to change his ways and serve the Lord, lest tragedy overtake him. Soon thereafter a squall struck the *Herminia* and capsized it, the crew barely escaping with their lives. Some years later a friend of Bates met Carpentier and asked if he knew the New Bedford captain. Carpentier "cursed and railed" against Bates, claiming that it was Bates' religious instruction that had brought about his misfortune.[31]

Closer to home than the many strangers that Joseph sought to evangelize was his brother Franklin, who had served with him on the same ship and since the mid-1820s had been alternating with him as captain of the *Empress,* each commanding the ship while the other had shore leave. On September 30, 1827, he dreamed that Franklin had died. "I immediately felt condemnation for not going to see him before to point him to my saviour."[32]

Four days previously he had written to Franklin that he feared that "the road that you are traveling leads to death and you have not the promise of a tomorrow." Joseph appealed to him that today is the day of salvation and that he stood "alone in [his] father's family" in not being a Christian. Franklin's young son had recently died, a similar crisis that Bates himself had gone through a few years before. "I have no doubt," appealed the recently converted evangelist, "but our dear little children are in heaven. This surely is a loud call for us to prepare to meet them."[33]

While his other outreach activities were important to him, Bates' primary evangelistic audience for the duration of his final voyage were the seven members of his crew, who met with him for daily prayers, kept an enforced Sunday, and were deluged with tracts and other Christian reading. Bates' concern for the spiritual condition of his men appears on nearly every page of his 1827-1828 logbook.

Unfortunately, he never got the response he desired. Two months into the voyage he complained that he hadn't seen the "alteration in my men which I expected." To him they appeared to be like "stony ground hearers," who seemed "to listen with attention but bring forth no fruit." And then there was "one of our number who appears to use his influence to destroy all serious impressions."[34]

But Bates' missionary activity did have its bright side. A little more than a month into the voyage one of his crew came to him with serious religious questions. Joseph was hopeful that all will "ketch the infection and be brought to know the mild scepter of king Jesus." But things didn't really begin to happen until the ship had turned toward home. On April 23, 1828, 25-year-old James Stubbs told Bates that "he felt determined to seek the Lord [and that] he had attempted a number of times and failed, but now he was determined if he could think there was any mercy for him." Stubbs had taken to Bible reading in all his spare time. By May 5 Bates could report that he believed that the crewman had been "born again." That evening the captain announced to the rest of the crew that one of their number had been converted. "Though they were aware something was the matter with him," Bates reported, "they looked somewhat amazed when I gave them my opinion about him." At that point the good captain "exorted them to flee to the outstretched arms of Jesus who was as willing to receive them as [He had] their shipmate."[35]

That one conversion began to have its effect. Three days later Bates wrote in his logbook that "J. S. appears very happy & two or three others [were] very serious." Within a few days he could report that two or three of his crew were "under pungent conviction." And two days after that he concluded that all of them prayed more or less. Near the end of the voyage he could report that "J. S. continues very happy. Says he loves the Bible so much that he fairly kisses it and calls it a blessed book." By June 1, two weeks before they made landfall on their homeward voyage, Bates believed that three of his seven men "are converted from the error of their ways. And the rest but one [were] enquiring" of the Lord. He prayed that they all might persevere until they found spiritual joy.[36]

THE CAPTAIN'S PERSONAL RELIGIOUS JOURNEY

Bates utilized his spare time on his last voyage (his first as a baptized Christian) not only to spend much time reading his Bible, praying, and exhorting others to a new life in Christ, but also to read widely in Christian literature. Among others, his logbook lists a work titled *Defence of Trinitarianism,* Seth Williston's *Five Discourses on the Sabbath* (read at least twice), the life of Elias Smith (one of the founders of the Christian Connexion), Jonathan Edwards on revivalism, and William Paley's *Natural Theology.*[37] Several times he refers to the excellent library of religious materials he had in his cabin. Apparently the voyage was not only one of evangelism but also of a self-tutored theological education.

Following his conversion, Bates had peace of mind "for weeks and months." But such contentment could not last forever for such a naturally introspective Christian. His logbook (which functioned somewhat like a diary) reports him as feeling "stupid about eternal things." He went on to note that "it does not seem to be faith that I lack so much as it does spiritual vigor to arouse me from this lukewarm state of lethargy [into] which I feel myself sinking. O Lord I desire still to put my trust in thee." On another occasion, after ascertaining his longitude and latitude, he wished he could determine his state before God as easily as he could the position of his ship.[38]

Bates appears to have had an apprehension-of-judgment obsession that often left him without any assurance of salvation. On August 28, 1827, for example, he wrote about "how necessary it is for me to strive to ascertain from time to time my true state and standing before God." Then again near the end of his long voyage he wrote that "I am far from being prepared to meet my judge, but still I felt somewhat resigned, and cherished a hope that it would be well with me."[39] That same lack of assurance and an orientation toward or preoccupation with divine judgment would also surface in his wife's periodic letters to the *Review and Herald* in the 1850s and 1860s. The same concern undoubtedly pushed Bates throughout his life to a works orientation and motivated the legalistic approach he would take toward such issues as the seventh-day Sabbath in the mid-1840s (see chapter 5).

Joseph, of course, did have his faults, even if one of them wasn't a lack of total dedication to his Lord. Repeatedly his logbook refers to an unruly tongue and a quick temper. His most disastrous experience along that line involved striking his cook for "contradicting me and disobeying my commands." As we might expect, he immediately prayed for both personal forgiveness and forgiveness for the cook.[40]

Set over against Bates' personal shortcomings was his profound dedication to his beliefs. Reading his daily jottings leaves one without the slightest doubt that Joseph Bates was a totally surrendered Christian.

One effect of his conversion was to draw him more intimately to his wife and children. While a certain closeness appears to have always been there, Bates' conversion definitely intensified it. "I found it much more trying," he wrote, "to part with my family and friends this time than ever before." That sentiment shows up from the first page of his logbook to the last. Bemoaning the fact that of their 10 years of marriage they had been separated for about seven and one half years, he committed himself to quitting the sea, hoping "we shall be permitted to spend the remainder of our days together and train up the dear offspring" that the Lord had given them.[41]

THE CONNEXION CONNECTION

As noted earlier, Bates' religious affiliation was with the Christian Connexion (Christian Church). He joined the Connexion against the wishes of his Congregationalist parents. Two of the deciding doctrines were those of the Trinity and baptism. His father, a deacon in the Congregational church, labored to convince him of the correctness of both the Trinity and infant baptism. Bates responded that the Bible teaches "that we must first believe and then be baptized" and that infants are incapable of believing. "Respecting the trinity," he concluded "that it was an impossibility for me to believe that the Lord Jesus Christ, the Son of the Father, was also the Almighty God, the Father, one and the same being." Although Bates, in harmony with J. V. Himes and others in the Christian Connexion, appears to have been confused regarding the traditional understanding of the Trinity, it is clear that he rejected the doctrine. As a result, Joseph decided to become part of the Christian Connexion because "they took the Scriptures for their only rule of faith and practice, renouncing all creeds." [42]

Within a short time Bates became a leading member of the Christian Connexion congregation in Fairhaven. Local records show him on March 12, 1832, to be one of the signers of a contract for the erection of a new church building. [43]

The fact that Bates joined the Christian Connexion at his baptism is important because the Connexionist understandings that he brought with him would do much to shape the theology of early Sabbatarian Adventism. That was doubly so since James White also came out of the Connexion. [44] It is therefore important to understand that movement.

Two basic pillars undergird the theology of the Christian Connexion. One, wrote William Kinkade in 1829, was the conviction that people "would take no other book for [their] standard but the *Bible.*" A second pillar was the concept of the "restoration of the ancient order of things. When I speak of the ancient order," Kinkade wrote, "I mean the order of the New Testament; one inch short of that will not satisfy me." Thus at the foundation of Christian Connexion beliefs was the desire to reclaim all the lost teachings of the New Testament. That perspective viewed the Reformation as having begun in the sixteenth century but not completed then. Rather, the Christian Connexion regarded reformation as an ongoing process in which God's people came ever closer to the complete teachings of the New Testament church.[45]

Bates enthusiastically accepted both the position of the Connexionists toward the Bible as being the only rule of faith and their anti-creedalism. He believed that once a church published a creed it became the standard rather than the Bible itself. Thereafter the creed shaped the church. His approach to the Bible was that we should read it just as we find it, that an open-minded study of the Scriptures will reveal its obvious meaning.[46]

One belief that both Bates and James White would bring into Sabbatarian Adventism from their Connexionist background was Antitrinitarianism. Joshua V. Himes, a leading Connexionist minister, outlined the movement's perspective on the Trinity in 1835. He noted that at first the Connexionists were in general Trinitarian but had moved away from that belief when they came to see it as "unscriptural." Himes noted that the word "Trinity" didn't appear in the Bible and thus must be a part of the medieval apostasy. He wrote that his coreligionists believed in "one living and true God, the Father almighty, who is unoriginated, independent, and eternal" and that "Christ is the Son of God, the promised Messiah and Savior of the world." His statement clearly has the Father alone as "unoriginated, independent, and eternal," thus implying that Christ had an origin, was dependent, and had been brought into existence by the Father. Kinkade held essentially the same position, even going so far as to argue that Christ was a created being.[47]

Early on in his religious experience Bates hadn't quite decided on the Trinity. But by the time of his baptism he had become fully antitrinitarian.[48]

Another Connexionist understanding that Bates came to accept was that of conditional immortality. Early in his experience he believed that people were born immortal. Thus he could write to his brother Franklin that their deceased baby boys were already in heaven. Likewise, in his 1827-1828 logbook he could speak of a dead man as having an "immortal soul" and refer to the crew from a sunken ship as already being in eternity and of his father as being in heaven.[49]

We don't know when or how Bates came to believe in immortality being a gift of God at the Second Advent, but that is the position he held by the mid-1840s. It is possible that he began to reach that belief through his study of the autobiography of Elias Smith, which he read during his last voyage. Smith's autobiography explicitly teaches the destruction of the wicked, an understanding integrally connected to conditional immortality. One of the founders of the Christian Connexion, Smith had become by 1808 a firm believer in both immortality as a gift and the utter destruction of the wicked at the time of the second death.[50]

Another important contribution of the Christian Connexion to Bates' developing understanding of Christian doctrine was its position on spiritual gifts. Kinkade, for example, argued that to say that such gifts ceased in the Christian era is the same as claiming that "God has abolished the order of the New Testament church." He went on to argue the perpetuity of spiritual gifts from the Bible.[51] That perspective helped make Bates open to the gift of prophecy in Ellen White in 1846.

Bates also brought the Connexionist attitude toward church organization with him into Adventism. The Christian Connexion vested ecclesiastical authority in local congregations tied together by essentially powerless associations. The movement, noted Himes in 1836, opposed any "infringement of Christian liberty." Thus "each church" or congregation is "an independent body, possessing exclusive authority to regulate and govern its own affairs."[52]

Joseph was expressing that ideal of church organization in 1847 when he defined a Christian church as "an assembly of congregations of *faithful men.*" Likewise in 1854, as Sabbatarian Adventism began to discuss organizing itself, Bates reflected the Connexionist mentality when he defined the church in congregational terms and spoke of moving toward correct gospel order as "restoration" or "restitution of all things, which God hath spoken by the mouth of all his holy prophets."[53]

A final Connexionist understanding that Bates would bring with him into Adventism was his theology of baptism. True to its Baptist heritage, the Christian Connexion uplifted baptism by immersion.[54]

Bates' conversion to Christianity became the central turning point in his life. It shaped the man and pointed him in a direction that would dominate the rest of his earthly existence. His early zeal in sharing his faith with his crew and others would continue to characterize him. That dedication drove him as a reformer, a Millerite leader, and later as a Sabbatarian Adventist. He was a persistent and tireless evangelist at heart.

His early religious experience also guided his later approach to religion. For the rest of his life he tended to focus on the judgment, emphasized the importance of Christian behavior to the point where it became legalism, and remained totally dedicated to the Bible and his understanding of its message.

Beyond that, his belonging to the Christian Connexion did much to shape the thinking of the man who would become Sabbatarian Adventism's first theologian. Such beliefs as the supreme place of the Bible, an openness to spiritual gifts, antitrinitarianism, baptism by immersion, congregational church organization, and conditional immortality became central to early Adventist theology. And beyond those specific items was the strategic concept of an ongoing religious reformation, that the Protestant Reformation had not concluded in the sixteenth century but would be a continuous process until the return of Christ. That restorationist perspective left Bates and the church he did so much to shape open to rediscovered Bible truths that Sabbatarian Adventists needed to recover as God led His people toward the apocalyptic climax of world history.

Before closing this chapter it should be reemphasized that Bates came to religion by the avenue of moral reform. His conversion did not quench that reform impulse. Rather, his experience energized and enlightened it. Thus the reform impulse not only led Bates to religion, it also flowed out from religion. It is to that topic that we turn in chapter 3.

---

[1] J. Bates, *Autobiography*, pp. 173, 233, 234; J. Bates to Honored Parents, Sept. 26, 1827.

[2] J. Bates, *Autobiography*, p. 97; J. Bates, "Experience in Health Reform," *Health Reformer*, July 1871, p. 20.

[3] J. Bates, "Experience in Health Reform," *Health Reformer*, July 1871, p. 21.

[4] *Ibid.*, p. 20.

[5] J. Bates, *Autobiography*, p. 143; J. Bates to E. G. White, Feb. 14, 1872.

[6] J. Bates, "Experience in Health Reform," *Health Reformer*, July 1871, p. 20; J. Bates, *Autobiography*, pp. 150, 167, 168, 179, 188.

[7] J. Bates, *Autobiography*, pp. 168, 172, 173; J. Bates to E. G. White, Feb. 14, 1872.

[8] J. Bates, *Autobiography*, p. 173.

[9] *Ibid.*, p. 174.

[10] J. Bates, Logbook, Aug. 31, 1827.

[11] J. Bates, *Autobiography*, pp. 27-31.

[12] *Ibid.*, pp. 113, 119.

[13] *Ibid.*, pp. 116, 117, 119.

14 *Ibid.,* pp. 179, 180.

15 *Ibid.,* p. 181.

16 *Ibid.,* pp. 181, 182.

17 *Ibid.,* pp. 183-185.

18 J. Bates, Logbook, Sept. 1, 1827; cf. Aug. 18, 1827.

19 *Ibid.,* Sept. 2, 1827.

20 J. Bates, *Autobiography,* p. 193. Bates' surviving logbook often mentions these excursions into the forest.

21 *Ibid.,* pp. 193, 186.

22 *Ibid.,* p. 201.

23 *Ibid.,* pp. 201, 202.

24 *Ibid.,* pp. 202, 203.

25 J. Bates, Logbook, Jan. 7, 1828; J. Bates, *Autobiography,* pp. 43, 44.

26 J. Bates, *Autobiography,* pp. 204-206.

27 *Ibid.,* pp. 208-213.

28 Michael Ooley, "The Logbook (1827-1828) of Captain Joseph Bates of the Ship *Empress,*" *Adventist Heritage* (Winter 1978), p. 7; Daly, "Joseph Bates' Logbook," p. 34.

29 J. Bates, Logbook, Dec. 4, 1827.

30 *Ibid.,* Oct. 7, 1827; Oct. 29, 1827; Nov. 29, 1827; Dec. 15, 1827; Feb. 2, 1828; Feb. 9, 1828; Jan. 28, 1828.

31 J. Bates to L. Carpentier, Feb. 10, 1828, in J. Bates, Logbook, Feb. 18, 1828; J. Bates, *Autobiography,* pp. 222, 223.

32 J. Bates, Logbook, Sept. 30, 1827.

33 J. Bates to Dear Brother, Sept. 26, 1827; cf. J. Bates to Honored Parents, Sept. 26, 1827.

34 J. Bates, Logbook, Oct. 14, 1827; May 4, 1828.

35 *Ibid.,* Sept. 20, 1827; April 24, 1828; April 26, 1828; May 5, 1828; May 6, 1828.

36 *Ibid.,* May 8, 1828; May 11, 1828; May 13, 1828; May 18, 1828; June 1, 1828.

37 *Ibid.,* Aug. 25, 1827; Oct. 17, 1827; Aug. 27, 1827; Mar. 9, 1828; April 13, 1828; April 20, 1828.

38 *Ibid.,* Oct. 13, 1827; May 22, 1828; cf. Oct. 28, 1827.

39 *Ibid.,* Aug. 28, 1827; May 30, 1828.

40 *Ibid.,* Oct. 16, 1827; March 29, 1828.

41 J. Bates, *Autobiography,* pp. 208, 209; J. Bates, Logbook, Feb. 16, 1828; see also Aug. 9, 1827; Aug. 16, 1827; Aug. 22, 1827; Dec. 12, 1827; April 9, 1828.

42 J. Bates, *Autobiography,* pp. 204, 205. In regard to the somewhat strange understanding of the Connexionists on the Trinity being a confounding of the persons of the Father and the Son, see J. V. Himes, *A Letter to a Methodist Minister in Defence of the Principles of the Christian Connection* (Union Mills, n.p., cir. 1830), pp. 8, 9.

43 Harris, *Old-Time Fairhaven,* p. 127.

44 See Wheeler, *James White,* pp. 29-36.

45 William Kinkade, *The Bible Doctrine of God, Jesus Christ, the Holy Spirit, Atonement, Faith, and Election: To Which Is Prefixed Some Thoughts on Natural Theology and the Truth of Revelation*

(New York: H. R. Piercy, 1829), pp iv, 331; J. Bates, *Autobiography*, p. 204. For historical treatments of Restorationism see Richard T. Hughes and C. Leonard Allen, *Illusions of Innocence: Protestant Primitivism in America, 1630-1875* (Chicago: University of Chicago Press, 1988); James DeForest Murch, *Christians Only: A History of the Restoration Movement* (Cincinnati: Standard Publishing, 1962); Milo True Morrill, *A History of the Christian Denomination in America, 1794-1911 A.D.* (Dayton, Ohio: Christian Pub. Assn., 1912).

[46] J. Bates, *Autobiography*, p. 204; J. Bates, *Opening Heavens*, p. 35; J. Bates, *The Seventh Day Sabbath, A Perpetual Sign, From the Beginning, to the Entering Into the Gates of the Holy City, According to the Commandment*, (New Bedford, Mass.: Benjamin Lindsey, 1846), p. 3.

[47] [Joshua V. Himes], "Christian Connexion," in *Encyclopedia of Religious Knowledge*, J. Newton Brown, ed. (Brattleboro: Fessenden and Co., 1836), p. 363; Kinkade, *The Bible Doctrine*, pp. 39, 131. For a helpful history of Seventh-day Adventism on the Trinity, see Woodrow Whidden, Jerry Moon, John W. Reeve, *The Trinity* (Hagerstown, Md.: Review and Herald Pub. Assn., 2002), pp. 190-231.

[48] J. Bates, *Autobiography*, pp. 204, 205; cf. J. Bates, *Vindication of the Seventh-day Sabbath*, p. 70.

[49] J. Bates to Dear Brother, Sept. 26, 1827; J. Bates, Logbook, Feb. 8, 1828; May 31, 1828; June 11, 1828.

[50] J. Bates, Logbook, Oct. 17, 1828; LeRoy Edwin Froom, *The Conditionalist Faith of Our Fathers: The Conflict of the Ages Over the Nature and Destiny of Man*, 2 vols. (Washington, D.C.: Review and Herald Pub. Assn., 1965, 1966), vol. 2, pp. 291-295, 675.

[51] Kinkade, *The Bible Doctrine*, pp. 332-340.

[52] "Conferences," *Christian Journal*, May 14, 1835, p. 14; [Himes], "Christian Connexion," in *Encyclopedia of Religious Knowledge*, pp. 362, 363. For an overview of the Connexionist contribution to early Adventism on church organization, see George R. Knight, *Organizing to Beat the Devil: The Development of Adventist Church Structure* (Hagerstown, Md.: Review and Herald Pub. Assn., 2001), pp. 15-18.

[53] J. Bates, *Second Advent Way Marks and High Heaps, or a Connected View, of the Fulfilment of Prophecy, by God's Peculiar People, From the Year 1840 to 1847*, (New Bedford, Mass.: Benjamin Lindsey, 1847), p. 25; J. Bates, "Church Order," *Review and Herald*, Aug. 29, 1854, pp. 22, 23.

[54] J. Bates, *Autobiography*, p. 205.

Chapter III

REFORMER ON THE LOOSE

CHAPTER 2 demonstrated that for Bates morality preceded religion. That is, before he "got religion" he had given up ardent spirits, wine, tobacco, and had begun to work on his swearing problem. The present chapter will note that in Bates' case morality also followed the acceptance of religion. The man would be a reformer for the rest of his life, and Christianity would shape and give meaning to those reforms.

As we might expect from a person of Bates' convictions, one of the first places he began his reform activity was on his own ship. The *Empress* set sail in August 1827 as a temperance ship. Unfortunately for the crew, they didn't discover that fact until they were 15 miles out to sea. And by then it was too late to turn back.

NO PLACE TO ESCAPE FROM CAPTAIN BATES

Bates on his last voyage not only believed his duty was to convert his crew to Christianity, but to make sure they behaved like Christians, even before they actually became one. At sunset on August 9 (the day of their departure from New Bedford), he assembled his crew and stated the rules and regulations that would govern the voyage. It must have been a shock to the rough, seagoing men who stood before him. First, they must show respect for each other by using their proper names rather than nicknames. Second, he would allow no swearing. That rule brought a response from William Dunn, who pointed out that he had always had that privilege. "Well," replied Bates, "you cannot have it here." He then quoted the third commandment. But, Dunn protested, he swore without thinking about it. "I can't help it, sir!" "Then I will help you to help it," Bates countered in a demonstration of firmness. Dunn, not yet satisfied, claimed that he was bound to swear in a difficult situation. If so, said the intransigent captain, he would be sent below in disgrace, and the other men would do his work.[1]

While those rules were radical enough for such men, the worst were yet to come. A third restriction had to do with Sunday. They would have no shore leave on it. "For," said Bates, "we shall observe the Sabbath on board in port." At that point the irrepressible Dunn, who by this time was beginning to feel a bit claustrophobic, responded that Sunday shore leave was the sailors' privilege and that he had always had such leave. "I know that very well," Bates replied, "but I cannot give you that liberty" because it would be a violation of the law of God. Rather, the crew could have Saturday for shore leave. That would also be the day that they prepared their clothes for the Sabbath, both in port and at sea.[2]

But the real bomb was yet to be dropped. The *Empress,* Bates announced, would be a temperance ship. There would be no liquor or intoxicating drinks on board, and if he could he would persuade them never to drink even when on shore.[3]

At that point Bates knelt down and dedicated himself and his crew to God. "The next morning, all but the man at the helm were invited into the cabin to join with us in our morning prayer." And Sunday was set aside for worship (led by Bates) and the reading of the Christian literature he had brought for that purpose.[4]

Such was the atmosphere of what must have been a strange voyage for the crew of the *Empress.* We don't know all their feelings, but one of the crew exclaimed that they were off to "a very good beginning." Dunn, of course, held that it was a very bad beginning.[5]

And how, we might ask, did the voyage turn out? Quite good if one is to believe Bates' published *Autobiography,* in which the men "appeared cheerful and willing to obey" and compared very favorably to those crews who returned from leave in "a turbulent and riotous condition." On the other hand, Bates had to reprove Dunn "once or twice during the voyage for drinking while he was on shore."[6]

The unpublished logbook tells us a somewhat different story. On Saturday, November 24, 1827, for example, Joseph reports that he let the men go to shore. But one was so intoxicated that Bates feared he might capsize the boat as they returned to the *Empress.* A second couldn't be found and had to be left on shore. Bates notes that I "lost my head" and "preached much . . . beyond that which is customary."[7]

Again, on December 25 he reported that he did not know what to do with some of his men. "Two of them are in the practice of getting drunk when an opportunity offers, which was the case yesterday. This morning I scolded severely but I fear it will not stop them. I even told one that I would set him on shore if he did not do better, but it appears to have no good effect. O Lord teach me by thy Holy Spirit how to govern them in a proper manner."[8]

At times Bates felt tension over his regulations, declaring to his log-book one time that "it does not seem right to keep them on board like prisoners." On another occasion he claimed to feel a "good deal tried in my mind . . . about keeping my men on board on the Sabbath." But, he reasoned, "when I look into the Word of God I feel justified notwithstanding they may think it is hard." He could not "permit them to profane God's holy Sabbath."[9]

All in all, however, he judged the experiment to be a success, noting to his satisfaction that all but one stayed with him after arriving in New York to discharge the cargo and that some even expressed a desire to sail again with him. Such was not to be, though. Bates had gone to sea for the last time. But the *Empress* wasn't finished. On its next voyage it sailed as a temperance ship under the captaincy of Bates' brother Franklin.[10]

Before moving away from the discussion of Bates' last voyage, we need to examine a bit more his growing understanding of the Sabbath. The voyage witnessed his reading at least twice Seth Williston's *Five Discourses on the Sabbath*. On the first reading Bates declared that he did not know that the Bible had so much to say about the Sabbath. He concluded that the Sabbath had been a divine command since the seventh day of creation, when God rested on it and sanctified it. Of course, he noted, it "was altered to the first day of the week" as a remembrance that on that day "our Saviour arose triumphant from the grave." He then went on to berate himself for polluting God's sacred Sunday. Six months later he went through Williston a second time, again remarking on how many texts Scripture had regarding God's holy day. A few weeks afterward he wrote that "the more I read and reflect on this holy day the more I am convinced of the necessity of keeping it entirely holy."[11]

Only once during his 1827-28 voyage did Bates go against his principles on Sabbathkeeping. On Sunday, March 9, 1828, he had to decide to sail from port when he had an opening or to wait for several days until the next opportunity. Finally he chose to hoist anchor. "This is what I never did before since I appeared on the Lord's side," he reported in his log-book. He suffered much for going against his convictions, claiming he wasn't absolutely sure if he had done right or wrong, given the extraordinary circumstances he faced at the time. On the other hand, he did know for sure that he had, as he put it, to a "great measure destroyed my peace of mind." The next two days found him personally ill and the ship in a fierce storm. He hoped, he wrote, that the experience "will teach me not to break the Sabbath." The experience continued to trouble Bates for the rest of the voyage.[12]

His sensitivity to the importance of the Sabbath would in his later life become a central issue. That would especially be true in 1845 when he came to an understanding of the sacredness of the seventh-day Sabbath and in 1846 and 1847 when he began to see the issue in the light of the prophecies of Daniel and Revelation. But it was in the 1820s that his ideas of the importance of the Sabbath and how one should keep it first surfaced in his mind.

A REFORMER IN AN AGE OF REFORM

In the matter of temperance reform Bates was not alone. Rather, he was an early participant in a movement that would gain momentum throughout the century, finally climaxing in 1918, with the passage of the eighteenth amendment to the United States Constitution, prohibiting the manufacture, transportation, and sale of alcoholic beverages.

Neither was Bates the only captain of a temperance ship in the late 1820s. Lyman Beecher in his influential *Six Sermons on the Nature, Occasions, Signs, Evils, and Remedy of Intemperance,* preached in 1825 and first published in 1826, noted that some ships were already being "navigated . . . without the habitual use of ardent spirits."[13]

Again, the president of the Medical Society of the Western District of New Hampshire reported in June 1827 (two months before Bates launched his temperance voyage) that a vessel belonging to one of his neighbors sailed from New England to South America and then to India, with no spirits being "allowed to the crew during the whole voyage." He had personally shipped three crews, telling the men beforehand that they would receive no grog. "It is," he concluded, "in the power of every ship owner to prevent the use of ardent spirit[s] on board his vessels."[14]

By the early 1830s the idea of temperance ships had spread rapidly. *The Sailors' Magazine and Naval Journal* published by the American Seaman's Friends Society reported 40 ships sailing from New Bedford in 1830 "with supplies of distilled liquor for medicinal use only," with that number rising to 75 a year later.[15]

The point at which Bates may have been in advance of other temperance ships was that he was against all alcoholic beverages, whereas some of the others appear to have only prohibited distilled (or ardent) spirits in contrast to fermented beverages with a much lower alcohol content. Bates, who was a purist on the topic, had had to fight that battle in the organizing of the Fairhaven Temperance Society soon after his baptism. The society at first prohibited only ardent spirits (rum, gin, brandy, and whiskey) but soon included all intoxicating beverages when one of its members showed up drunk from fermented cider.[16]

The temperance movement was only one of the reforms in the period running from 1830 to 1860. Henry Steele Commager, who sees that period as the "era of reform," noted that "it was a day of universal reform— a day when almost every man you met might draw a plan for a new society or a new government from his pocket; a day of infinite hope and infinite discontent."[17]

Reform societies arose in the early nineteenth century in almost every conceivable area of human interest. Societies organized for the abolition of slavery and war; the promotion of public education; better treatment of the deaf, blind, mentally incapacitated, and prisoners; the equality of the sexes; and so on. There were hundreds of such groups, including the American Vegetarian Society. The first half of the nineteenth century was awash in organizations aimed at individual and social perfection. Such associations existed not at the edges of American society, but at its very heart. Ralph Waldo Emerson, tongue-in-cheek, mused that "even the insect world was to be defended, and a society for the protection of ground-worms, slugs, and mosquitoes was to be incorporated without delay."[18]

The purpose of the reforms from a Christian perspective was to bring in the millennium—that thousand year period in which the world would get better and better until after the 1,000 years when Christ would come.

Charles Finney, the greatest American evangelist of the day, set forth the prevailing view when he penned in 1835 that "if the church will do her duty, the millenium [sic] may come in this country in three years."[19]

Some of those reform movements would affect Bates more than others. He undoubtedly took an interest in the spate of legislation in the late 1820s and early 1830s aimed at protecting Sunday sacredness.[20] But of much more immediate impact to him was the health reform movement, represented by such individuals as Sylvester Graham. Graham proposed a vegetarian diet, bread made with whole wheat, and dispensing with butter, milk, rich gravies, spicy condiments, and "all stimulants of every sort and kind, as tea, coffee, wine, tobacco (in all its forms), cider, beer," and so on. He suggested that people should drink nothing but pure soft water and that they should never eat between meals. In addition, he advocated the avoidance of medicine and the adoption of regular sleeping and bathing and exercise in the open air. Bates was familiar with Graham's writings and cites them as to the fact "'that both tea and coffee are among the most powerful poisons of the vegetable kingdom.'"[21]

BATES AND HEALTH REFORM

Earlier we noted that Bates had begun his health reform journey before he became a Christian. In 1821 he had given up ardent spirits, wine in 1822, tobacco in 1823, and all other forms of alcohol in 1824. Then in about 1831 he swore off tea and coffee because "it is poison." "It had such an effect on my whole system," he wrote, "that I could not rest nor sleep until after midnight."[22]

Next to go were flesh foods. "In February 1843," he recalled, "I resolved to eat no more meat. In a few months after, I ceased using butter, grease, cheese, pies, and rich cakes." Bates had first become alerted to the advantages of a vegetarian diet in 1820 when he discovered that two potato-eating Irish laborers could outwork seven or eight of his meat-eating men. Later, such writers as Graham undoubtedly led him further toward a complete vegetarian diet.[23]

When James White first met Bates in 1846 the ex-seaman's diet consisted of "only plain bread and cold water." He wouldn't eat "fruits and nuts because of the custom to eat them between meals." It wasn't until the mid-1860s that Joseph added those items to his diet. As a result, White reported, many thought Bates might starve to death. But in 1846 the 54-year-old was in vigorously good health. "He was the last man to be picked out of the crowd as one who had endured the hardships and exposure of sea life, and who had come in contact with the demoralizing influences of such a life for more than a score of years. It had been eighteen years since he left the seas, and during that time his life of rigid temperance in eating, as well as in drinking, and his labors in the pure sphere of moral reform, had regenerated the entire man."[24]

The above discussion makes it quite evident that Bates was already a thoroughgoing health reformer by the time of the formation of the Sabbatarian Adventist movement during the late 1840s. In that matter he stood somewhat alone among the founders. As a result, he decided the best way to maintain unity was not to push his health views. After all, they had more important issues to convert people to, such as the seventh-day Sabbath and its place in apocalyptic history. As a result, he chose to remain quiet on health reform. "When asked why he did not use these things," James White noted, "his usual reply was, 'I have eaten my share of them.' He did not mention his views of proper diet in public at that time, nor in private, unless questioned upon the subject." It would not be until about 1863 when the Seventh-day Adventist Church (following the lead of Ellen White) began to advocate health reform as a part of its message that Bates began to speak freely on the topic.[25]

But that doesn't mean that he had been totally silent on health reform before that time. In 1849, for example, in his book on the seal of God he advocated the sacrificing of tobacco and alcohol because they neither nourish one's body or glorify God. Beyond that, nothing would enter the holy city that defiles. On the opposite side, he recommended that "good wholesome food is all that we require to sustain these bodies." That same year we find him rejoicing that "the pipes and tobacco are traveling out of sight fast" in response to his preaching. Again in 1852 Bates urged that Adventist meetings should provide plain healthy food rather than rich dishes.[26]

Even after the church began to advocate health reform in 1863 to 1865 we find Bates to be rather low keyed on the topic, something rather surprising given his forcefulness with his crew on the *Empress*. Along that line, James White pointed out that "it might be supposed that he would be exacting and overbearing in his efforts to reform others." And while it is true that Bates could state his position forcefully, White added, "after he had set forth principles, and urged the importance of obedience to them, he was willing to leave his hearers free to decide for themselves."[27]

In that gentle approach Bates was the opposite of D. W. Revis' Aunt Permelia O'Bryan who was "a strict old-time health reformer, an ardent disciple of one Dr. Trall. 'Cold water and two plain meals a day' was her hobby, and she rode it hard. Also everyone else in her home was compelled to ride the same steed."[28]

An illustration of Bates' more gentle approach took place in 1866. "Several years ago," he wrote in 1872, "I was with the church in Vassar, Tuscola County, Michigan, and was invited to address them, and more especially their children, in a barn on the 4th of July, and dine with them. The tables were soon up and loaded with inviting eatables, and I was invited to ask the blessing. The swine's flesh I knew was abominable, and unclean from creation (Genesis 7:2, 8) and God had positively forbidden the use, eating or touching of it by *law*. . . . I therefore quietly distinguished, and asked the blessing on the clean, nutritious, wholesome, lawful food. Some whispered, and some smiled, and others looked, and so on." Not surprisingly, we find Bates reporting a week after the Vassar meeting that he taught the subject of health reform to the congregation in the hope that "they will continue to learn how to live, and not be behind any of the churches in discharging their whole duty."[29]

As a result of his healthful living, Bates was the only one of the founders of Sabbatarian Adventism largely free of sickness. His first serious and prolonged illness appears to have hit him in 1859, when the 67-year-old evangelist found himself so sick that he couldn't preach. After a three hour train trip on the way home, he tells us, he took the water pail at the station house "and drank water enough to quench in part, the fire that seemed to be consuming my very vitals." A month later he reported that he was still recovering.[30]

Whether related to his 1859 illness we do not know, but the summer of 1860 found the intrepid traveler again laid up for several weeks with what appears to be the same problem. His rather surprised wife wrote that "Mr. Bates has been sick again with that Michigan scourge, fever, and ague [chills—he may have had malaria]. His health seems to be failing him. It seems strange indeed to have him sick. He has always enjoyed such perfect health. . . . I hope my kind Heavenly Father will continue to bless until he is restored to perfect health."[31]

After those two bouts of severe sickness, Bates may have wondered if his evangelistic days were over. But such would not be the case. He would continue his incessant itinerary for another 11 years. And during that time he would take time out to raise money for the Whites and John Loughborough (his much younger colleagues), who were recooperating at the health reform institute in Dansville, New York, at a time when the General Conference committee could not meet for almost a year because of the illnesses of the majority.[32]

James White (who died at age 60) would later write that in Bates' seventy-ninth year he "stood as straight as a monument, and could tread the side-walks as lightly as a fox." Beyond that, White noted that Bates claimed "that his digestion was perfect, and that he never ate and slept better at any period of his life."[33]

The fruits of healthful living appear to have paid off in the life of the man who can justly be set forth as Sabbatarian Adventism's first health reformer. But that crusade was only one of many in Bates' experience.

A BROAD-BASED REFORMER

One thing Bates hoped to achieve after returning from the sea was to forward the cause of moral reform. One of the projects he helped establish was the Fairhaven Seaman's Friend Society "for the moral improvement of seamen" in 1832. The document of incorporation has Bates' signature at the top of the list.[34]

Other causes that attracted his sponsorship in the early 1830s were foreign missions and the American Tract Society. But his enthusiasm for the latter society began to wane "when they manifested their unwillingness and determination not to publish any tracts in favor of the downtrodden and oppressed slave in their own land, when they were solicited by antislavery men to do so. It became manifest and clear that their professed unbounded benevolence embraced the whole human race, of all colors and complexions, except those who were suffering under their task-masters, and perishing for lack of religious knowledge within the sound of their voice, in their own churches, and by their firesides."[35]

In terms of racial issues, Bates early on became interested in the work of the American Colonization Society, which proposed to establish colonies in Africa for free people of color residing in the United States (a program later favored by such people as Abraham Lincoln and Harriet Beecher Stowe—author of *Uncle Tom's Cabin*—and many others in prominent positions). But that support disappeared with the rise of the abolitionist movement in the early 1830s. The abolitionists sought the immediate emancipation of all Blacks. That, however, was just what the colonizationists feared most, since "emancipation would saddle the nation with an intolerably large, unassimilable free black population." At that point many, including Bates, began to see the colonization movement as less than genuine. They began to believe that the colonizers were more interested in their own convenience than in the rights of the slaves. Thus abolitionist James G. Birney could claim that the Colonization Society acted as "an opiate to the consciences."[36]

The persecution of abolitionists in the early 1830s was severe, resulting in mob action, arson, and even murder. Such hostility shook Bates, who came to the conviction that the colonization societies were "the worst enemies of the free people of color," and that the societies desired to perpetuate slavery in the slave-holding states.[37]

Bates decided that he must cast his lot with the persecuted abolitionists. "I then began to feel," he wrote, "the importance of taking a decided stand on the side of the oppressed. My labor in the cause of temperance had caused a pretty thorough sifting of my friends, and I felt that I had no more that I wished to part with; but duty was clear that I could not be a consistent Christian if I stood on the side of the oppressor, for God was not there. Neither could I claim his promises if I stood on neutral ground. Hence my only alternative was to plead for the slave, and thus I decided."[38]

So it was that in the early 1830s he joined about 40 of his fellow citizens to form the Fairhaven Antislavery Society as an auxiliary to the New England Antislavery Society. That move, he noted, brought "down the wrath of a certain class of our neighbors," who called opposition meetings, denounced the antislavery party in "very severe terms," and threatened to break up its gatherings. Thus things were not any different for abolitionists in Fairhaven than in other parts of the northern United States in the early 1830s before the antislavery crusade became popular.[39]

Joseph was unsparing in his condemnation of slavery. Many of his remarks arose in response to the United States' war with Mexico from 1846 to 1848, which he, along with many other New Englanders, interpreted as an action to extend slave territory. In that context he referred to the United States as a "land of blood and slavery" and as a "heaven-daring, soul-destroying, slave-holding, neighbor-murdering country."[40]

His abolitionism put him in the same camp with such future Millerite leaders as Joshua V. Himes, Charles Fitch, and George Storrs, all active in the antislavery movement. All of those men, like Bates, also participated in other reform causes. Bates notes that he and Himes had worked closely in several reforms.[41]

One cause that both Bates and Himes were active in was the manual-labor school movement. In 1835 Himes initiated the establishment of a manual-labor school where boys could receive a book education and learn a trade at the same time. Meanwhile, their work would pay the costs involved. About the same time, Bates reports, I "erected a school-house on my place, in which I designed to have a manual-labor school for youth." His aim was to plant mulberry trees so that he could start a silk-worm industry, a project that captured the imagination of many American entrepreneurs during the 1830s.[42]

The manual-labor school movement was a widespread reform of the day. At the forefront of the concept were such institutions as Oberlin College in Ohio, founded in 1833 as a school that sponsored not only work/study programs, but such causes as abolitionism, equal rights for women, and Grahamite vegetarianism.[43]

It should be noted that the members of the radical, reformist wing of New England Protestantism, of which Bates was a part, tended to be interlocked with each other in a multiplicity of social issues in the 1830s. That unity would come to a halt in the 1840s when Bates, Himes, and many of the other reformers accepted what they believed to be the ultimate solution to all human injustice. Their new beliefs would separate them from the main line of social reform in their day, to the disgust of William Lloyd Garrison and others who had once worked with them. It is to that new movement that we turn in chapter 4.

Meanwhile, the late 1820s and the 1830s proved to be an important developmental period in Bates' life. During those years he not only became an initiator in social causes, but, more importantly, he learned to stand against the majority on unpopular issues. That was important since he would be doing more of the same for the rest of his life.

---

[1] J. Bates, Logbook, Aug. 9, 1827; J. Bates, *Autobiography,* pp. 209, 210; see also Logbook, Oct. 22, 1827; Godfrey T. Anderson, "The Captain Lays Down the Law," *New England Quarterly,* XLIV (June 1971), pp. 305-309.

[2] J. Bates, *Autobiography,* p. 210; cf. J. Bates, Logbook, Oct. 3, 1827.

[3] J. Bates, *Autobiography,* p. 211.

[4] *Ibid.,* p. 211; J. Bates, Logbook, Aug. 10, 1827.

[5] J. Bates, Logbook, Aug. 9, 1827.

[6] J. Bates, *Autobiography,* pp. 212, 221, 222, 229.

[7] J. Bates, Logbook, Nov. 24, 1827.

[8] *Ibid.,* Dec. 25, 1827.

[9] *Ibid.,* Nov. 24, 1827; Dec. 9, 1827.

[10] J. Bates, *Autobiography,* pp. 228, 230.

[11] J. Bates, Logbook, Aug. 27, 1827; Mar. 9, 1828; Mar. 16, 1828; May 4, 1828.

[12] *Ibid.,* Mar. 9, 1828; Mar. 11, 1828; cf. Mar. 16, 1828.

[13] Lyman Beecher, *Six Sermons on the Nature, Occasions, Signs, Evils, and Remedy of Intemperance,* 4th ed. (Boston: T. R. Marvin, 1828), p. 22.

[14] *Permanent Temperance Documents of the American Temperance Society* (Boston: Seth Bliss, 1835), vol. 1, pp. 21, 22.

[15] Quoted in Anderson, *Outrider of the Apocalypse,* p. 39.

[16] J. Bates, *Autobiography,* pp. 206, 207. For helpful treatments of the nineteenth-century temperance movement see W. J. Rorabaugh, *The Alcoholic Republic: An American Tradition* (New York: Oxford University Press, 1979); J. C. Furnas, *The Life and Times of the Late Demon Rum* (New York: Capricorn, 1973).

[17] Henry Steele Commager, *The Era of Reform, 1830-1860* (Princeton, N.J.: D. Van Nostrand, 1960), p. 7.

[18] Emerson quoted in Robert H. Abzug, *Cosmos Crumbling: American Reform and the Religious Imagination* (New York: Oxford University Press, 1994), p. vii. For helpful treatments of the reform era see Ronald G. Walters, *American Reformers, 1815-1860,* rev. ed. (New York: Hill and Wang, 1997); Charles I. Foster, *An Errand of Mercy: The Evangelical United Front, 1790-1837* (Chapel Hill, N.C.: University of North Carolina Press, 1960).

[19] Charles G. Finney, *Lectures on Revivals of Religion* (New York: 1835), p. 282, quoted in William G. McLaughlin, Jr., *Modern Revivalism: Charles Grandison Finney to Billy Graham* (New York: Ronald Press, 1959), p. 105.

[20] See Anson Phelps Stokes, *Church and State in the United States,* 3 vols. (New York: Harper and Brothers, 1950), vol. 2, pp. 12-20; William Addison Blakely, ed., *American State Papers on Freedom in Religion* (Washington, D.C.: Review and Herald Pub. Assn., 1943), pp. 187-208.

[21] "The Graham System, What Is It?" *The Graham Journal of Health and Longevity,* vol 1, 1837, p. 17; J. Bates, *Autobiography,* p. 234.

[22] J. Bates, "Experience in Health Reform," *Health Reformer,* July 1871, p. 21; J. White, ed., *Early Life and Later Experience and Labors of Elder Joseph Bates,* p. 314; J. Bates to E. G. White, Feb. 14, 1872; J. Bates, *Autobiography,* p. 234.

[23] J. Bates, *Autobiography,* pp. 138, 139; J. Bates, "Experience in Health Reform," *Health Reformer,* July 1871, p. 21; J. Bates, "My Experience in the Health Reform," *Health Reformer,* Feb. 1868, p. 120.

[24] J. White, ed., *Early Life and Later Experience and Labors of Elder Joseph Bates,* pp. 311, 312; J. White, *Bible Hygiene* (Battle Creek, Mich.: Good Health Pub. Co., 1890), pp. 252.

[25] J. White, *Bible Hygiene,* pp. 252, 253.

[26] J. Bates, *A Seal of the Living God: A Hundred and Forty-Four Thousand of the Servants of God Being Sealed, in 1849* (New Bedford, Mass.: Benjamin Lindsey, 1849), pp. 67, 68; J. Bates to Bro. and Sis. Hastings, Sept. 25, 1849; [J. White], "The Conference," *Review and Herald,* Mar. 23, 1852, p. 108.

[27] J. White, *Bible Hygiene,* p. 253.

[28] D. W. Reavis, *I Remember* (Washington, D.C.: Review and Herald Pub. Assn., n.d.), p. 32.

[29] J. Bates to E. G. White, Feb. 14, 1872; J. Bates, "Report From Bro. Bates," *Review and Herald,* July 24, 1866, p. 61.

[30] J. Bates, "Meetings in Ionia and Livingston Counties," *Review and Herald,* Nov. 3, 1859, p. 188; J. Bates, "Note from Bro. Bates," *Review and Herald,* Dec. 1, 1859, p. 16.

[31] J. Bates, "Reply," *Review and Herald,* Sept. 4, 1860, p. 128; P. Bates to Sis. Below, Aug. 12, 1860.

[32] J. Bates, "Letter of Condolence," *Review and Herald,* Nov. 21, 1865, p. 200.

[33] J. White, *Bible Hygiene,* pp. 254, 255.

[34] J. Bates, *Autobiography,* pp. 230, 231; Harris, *Old-Time Fairhaven,* p. 170.

[35] J. Bates, *Autobiography,* pp. 231, 232.

[36] *Ibid.,* p. 232; James Brewer Stewart, *Holy Warriors: The Abolitionists and American Slavery* (New York: Hill and Wang, 1976), pp. 29, 43.

[37] J. Bates, *Autobiography,* pp. 233, 235.

[38] *Ibid.,* p. 236.

[39] *Ibid.,* pp. 236, 237. For helpful treatments of the tensions between the colonizers and the abolitionists, see Leonard L. Richards, *"Gentlemen of Property and Standing": Anti-Abolition Mobs in Jacksonian America* (New York: Oxford University Press, 1970); Stewart, *Holy Warriors,* pp. 33-73.

[40] J. Bates, *Vindication of the Seventh-day Sabbath,* p. 88; J. Bates, *Second Advent Way Marks and High Heaps,* p. 48.

[41] J. Bates, *Autobiography,* p. 250. See also Ronald D. Graybill, "The Abolitionist-Millerite Connection," in Ronald L. Numbers and Jonathan M. Butler, eds., *The Disappointed: Millerism and Millenarianism in the Nineteenth Century* (Bloomington, Ind.: Indiana University Press, 1987), pp. 139-152.

[42] J. V. Himes, "Education," *Christian Journal,* Jan. 7, 1836, p. 1; Morrill, *A History of the*

Christian Denomination, p. 162; J. Bates, *Autobiography,* pp. 242, 243.

[43] Robert Samuel Fletcher, *A History of Oberlin College From Its Founding Through the Civil War,* 2 vols. (Oberlin, Ohio: Oberlin College, 1943); George R. Knight, "Oberlin College and Adventist Educational Reforms," *Adventist Heritage,* 8 (Spring 1983): 3-9.

CHAPTER IV

THE ULTIMATE REFORM: MILLERISM

A MAJOR transition of the first magnitude took place in Bates' life in 1839 when he accepted Millerite Adventism. William Miller had concluded from an examination of the time prophecies of Daniel and Revelation that Jesus would return to earth "about the year 1843." He had first come to that conclusion in 1818, but didn't start preaching it until the early 1830s. Yet it wasn't until the late thirties that his ideas made much headway. The most significant acquisition to the movement was Joshua V. Himes, a leading minister of the Christian Connexion, who began to accept Miller's message in December 1839. In the 1840s Himes would transform Millerism from being a rather backwoodsy movement into a nationwide and even worldwide phenomenon.[1]

BATES BECOMES A MILLERITE

Bates first encountered the concept of Christ's soon return through a local preacher. But that idea didn't make much progress in his mind until 1839. In the fall of that year he heard about Miller preaching in the state of New York that Christ would come about 1843. When Bates objected to the idea, someone told him that Miller used a great deal of Scripture to prove his point. Soon thereafter a Christian Connexion preacher identified as Elder R. invited Bates to hear him preach on the second coming of Christ. Bates attended and became "deeply interested." He was "very much surprised to learn that any one could show anything about the *time* of the Saviour's second coming." On the way home after Elder R's first lecture, Bates declared "*'That is the Truth'*" to his wife, who was also developing an interest.[2]

His next step was to obtain Miller's *Evidence From Scripture and History of the Second Coming of Christ, About the Year 1843,* a book of printed lectures. He was especially interested in Miller's treatment of Daniel's prophetic time periods. Bates wholeheartedly accepted Miller's teaching, thus becoming, as Everett Dick points out, "the earliest of all those who later became Seventh-day Adventists, to embrace and participate in the advent movement."[3]

Millerite Adventism progressively became the dominating influence in Bates' life, eventually usurping the time that he had previously devoted to social reform. At that point some of his friends asked him why he no longer attended the meetings of the temperance and abolitionist societies that he had been instrumental in starting. "My reply was," Bates told them, "that in embracing the doctrine of the second coming of the Saviour, I found enough to engage my whole time in getting ready for such an event, and aiding others to do the same, and that all who embraced this doctrine would and must necessarily be advocates of temperance and the abolition of slavery."[4]

Bates went on to tell his friends that "much more could be accomplished in working at the fountainhead" of the problem. After all, the vices that the various reform societies sought to eradicate were the product of a sinful existence. But when Christ returned there would be a "sudden and total obliteration of evil." Thus Millerism became for Bates what David Rowe has termed "the ultimate reform." For the Millerites, "corrupt humanity could not reform corruption." But the advent of Christ would circumnavigate that difficulty.[5]

Nor was Bates alone in such opinions. Himes and several other active reformers moved their focus from the social causes of the day to what they saw as the ultimate solution.

William Lloyd Garrison, a foremost abolitionist, found himself frustrated beyond measure when such talented leaders converted to Millerism. "Multitudes," he penned, "who were formerly engaged in the various moral enterprises of the age, have lost all interest in works of practical righteousness, and think and talk of nothing else but the burning up of the world.—Deluded people!" Again, he commented, "A considerable number of worthy abolitionists have been carried away by it [Millerism], and, for the time being, are rendered completely useless to our cause. But the delusion has not long to run."[6]

On one point, Garrison's critique was in error. Millerites had not lost "all interest in works of practical righteousness." Rather, they had lost faith in human ability to achieve a sufficient solution. Whereas Garrison taught that the best way to prepare for the millennium was to work for it in the present, and whereas Oberlin College's Henry Cowles believed that it was a "dreadful mistake" to think that "God will bring in the Millenium [sic] by a sort of miracle . . . without human agency," the Millerites held the Second Advent to be an immediate solution to slavery and all other problems.[7]

In essence, what was taking place was the confrontation of two conflicting millennial views, with a significant sector of the reform movement shifting from a postmillennial belief to premillennialism. Bates was a part of that major ground shift.

A MILLERITE ACTIVIST

Joseph was never one to sit on the sidelines. Throughout his long life he threw himself into whatever projects currently interested him. His activist stance was certainly true of his Millerite experience, during which he functioned as one of the movement's most prominent lay leaders.

The fact that Himes had lived in the New Bedford/Fairhaven community for several years in the early 1820s and had during that period belonged to the same Christian Connexion congregation as Prudence Bates had put him and Joseph Bates into early contact with each other. As Bates points out, he had been "intimately acquainted" with Himes and had "associated with him in the reforms of the day."[8] With those connections in mind, it is little wonder that we find Bates being pulled toward the center of the Millerite movement once Himes had in essence taken over as its director and manager.

One of Bates' first "official" positions in the Millerite movement began in mid-1840 when he became a circulation agent for its main periodical—the *Signs of the Times*. It was in that position that he brought H. S. Gurney into Millerism. Gurney notes that Bates was soliciting subscriptions for the *Signs* when he stopped by his blacksmith shop. Although Gurney had heard about Miller and his teachings, he didn't know much about them. His subscription "afforded me great help in my investigation of the second advent doctrine."[9] The two men, both from the New Bedford area, would soon team up as traveling evangelistic partners for the duration of the Millerite movement and for the early years of Sabbatarian Adventism.

October 1840 witnessed a major step in the development of Millerite Adventism. That month saw the meeting of the first "General Conference of Christians expecting the advent of our Lord Jesus Christ." "The object of the Conference," noted the announcement, "will not be to form a new organization in the faith of Christ; . . . but to discuss the whole subject faithfully and fairly, in the exercise of that spirit of Christ, in which it will be safe immediately to meet him at the judgment seat." The notice listed Bates as one of the 16 men calling for the meeting. The session appointed Bates, along with Himes and Josiah Litch (both of whom would be prominent leaders in the Millerite movement) and two others, to the committee in charge of arrangements. Interestingly enough, the *Christian Herald and Journal* (a leading periodical of the Christian Connexion) published a favorable report of the Boston meeting, listing Bates as a member of the business committee.[10] That harmonious relationship would deteriorate in the next few years, and Bates would have to decide where his true allegiance belonged.

Unfortunately for Bates and many others who had never met the man, William Miller was unable to attend the first Millerite general conference because of illness. Bates remedied his lack of a personal acquaintance with Miller by arranging for him to present a series of lectures at the Fairhaven Christian Church from March 15 to 18, 1841. At first he committed himself to giving up his seat so that nonbelievers in the Advent doctrine could hear Miller. But Bates soon repented. "After hearing his first lecture," he tells us, "I felt that I could not be denied the privilege of hearing the whole course, for his preaching was deeply interesting, and very far in advance of his written lectures." The meetings created quite a stir in the city and many were convicted. The next week Miller lectured two miles away in New Bedford, where several clergy expressed their agreement with his message.[11]

Bates served as an assistant chairman at the second general conference of Millerite Adventism, which met at Lowell, Massachusetts, from June 15 to 17, 1841. But it was at the Boston general conference in May 1842 that he would reach his apex of leadership in the Millerite movement. The 1842 conference was a pivotal event in Millerite history. Everett Dick characterizes it as "one of the most important gatherings ever held in the history of the advent movement." And David Arthur states that "the time for discussion had ended, the time for unquestioning propagation had begun."[12]

Under Bates' chairmanship the conference took three steps that would change the very nature of Millerite Adventism. The first involved coming out solidly for 1843 as the year of the end of the world. The conference leaders believed it was imperative to take a strong stand on the date "because of the stupidity of the Church on the subject and the shortness of the time we have to work." Until then the movement had remained divided on whether it should be somewhat precise regarding the date. Thus this decision was of major importance in committing Millerism to a timetable that would soon bring it into conflict with the denominations in which the movement's adherents still held their church membership.[13]

Second, since other religious groups had used them successfully, the conference decided to hold camp meetings in various localities. The delegates believed they would be "criminally negligent" not to utilize such meetings for spreading the message that Christ was coming in 1843. The holding of ever more frequent camp meetings would do much in the next two-and-one-half years to bring Millerite Adventism to the population of the northern states.[14]

The third major event of the May 1842 meeting was the presentation by Charles Fitch and Appolos Hale of an 1843 prophetic chart that graphically portrayed the prophecies of Daniel and Revelation and provided several ways of calculating the year of the end as 1843. Bates believed that Fitch and Hale had fulfilled the prophecy of Habbakuk 2:2: " 'Write the vision and make it plain upon tables, that he may run that readeth it.' "[15]

Joseph would be an ardent proponent of prophetic charts for the rest of his life, often displaying them in public places so that he could draw a crowd for his lecture. At one time, for example, he hung up his chart in the passenger cabin of a Long Island steamer headed for Massachusetts. "By the time we had sung an advent hymn," he reported, "a large company had collected, who began to inquire about the pictures on the chart. We replied, if they would be quietly seated, we would endeavor to explain." After they hit a storm, both preacher and congregation had to debark and to finish their journey by train. But Bates didn't give up. He and his trusty chart continued the message until they arrived at Boston station.[16]

One of his more interesting itineraries as a Millerite lecturer took place in early 1844 when he and Gurney decided to preach the message in the slaveholding state of Maryland. They may have gone in response to repeated appeals from the South for lectures on the Second Advent. The general conference held in May 1843 in New York sympathized with the need but decided to send only literature and not any preachers, since "the existing prejudices and jealousies of the South on the subject of slavery, renders it difficult and next to impossible" to fill those requests. The fact that most of the Millerite leaders had ties to abolitionism certainly didn't help matters.[17]

Past experience seemed to bear out the fears of the New York conference. After all, George Storrs (an ardent abolitionist) had been mobbed that very month in Norfolk, Virginia.

It was in that context that Bates and Gurney made their decision to head south, although Gurney at first intended to accompany Bates only as far as Philadelphia. People told Bates that if he tried preaching in the South "the slaveholders would kill me for being an abolitionist." They also warned him that travel was difficult in the winter and that he was a stranger to the culture. His friends asked him what he hoped to accomplish. But problems or not, Bates was under conviction. He could only reply that "God knows best."[18]

After experiencing some modest success in Maryland, he found himself challenged and denounced by a Methodist lay leader who attacked the "doctrine of the Advent in a violent manner." In the midst of his attack the man "began to talk about *riding us [out of town] on a rail*. I said," replied Bates, "'We are ready for that, sir. If you will put a saddle on it, we would rather ride than walk.' This caused such a sensation in the meeting that the man seemed to be at a loss to know which way to look for his friends. I then said to him, 'You must not think that we have come six hundred miles through the ice and snow, at our own expense, to give you the Midnight Cry, without first setting down and counting the cost. And now, if the Lord has no more for us to do, we had lief [gladly] lie at the bottom of the Chesapeake Bay as anywhere else until the Lord comes. But if he has any more work for us to do, you can't touch us!'" The *Newark Daily Advertiser* in reporting the incident noted that "the wreck of matter and the crush of worlds is but a small consideration to one who can take things so coolly as this."[19]

On another occasion on that same Maryland tour, a southern judge accosted Bates, saying that he understood that Bates was an abolitionist

who had come "'to get away our slaves.'" "'Yes, Judge,'" Bates replied, "'I am an abolitionist, and have come to get your slaves, and *you too!* As to getting your slaves *from* you, we have no such intention; for if you should give us all you have (and I was informed he owned quite a number), we should not know what to do with them. We teach that Christ is coming, and we want you all saved.'"[20]

At yet another time on this tour Bates heard from the local postmaster that the area ministers were so enraged with the two itinerants that they were talking about having them imprisoned before nightfall. "'Please give them our compliments,'" quipped Bates, "'and tell them we are all ready; the jail is so nearly connected with our place of meetings that they will have but little trouble to get us there!'" Bates went on to note that his real fear was not so much going to jail "as that these ministers would influence the people to shut us out from giving them the Advent message."[21]

Bates and Gurney were especially gratified in being able to give their message to slaves. At times they even walked from one appointment to another so that they would be able to talk to the slaves they met outside of the hearing of other Whites. And what was the response? "The poor slaves feasted upon it [the advent message], especially when they learned that the Jubilee was so near at hand. They seemed to drink it down as the ox drinks water, and from what I have since heard, I believe that many of them will be ready when Jesus comes."[22]

Not only did Bates publicly advocate the soon coming of Christ, but he also did so privately. He especially had a deep concern for his family. For example, on December 24, 1842, he wrote to his sister Sophia Bourne pleading with her to prepare for Christ's coming. "My anxiety for your complete salvation," he told her, "prompts me to give you the light which I fully believe God by his Spirit and word has imparted to my mind within a few weeks, taking history for the proof of the fulfillment of prophecy." Based on his understanding of the 1290 and 1335 days of Daniel 12, he had concluded that the Advent would take place on February 15, 1843, or six or seven weeks from the time he penned the letter. At that time he believed the righteous would rise to meet Christ in the air, while the wicked would remain on earth until the end of the 2300 day prophecy of Daniel 8 in April, at which time God would pour out the vials of His wrath.[23]

While Bates praised God for what was coming, he feared that his sister might think he was "crazy." To that sentiment he responded, "I feel and believe that I am coming to my senses. O what a tremendous hour this will be to the wicked. Let us see to it my dear sister that we are prepared for that eventful hour." Prudy, he added, joined him in his warning. On the letter a note is scribbled that Sophia needs to warn some of their other relatives.[24]

A GLIMPSE OF THE THREE ANGELS OF REVELATION 14

Before moving to the climax of the Millerite movement in 1844 it is important to examine its understanding of the three angels' messages of Revelation 14, since they would find a central place in Bates' Sabbatarian theology in the years after the Millerite disapointment of October 1844.[25]

In retrospect, it seems that Revelation 14 should have been a central passage in Millerite Adventism, since verses 6 to 12 provide a sequence of three consecutive messages that need to be given before the great Second Advent harvest in verses 14 to 20. But that focus wasn't there. That doesn't mean that the Millerites totally neglected the messages, but rather that they never emphasized them to the extent we might have expected, given their strategic position in the flow of the book of Revelation. Alberto Timm in his doctoral study concluded that Millerite authors dealt more fully with the first and second angels' messages than with the third.[26]

Timm points out that the Millerites defined the work of the first angel of Revelation 14:6, 7 from the perspective of its two main components. Up into the early 1840s they tended to stress that the mission of the first angel involved the preaching of "the everlasting gospel" to every part of the world, a task, they believed, that had been undertaken by the missionary and Bible societies that had arisen since the 1790s in Daniel's time of the end. The early 1840s, however, saw the emphasis change to "the hour of God's judgment," a message that Miller claimed would be proclaimed until "Christ shall actually come to judge the quick and dead at his appearing and kingdom."[27]

Thus in later Millerite understanding the hour of God's judgment was an executive judgment that would take place at the Second Advent. Bates accepted that position, but he did not neglect the earlier focus. To his mind the Millerites had already accomplished the worldwide preaching of the gospel message when they had sent their literature throughout the world during the early 1840s.[28] That belief would leave Bates and other Sabbatarian believers in the late 1840s with an extremely restricted view of their mission.

What is important to understand at this point in our discussion is that Bates and others believed that the first angel's message had been given through the Millerite outreach. That conclusion brings us to the second angel's message of Revelation 14:8, dealing with the fall of Babylon.

The central person in the development of the theology of the second angel was Charles Fitch, a leading Millerite minister. Up to 1843 Millerite authors generally accepted the Protestant tradition of identifying Babylon with the Roman Catholic Church. But by that year the ever increasing assertiveness of the Millerites, who still held membership in the various denominations, was bringing the situation in many churches to a crisis point. It was one thing to preach Miller's 1843 message when the Second Advent was some years off. But it was quite another thing when the proposed time began to loom on the horizon. An idea that seemed harmless enough in the late 1830s threatened to disrupt both churches and society by 1843. The developing "boundary crisis" was highlighted by the firm Millerite belief that God's demands took precedence over those of the church community. Thus the Adventists believed themselves bound by duty to sound their warning of the imminent end of the world even in congregations and denominations that did not want to hear it.[29]

The result was predictable. The various churches began to disfellowship Millerite "agitators," and Second Advent ministers began to lose their pulpits.

It was in that context that Fitch in July 1843 began to sound the second angel's message. On July 26 he published what became one of the most famous Millerite sermons, based on Revelation 18:1-5 and 14:8. After identifying Babylon as the antichrist, Fitch went on to suggest that "whoever is opposed to the PERSONAL REIGN of Jesus Christ over this world . . . is *Antichrist.*" That, he held, included both Roman Catholics *and* those Protestants who rejected the teaching of the premillennial soon coming of Christ. The Protestant churches had fallen in the sense that they, like their Catholic forerunner had become oppressive. Fitch then went on to proclaim that "to come out of Babylon is to be converted to the true scriptural doctrine of the personal coming of the kingdom of Christ."

He saw no way that one could avoid the advent truth and be a Christian. Thus, he appealed, "if you are a Christian, *come out of Babylon!* If you intend to be found a Christian when Christ appears, *come out of Babylon,* and come out Now!"[30]

With Fitch's call to abandon Babylon we have the beginning of Millerite separatism.[31] It was a time when advent believers, either through being excommunicated from their churches or having voluntarily left them, began to form identifiable adventist congregations.

Bates was a part of that exodus. He reports that some in his Christian Connexion congregation asked him to stop talking so much about the Second Advent. "'We like to hear you exort and pray,'" he reports them as saying, "'but we don't like to hear you say so much about the second coming of Christ, and the time.'" Then, after a pastor arrived who was against the advent message, Bates joined 32 members who withdrew to form an adventist congregation.[32]

Denominational periodicals, as we would naturally expect, saw the withdrawal of the Millerites as an irresponsible move. "It can no longer be doubted," reported the major Connexionist periodical, "that it is now the settled policy of certain leading *Adventists* to break up the churches of every class, as far as possible and build up a new sect of disorganizers with the fragments." They "proclaim themselves out of Babylon—free from all church connexion."[33] Bates, by way of contrast, would argue for the rest of his life that the second angel's message was an important step in the unfolding of Bible prophecy that God wanted proclaimed before Christ's return.

Whereas the first two angels' messages found some prominence in Millerite Adventism, Bates was quite right in noting that the movement had largely neglected the third message (Rev. 14:9-12).[34] And those few authors who did treat it saw the third message as the judgment pronounced on the worshipers of the beast. That was the position Bates would argue in 1847, although we should point out that he at that time restricted the third angel to verses 9-11, with the all-important verse 12 describing something that followed the completion of the work of the third angel.

The message of the three angels would be absolutely central to the Sabbatarian theology that Bates developed in 1846 and 1847. He would build upon Millerite understandings, but he would also transcend them in giving them a sequential emphasis not found in Millerite discussions and in stressing the third message, especially as it related to Revelation 14:12. We will return to this subject in chapters 7 and 9.

THE YEAR OF THE END OF THE WORLD

William Miller had never wanted to be too specific on the time of the Advent. He merely stated that to the best of his calculations it would be "about the year 1843." But by December of 1842 his followers began pressing him to be more precise. Thus in the very month that Bates calculated that Christ would come on February 15, 1843, Miller concluded that the Advent would take place between March 21, 1843, and March 21, 1844.[35]

Miller's dates left some room for flexibility. But as March 1844 approached excitement mounted among the Adventist believers. It was during that time that Bates sold his home so that he could pay his debts and could say that he "owed 'no man anything'" when Christ returned.[36]

The New Bedford office of the Register of Deeds records that Bates sold his home on February 6, 1844, for $4,500. About that same time he disposed of most of the rest of his property. What funds remained after he took care of his debts he then used to sponsor himself and others in preaching the advent message. Having once been quite well off financially, the ex-captain would live near the edge of poverty for the rest of his life. But that condition never stopped him from traveling and publishing for the forwarding of his religious beliefs. His favorite motto was "The Lord will provide."[37]

Needless to say, the final date for Miller's year of the end of the world came and went, leaving the disappointed Millerites still on Earth. After the passing of the last possible spring date, Bates tells us, "those who felt the burden of the message were left in deep trial and anguish of spirit." On the other hand, the non-Adventist public "were exulting with joy because of the failure of their calculation."[38]

The late spring and summer of 1844 was a difficult time for the advent believers. But they took some hope from Habakkuk 2:2, 3; Matthew 25:5; and Hebrews 10:36-39 that suggested they were in the tarrying or waiting time. "For the vision is yet for an appointed time," they read in Habakkuk, "but at the end it shall speak, and not lie: though it tarry, wait for it; because it will surely come."[39]

The next turning point came during a camp meeting at Exeter, New Hampshire, in mid-August 1844. Bates later claimed that he had a premonition that new light would emerge there; something that would give new impetus to the work of proclaiming the Advent. It was a difficult camp meeting, with neither speakers nor people having any assurance of where they were in prophetic history. The preaching may have been good, but it "failed to move the people." An unhealthy listlessness had settled over the believers despite the enthusiastic efforts of the leaders to buoy them up.[40]

Under those circumstances, participant James White tells us, Bates was doing his best in the pulpit as he preached the well-worn advent message to the people. Suddenly Mrs. John Couch interrupted him in midsermon when she stood to her feet and addressed both preacher and audience. "'It is too late, Bro. [Bates],' she called out. 'It is too late to spend our time upon these truths, with which we are familiar, and which have been blessed to us in the past, and have served their purpose and their time. . . . It is too late, brethren, to spend precious time as we have since this camp-meeting commenced. Time is short. The Lord has servants here who have meat in due season for his household. Let them speak, and let the people hear them.'"[41]

That "servant" was her brother Samuel S. Snow, heretofore a minor player in the Millerite movement. But Snow's presentation at Exeter thrust him to the center of the climactic phase of Millerism. His contribution centered on a new interpretation of Daniel 8:14 and the cleansing of the sanctuary.

Snow argued on the basis of scriptural typology that the Millerites had been in error in looking for the fulfillment of the 2300 days of Daniel 8:14 (which they equated with the second coming of Christ) to take place in the spring of 1844. Viewing the Old Testament ceremonial sabbaths as types and the ministry of Christ as antitype, Snow demonstrated from the New Testament that the feasts of Passover, First Fruits, and Pentecost had been fulfilled at the exact time in the year as in the annual celebration. "God is an *exact time keeper*," he reasoned. Snow then pointed out that "those types which were to be observed in the 7th month, have never yet had their fulfillment in the antitype."[42]

He next connected the annual day of atonement with the second coming of Jesus. Combining that finding with his conclusion that the 2300 day prophecy of Daniel 8:14 ended in 1844 (rather than 1843), Snow proclaimed that Christ would arrive on "the *tenth day* of the *seventh month*" of "the *present* year, 1844." Thus the Millerites began to look to October 22, 1844, as the fulfillment of Daniel 8:14.

It would be the day that the sanctuary (earth) would be cleansed (by fire), the day that Christ would come in the clouds of heaven.[43]

Snow's message took Adventism by storm. "When that meeting closed," Bates reported, "the granite hills of New Hampshire rang with the mighty cry, *Behold the Bridegroom cometh, go ye out to meet him!* As the stages and railroad cars rolled away through the different States, cities, and villages of New England, the rumbling of the cry was still distinctly heard. Behold the Bridegroom cometh! Christ is coming on the tenth day of the seventh month! Time is short, get ready, get ready!!" James White would note that the preaching of the seventh month message had an "almost irresistible" power.[44]

Looking back from October 30, Himes and the other editors of the *Advent Herald* in speaking of the seventh month movement wrote that "there seemed to be an irresistible power attending its proclamation, which prostrated all before it. It swept over the land with the velocity of a tornado, and it reached hearts in different and distant places almost simultaneously, and in a manner which can be accounted for only on the supposition that God was [in] it." Saying the same thing in a different manner, Bates wrote that "'the advent ship was making such rapid onward progress under her cloud of well-trimmed sails, that all the opposition of currents and adverse winds could not check her career.'"[45]

Millerism had reached its climactic phase. Believers with all their hearts expected Christ to appear on October 22. Bates, who by now was dirt poor, had a small crop of potatoes in the ground. His neighbors wanted to buy them, but he wouldn't sell. "'It would not be right to sell them to you,'" he told them, "'when I know that you will not receive benefit from them. Let them remain in the ground as a witness of my faith in the Master's immediate return to the earth.'"[46]

Believers awaited the Advent with full faith in its certainty. But Christ did not return. The effect on the people and the movement was crippling. Not only were they totally disappointed, but unbelievers scoffed as never before. Miller observed a few weeks later that "it seemed as though all the demons from the bottomless pit were let loose upon us. The same ones and many more who were crying for mercy two days before, were now mixed with the rabble and mocking, scoffing, and threatening in a most blasphemous manner."[47]

In like manner, Henry Emmons wrote: "I waited all Tuesday [October 22] and dear Jesus did not come;—I waited all the forenoon of Wednesday, and was well in body as I ever was, but after 12 o'clock I began to feel faint, and before dark I needed some one to help me up to my chamber, as my natural strength was leaving me very fast, and I lay prostrate for 2 days without any pain—sick with disappointment."[48]

Bates noted that "the effect of this disappointment can be realized only by those who experienced it." "Hope sunk and courage died."[49]

He later told John O. Corliss that he had only a few pennies left and that he had purposely allowed his provisions to run out. As a result, on the morning of October 23 he had to buy some flour and other items for his family. "'The boys of the street,'" he recalled, "'followed and hooted after me, and men pointed the finger of scorn at me, saying, "I thought you were going up yesterday."'" "'You can have no idea of the feeling that seized me. I had been a respected citizen, and had with much confidence exhorted the people to be ready for the expected change. With these taunts thrown at me, if the earth could but have opened and swallowed me up, it would have been sweetness compared to the distress I felt.'"[50]

The fact that Bates' only living son had sailed on October 21 as a crew member of the whaler *Marcus* probably didn't help his distress.[51] The boy was 14, almost a year younger than his father had been when he first went off to sea. The date is probably no accident. Being a typical teenager, the son was undoubtedly sick and tired of hearing his parents' preachings. Obviously leaving home as an unbeliever, he could have done nothing more calculated to hurt his father.

POST-DISAPPOINTMENT ADVENTISM: A TIME OF TENSION AND DISORGANIZATION

"Disorientation" and "disarray" are two words that help us capture the situation of Millerite Adventism after October 22, 1844. Whereas once the movement had known exactly where it was going and what it stood for, now it was in a state of uncertainty. What Adventists would later call the scattering time had arrived. As Bates put it, after the disappointment "some turned away and gave . . . up" their Adventist beliefs, "while a large majority continued to teach and urge that the days were not ended. Still others believed that the days had ended, and that duty would soon be made plain."[52]

The most basic theological dividing line among the various post-disappointment sectors of Adventism centered on whether anything had happened in October 1844. Those advocating that the date had fulfilled no prophecy became known as "open door" Adventists, while those claiming that it had some kind of a prophetic fulfillment were viewed as "shut door" Adventists. Thus one meaning for shut door was that October 22 had completed some aspect of prophecy. But that definition didn't exhaust the meaning of the terms for the Adventist community.

The open and shut door labels came from the Millerite understanding of Matthew 25:10, which states that when the bridegroom arrived the wise virgins went into the marriage with him while the door closed to all the rest. Miller, understanding the coming to the marriage to be the Second Advent, interpreted the closing of the door to be the ending of probation. Following Miller's lead, the 1842 Boston general conference of Millerite Adventists had resolved "that the notion of a probation after Christ's coming, is a lure to destruction, entirely contradictory to the word of God, which positively teaches that when Christ comes the door is shut, and such as are not ready can never enter in." Along that line of logic, and still believing that prophecy had met a fulfillment on October 22, Miller wrote on November 18, 1844, that "we have done [finished] our work in warning sinners."[53]

In short, the real issue was whether October 1844 represented the completion of some prophecy, with the shut door believers in the affirmative and the open door advocates in the negative. Those understandings had an intimate connection to concepts of mission. The open door Adventists came to believe in early 1845 that they still had a task of warning the world of impending doom, while the shut door Adventists concluded that they had completed their responsibility to humanity and that their only duty was to stir up and instruct other Adventists who had been in the 1844 movement.[54]

At first, Himes continued to have faith in the validity of the October movement. On October 30, 1844, for example, he wrote to Bates that it had been a blessing to him and that their faith had condemned the world. But he would soon conclude that October 1844 had no prophetic significance. Holding that they had been correct as to the event to take place at the end of the 2300 days of Daniel 8:14 (i.e., the second coming of Jesus), he reasoned that they had been wrong on the time calculation. On November 5, 1844, Himes stated that "we are now satisfied that the authorities on which we based our calculations cannot be depended upon for *definite* time." Although "we are near the end, . . . we have no knowledge of a *fixed date* or *definite time,* but do fully believe that we should watch and wait for the coming of Christ, as an event that may take place at any hour." Under Himes' leadership, his group took steps to organize itself into a distinct Adventist body at Albany, New York, in April 1845. By that time, in order to escape the fanaticism of some of the shut door Adventists, Miller had moved to the open door camp.[55]

For the rest of his life Bates would interpret the Albany experience as one of apostasy from biblical teaching. "I cannot help believing still," he wrote in May 1845, "that our position is right respecting the *cry at midnight,* and that we have been to the marriage and the door is shut—not half or three-quarters of the way—but effectually. And our fallen brethren [the Albany Adventists] will soon see their sad mistake!"[56] Bates would later devote much of his writing energy to what he considered to be the serious mistake made by the Albany group (see especially *Second Advent Way Marks and High Heaps,* [1847]). We will return to that topic in chapters 8 and 9.

Whereas the open door Adventists were able to unify at Albany, the shut door understanding eventually gave birth to two quite distinct orientations. The first, the "spiritualizers," got its name from the fact that it offered a spiritualized interpretation of the October 22 event. Concluding that the Millerites had been correct on both the time and the event predicted at the end of the 2300 days, the spiritualizers inferred that Christ had returned on October 22. That Advent, however, had been a spiritual coming to the hearts of the believers rather than a visible appearing in the clouds of heaven. Fanaticism and charismatic excesses plagued the ranks of the spiritualizers. In early 1846 Bates would publish his first book, *The Opening Heavens,* to combat their teachings. We will return to that topic in chapter 9.

The second strand of shut door Adventism agreed with the spiritualizers on the fulfillment of the 2300 day prophecy of Daniel 8:14 on
October 22, but disagreed with them on the nature of the event. In short,
the latter reasoned that the Millerites had been correct on the time but
wrong on what would take place. It is to this group that Bates belonged.

Millerite Adventism may have ended with a great disappointment for
Bates, but it was also one of the formative episodes in his life. Millerism
provided him with an apocalyptic focus that would shape his thinking
and his evangelism for the rest of his life. That apocalyptic focus will be at
the center as subsequent chapters reveal Bates' contribution to
Sabbatarian Adventism and later Seventh-day Adventism as the movement's first theologian and first historian.

---

[1] George R. Knight, *Millennial Fever and the End of the World: A Study of Millerite Adventism* (Boise, Idaho: Pacific Press Pub. Assn., 1993), pp. 70-73; William Miller, *Evidence From Scripture and History of the Second Coming of Christ, About the Year 1843* (Boston: Joshua V. Himes, 1842).

[2] John O. Corliss, "The Message and Its Friends—No. 2: Joseph Bates as I Knew Him," *Review and Herald*, Aug. 16, 1923, p. 7; J. Bates, *Autobiography*, pp. 243, 244.

[3] J. Bates, *Autobiography*, p. 244; Dick, *Founders of the Message*, p. 125.

[4] J. Bates, *Autobiography*, p. 262.

[5] *Ibid.*; David L. Rowe, *Thunder and Trumpets: Millerites and Dissenting Religion in Upstate New York, 1800-1850* (Chico, Calif.: Scholars Press, 1985), pp. 91, 92.

[6] W. L. Garrison to Elizabeth Pease, Apr. 4, 1843; W. L. Garrison to Henry C. Wright, Mar. 1, 1843.

[7] "Thoughts on the Second Advent," *The Liberator*, July 22, 1842, p. 116; H. Cowles, "The Millenium [sic]—No. 11," *Oberlin Evangelist*, July 7, 1841, p. 110.

[8] Isaac C. Wellcome, *History of the Second Advent Message and Mission, Doctrine and People* (Yarmouth, Maine.: I. C. Wellcome, 1874), p. 89; J. Bates, *Autobiography*, p. 250.

[9] H. S. Gurney, "Recollections of Early Advent Experience," *Review and Herald*, Jan. 3, 1888, p. 2.

[10] "A General Conference on the Second Coming of the Lord Jesus Christ," *Signs of the Times*, Sept. 15, 1840, p. 92; *The First Report of the General Conference of Christians Expecting the Advent of the Lord Jesus Christ* (Boston: Joshua V. Himes, 1841), p. 14; "A Conference Upon the 2d. Advent of Christ," *Christian Herald and Journal*, Oct. 29, 1840.

[11] J. Bates, *Autobiography*, pp. 253-256; Harris, *Old-Time Fairhaven*, pp. 127, 128.

[12] *Second Report of the General Conference of Christians Expecting the Advent of the Lord*

Jesus Christ (Boston: Joshua V. Himes, 1841), p. 2; Everett N. Dick, *William Miller and the Advent Crisis, 1831-1844* (Berrien Springs, Mich.: Andrews University Press, 1994), p. 29; David T. Arthur, "Millerism," in Edwin S. Gaustad, ed., *The Rise of Adventism: Religion and Society in Mid-nineteenth-century America* (New York: Harper & Row, 1974), p. 161.

[13] "Boston Second Advent Conference," *Signs of the Times,* June 1, 1842, pp. 68, 69.

[14] *Ibid.*

[15] *Ibid.*; J. Bates, *Autobiography,* pp. 262, 263.

[16] J. Bates, *Autobiography,* pp. 292, 293; cf. p. 287.

[17] J. Bates, *Second Advent Way Marks and High Heaps,* p. 14; "New York Conference," *Signs of the Times,* May 17, 1843, p. 85; J. Bates, *Autobiography,* p. 277.

[18] J. Bates, *Autobiography,* p. 277; J. Bates, *Second Advent Way Marks and High Heaps,* p. 14.

[19] J. Bates, *Autobiography,* p. 279; The *Newark Daily Advertiser* published the story on March 2, 1844. See Francis D. Nichol, *The Midnight Cry* (Washington, D.C.: Review and Herald Pub. Assn., 1944), p. 197. The story was first reported in the Baltimore *Patriot.*

[20] J. Bates, *Autobiography,* p. 281.

[21] *Ibid.,* p. 284.

[22] *Ibid.,* pp. 283, 285; J. Bates, *Second Advent Way Marks and High Heaps,* p. 13.

[23] J. Bates to Dear Sister [Sophia Bourne], Dec. 24, 1842.

[24] *Ibid.*

[25] For discussion of Millerism on the three angels, see Timm, "The Sanctuary and the Three Angels' Messages," pp. 52-65; P. Gerard Damsteegt, *Foundations of the Seventh-day Adventist Message and Mission* (Grand Rapids, Mich.: Eerdmans, 1977), pp. 45-48.

[26] Timm, "The Sanctuary and the Three Angels' Messages," p. 64.

[27] *Ibid.,* p. 53, 54; William Miller, *Wm. Miller's Apology and Defence* (Boston: J. V. Himes, 1845), pp. 30, 31.

[28] J. Bates, *Autobiography,* pp. 263, 269.

[29] For discussions of the "boundary crisis" and the second angel's message, see Knight, *Millennial Fever,* pp. 141-158.

[30] Charles Fitch, *"Come Out of Her, My People"* (Rochester, N.Y.: J. V. Himes, 1843), pp. 9-11, 18, 19, 24.

[31] See David Tallmadge Arthur, "'Come Out of Babylon': A Study of Millerite Separatism and Denominationalism, 1840-1865," Ph.D. dissertation, University of Rochester, 1970.

[32] J. Bates, *Autobiography,* p. 261; Harris, *Old-Time Fairhaven,* p. 128.

[33] "The Church in Haverhill, Mass.," *Christian Herald,* Mar. 28, 1844.

[34] J. Bates, *Autobiography,* pp. 301, 302.

[35] J. Bates to Dear Sister [Sophia Bourne], Dec. 24, 1842; William Miller, "Synopsis of Miller's Views," *Signs of the Times,* Jan. 25, 1843, p. 147.

[36] J. Bates, *Autobiography,* p. 277.

[37] Register of Deeds, New Bedford, Mass., Feb. 6, 1844. Cited in Anderson, *Outrider of the Apocalypse,* p. 50; Arthur Whitefield Spalding, *Origin and History of Seventh-day Adventists,* 4 vols. (Washington, D.C.: Review and Herald Pub. Assn., 1961), vol. 1, p. 123.

[38] J. Bates, *Autobiography,* p. 294.

[39] See Knight, *Millennial Fever,* pp. 165-178 on the tarrying time.

[40] J. Bates, *Autobiography,* p. 297; J. White, *Life Incidents* (Battle Creek, Mich.: Seventh-day Adventist Pub. Assn., 1868), p. 159.

[41] J. White, *Life Incidents,* pp. 159, 160; J. O. Corliss, "The Message and Its Friends—No. 2: Joseph Bates as I Knew Him," *Review and Herald,* Aug. 16, 1923, p. 7. It should be noted that the Exeter accounts by Bates and White vary, but their main point is the same; that the Exeter camp meeting changed the direction of Millerism.

[42] S. S. Snow, *The True Midnight Cry,* Aug. 22, 1844, pp. 1-4.

[43] *Ibid.;* "The Exeter Campmeeting," *Advent Herald,* Aug. 21, 1844, p. 20.

[44] J. Bates, *Second Advent Way Marks and High Heaps,* pp. 30, 31; J. White, *Life Incidents,* p. 166; cf. J. Bates, *Autobiography,* p. 298.

[45] "The Advent Herald," *Advent Herald,* Oct. 30, 1844, p. 93; J. O. Corliss, "The Experiences of Former Days—No. 2," *Review and Herald,* Aug. 4, 1904, p. 9.

[46] J. O. Corliss, "The Message and Its Friends—No. 2: Joseph Bates as I Knew Him," *Review and Herald,* Aug. 16, 1923, p. 7.

[47] William Miller to Bro. Orr, Dec. 13, 1844.

[48] Henry Emmons, "Letter from Bro. Emmons," *Day-Star,* Oct. 25, 1845, p. 6.

[49] J. Bates, *Autobiography,* p. 300.

[50] J. O. Corliss, "The Experiences of Former Days—No. 3," *Review and Herald,* Aug. 11, 1904, p. 8; J. O. Corliss, "The Message and Its Friends—No. 2: Joseph Bates as I Knew Him," *Review and Herald,* Aug. 16, 1923, p. 7.

[51] Melville Whaling Room, New Bedford Public Library. Cited in Anderson, *Outrider of the Apocalpyse,* p. 59.

[52] J. Bates, *Autobiography,* p. 300.

[53] Miller, *Evidence From Scripture and History* (1842 ed.), p. 237; (1836 ed.), p. 97; "Boston Second Advent Conference," *Signs of the Times,* June 1, 1842, p. 69; W. Miller, "Letter From Bro. Miller," *Advent Herald,* Dec. 11, 1844, p. 142.

[54] For a discussion of the three major branches of post-1844 Adventism, see Knight, *Millennial Fever,* pp. 236-325.

[55] J. V. Himes to J. Bates, Oct. 30, 1844, published in *Review and Herald,* Dec. 1850, p. 23; J. V. Himes, "Prophetic Times," *Midnight Cry,* Nov. 7, 1844, p. 150.

[56] J. Bates, "Letter From Bro. Joseph Bates," *Jubilee Standard,* May 29, 1845, p. 90; cf. J. Bates, "Letter From Bro. Bates," *Jubilee Standard,* June 12, 1845, p. 110.

CHAPTER V

BATES GETS THE SABBATH

L IKE most other Millerites, Bates suffered from not only disappointment but also confusion as 1844 moved into 1845. He belonged to that group that held that October 1844 fulfilled prophecy, but in early 1845 he was at a loss as to where they were in prophetic time or what God's will was for the future. Over the next two or three years he would continue to study his Bible as he sought to make sense out of his situation.

A major step forward in clarification took place in February 1845 when Bates accepted the seventh-day Sabbath after reading an article on the topic by T. M. Preble. A growing understanding of the Sabbath would eventually lead Bates into a fuller grasp of the end-time prophecies of Daniel and Revelation. But before we examine that, we need to look at the Sabbath in Millerism.

MILLERISM AND THE SEVENTH-DAY SABBATH

An interest in the seventh-day Sabbath among Adventists had originated before the October disappointment. J. A. Begg, a student of prophecy in Scotland, had first called it to their attention early in 1841. It is not known if Begg was a Seventh Day Baptist, but he did publish several articles and books through them beginning in the mid-1840s.[1]

The real push for the Sabbath in Millerism came from the Seventh Day Baptists. The first known attempt of that group to influence the Millerites took place in April 1842, but the *Signs of the Times* editors refused to publish the article, writing that "we wish to have no controversy with 'Seventh Day Baptists,' on the subject of the Sabbath."[2]

However, a felt need to spread the message of the Sabbath had begun building among Seventh Day Baptists.[3] The denomination had generally not been very aggressive, but that changed when their 1841 General

Conference session concluded that evangelism on the topic of the Sabbath was "required" by God. Then in 1842 the denomination's tract society "began publishing a series of tracts with the objective of 'introducing the Sabbath' to the 'Christian public.'" At their 1843 general conference session they once again resolved that it was their "solemn duty" to enlighten their fellow citizens on the topic.[4]

Their efforts had some positive results. At their 1844 meeting the Seventh Day Baptists thanked God that "a deeper and wider-spread interest upon the subject has sprung up than has ever before been known in our country." Part of that interest had developed among the Millerites. As a result, the *Sabbath Recorder* reported in June 1844 "that considerable numbers of those who are looking for the speedy appearance of Christ, have embraced the seventh day, and commenced observing it as the Sabbath." The *Recorder* went on to suggest that obedience to the Sabbath was part of "the best preparation" for the Advent.[5]

We do not know exactly what the *Recorder* meant by saying that "considerable numbers" of Millerites had begun to keep the Sabbath by the summer of 1844, but we do know that the issue of the seventh-day Sabbath had become problematic enough by September for the Millerite *Midnight Cry* to publish two articles on the topic. "Many persons," we read, "have their minds deeply exercised respecting a supposed obligation to observe the seventh day." The editors decided that *"there is no particular portion of time which Christians are required by law to set apart as holy time."* But "if this conclusion is incorrect, then we think the seventh day is the only day for the observance of which there is any law." The final article concluded with the thought that the "seventh-day brethren and sisters . . . are trying to mend the old broken Jewish yoke, and put it on their necks, instead of standing fast in the liberty wherewith Christ makes free." The article also suggested that Christians should call Sunday the Lord's day rather than Sabbath.[6]

The Seventh Day Baptists responded to the *Midnight Cry* articles by noting that "the new discovery of the Second Advent believers, which makes it morally certain to them that Christ will come on the tenth day of the seventh month, has probably unfitted their minds in a great measure for the consideration of the claims of the Sabbath upon their attention."[7]

Among those Seventh Day Baptists who interacted with the Millerites one of the more significant is Rachel Oaks. By early 1844 she had not only accepted the advent message, but she had also shared her Sabbath perspective with the Adventist congregation in Washington, New Hampshire, where her daughter (who married Cyrus Farnsworth) was a member.[8]

While at Washington, Oaks began to agitate the Sabbath issue. Her first convert, apparently, was her brother-in-law, William Farnsworth, the man who, it is claimed, had convinced her on the Millerite teachings. F. W. Bartle recalled another person who was brought to the Sabbath by her. Frederick Wheeler, a neighbor of Bartle's, told him that he had preached a sermon in the Washington church in which he remarked that all persons confessing communion with Christ should "be ready to follow Him, and obey God and keep His commandments in all things." Later Rachel Oaks reminded Wheeler of his remarks. "'I came near getting up in the meeting at that point,' she told him, 'and saying something.' 'What was it you had in mind to say?' he asked her. 'I wanted to tell you that you would better set that communion table back and put the cloth over it, until you begin to keep the commandments of God.' Elder Wheeler told me that these words cut him deeper than anything that he had ever had spoken to him. He thought it over, and soon he began to keep the Sabbath." That was apparently in March 1844. Subsequently several members of the Washington congregation joined Wheeler and William Farnsworth in observing the seventh-day Sabbath.[9]

BATES ACCEPTS THE SABBATH

But more significant than the conversion of any of the people in Washington, New Hampshire, was that of Thomas M. Preble, who was serving as the pastor of a Free Will Baptist congregation in nearby Nashua when he came into contact with Millerism in 1841. The exact connection is unclear, but Preble probably got the Sabbath from Wheeler, whose Washington congregation was about 35 miles from his home. He began to observe it about August of 1844.[10]

We have no record of any publications from Preble on the Sabbath issue before the October disappointment, although it is probable that he was a part of the agitation that resulted in the several responses published in the *Midnight Cry* in September to put a damper on the discussion of the seventh day. But in early 1845 he came out strong on the topic, publishing an article on the Sabbath in the *Hope of Israel* on February 28. He concluded his study by noting that "all who keep the first day for '*the Sabbath*,' are [the] *Pope's Sunday-keepers!!* and GOD'S SABBATH-BREAKERS!!!" "If I had but one day on this earth to spend," he declared, "I would give up error for truth, as soon as I could see it. May the Lord give us wisdom, and help us to keep all 'his commandments that we may have right to the tree of life.' Rev. 22:14." A 12-page pamphlet entitled *A Tract, Showing that the Seventh Day Should be Observed as the Sabbath, Instead of the First Day; "According to the Commandment"*[11] soon followed the article.

By April 1845 Bates had discovered Preble's article on the Sabbath in the *Hope of Israel*. He "read and compared" Preble's evidence "with the Bible" and became convinced "that there never had been any change" of the Sabbath to the first day of the week. "THIS IS TRUTH!" he declared to himself. And "in a few days," he reports, "my mind was made up to begin to keep the fourth commandment."[12]

Soon after making that commitment, Bates traveled to Washington, New Hampshire, to meet with Wheeler, the Farnsworth brothers, and other Adventists who had accepted the Sabbath. Wheeler's son George reports that Bates arrived at about 10:00 in the evening, "after the family were all in bed." George heard his father let someone in. And during the night he woke from time to time to hear their voices. "They talked all night long. When George and the hired man came down in the morning, they were introduced to Elder Bates, from Massachusetts." They discussed the topic until noon, perhaps with the Farnsworths and others included. At that point Bates headed home. H. S. Gurney tells us that Bates' trip to New Hampshire took place in April or May 1845.[13]

It was upon arriving home that Bates accosted James Madison Monroe Hall on the bridge linking Fairhaven to New Bedford and in response to Hall's query of "'Captain Bates, what is the news?'" told him that "'the news is, the seventh-day is the Sabbath and we ought to keep it.'" That led Hall and his wife into a Bible study on the topic. Within two weeks they also observed the Sabbath.[14]

Soon after meeting Hall on the bridge, the tireless Bates, H. S. Gurney reports, "came into our meeting with a little tract [undoubtedly Preble's] showing that we were keeping the wrong day for the Sabbath. He said he had examined it, and found it to be the truth, and he was going to keep the seventh day according to the commandment. A few of us investigated the subject, and came to the same conclusion."[15]

Gurney later reported that the Halls were Bates' first two converts to the Sabbath, while he was the third. In appreciation, the Halls named their only son Joseph Bates Hall. Gurney, for his part, would often accompany Bates on evangelistic tours, and at least once secretly paid the publisher for the printing of one of his friend's books when the captain had no funds.[16]

After his initial flush of excitement, Bates went through a period of doubt on the issue. "Contrary views did, after a little," he wrote in 1846, "shake my position some, but I feel now that there is no argument nor sophistry that can becloud my mind again this side of the gates of the Holy City." We see his temporary lack of conviction on the Sabbath illustrated by the fact that he reported in June 1845 that he and about 30 other shut door Adventists were meeting every "Sunday" as they awaited the Lord of the harvest.[17]

Merlin Burt appears to be correct when he attributes Bates' temporary doubts on the Sabbath to the fact that most of the Adventist proponents of Sabbath from mid-1845 up through early 1846 belonged to the fanatical wing of shut door Adventism and had moved the Sabbath away from Preble's emphasis on its relation to creation and the Ten Commandments, attaching it instead to some of their more questionable practices related to improper expressions of the holy kiss and mixed-gender foot washing. As Burt points out, Bates would be at the forefront in mid-1846 in both combating the errors of the fanatical wing of the shut door Adventists and in restoring the Sabbath emphasis to its relationship to creation and the Ten Commandments.[18]

At any rate, it appears that Bates' wavering over the Sabbath lasted only for a brief period. Gurney wrote in September 1845 that their Fairhaven/New Bedford group were "keeping his commandments, and expect in a few days, the return of their King." Bates would never again even begin to slip away from the Sabbath. Oral testimony has it that Bates would sit in prayer and testimony meetings, and, clapping his hands, exclaim with joy, "'Oh, how I do love this Sabbath!'" For him it was a preparation for that day when God would translate all His people from earth to heaven.[19]

Not everyone shared his enthusiasm for the Sabbath, however. His wife, for example, didn't accept the Sabbath until late 1850, even though Bates had written book after book on the topic and must have badgered her constantly. But he persevered and "kept the Holy Sabbath alone." Fairhaven tradition, reports Arthur Spalding, has it that "Captain Bates used to take his wife in their carriage to the Christian church on Sunday, but he himself would not enter to worship 'on the pope's Sabbath'; he would return for her after church."[20] That tradition harmonizes with everything we know about Bates.

Preble was another who had varying feelings toward the Sabbath. "After conscientiously observing the seventh day for the Sabbath, for about three years," he wrote in 1849, "I have seen satisfactory reasons for giving it up, and now keep the first day, as heretofore." In 1867 he published *The First-day Sabbath: Clearly Proved by Showing that the Old Covenant, or Ten Commandments, Have been Changed, or Made Complete, in the Christian Dispensation.*[21]

Commenting on the book from a Seventh-day Adventist perspective, Uriah Smith wrote that "the readers of the Review [sic] are already acquainted with the style in which Eld. P. has heretofore treated this question; and from the tenor of the foregoing notice, we have reason to suppose that he has not improved upon his former effort." In short, as we might expect, the Sabbatarians were happier with Preble's 1845 booklet on the seventh-day Sabbath. Preble's brother-in-law doubted his sincerity in the change back to Sunday. According to him, Preble had become the administrator of a large estate, and when the Sabbath interfered with his business, he gave it up. "The no law theory was his after excuse in the matter."[22]

But even though Preble rejected the Sabbath in his personal experience, he made an impact in the heart and mind of Joseph Bates that would eventually find itself in the core of an apocalyptic message that would spread to the far corners of the earth. But Bates, Adventism's apostle of the Sabbath, wouldn't be the only major leader of Sabbatarian Adventism to be influenced by Preble's 1845 tract. In the spring of that year (soon after Bates first read Preble) it fell into the hands of 15-year-old John Nevins Andrews and converted him on the topic of the seventh day. Andrews would later become Adventism's major scholar on the Sabbath, publishing the first edition of his important *History of the Sabbath and First Day of the Week* in 1873.[23]

And what happened to Rachel Oaks, the person who probably brought the Sabbath indirectly to Preble? She observed the Sabbath for the rest of her life, but did not join the Seventh-day Adventist Church because of certain rumors she had heard about James and Ellen White. Those rumors were cleared up in late 1867 or early 1868 and she was baptized a short time before her death. "She sleeps," S. N. Haskell wrote in her obituary, "but the result of her introducing the Sabbath among Adventists lives."[24]

THE LEGALISTIC TEMPTATION

No one can have the slightest doubt about Bates' devotion to the seventh-day Sabbath from 1846 to the end of his life. But his understanding of the Sabbath in relation to the plan of salvation is much less clear.

On the one hand, the good captain comes across as extremely legalistic. "Doing these commandments saves the soul." "The keeping of GOD'S SABBATH HOLY SANCTIFIES AND SAVES THE SOUL! but the keeping of one, or all the other nine without it will not." "We must keep the whole [law] if we would be saved." "God's children are to be saved, if at all, by doing or keeping the commandments." Such representative statements imply a serious legalism.[25]

One of Bates' favorite texts to support his legalistic approach to the Sabbath is the account of the rich young ruler in Matthew 19. Repeatedly Bates goes back to that story to make his point. "The young man came and said unto him, 'Good Master, what good thing shall I do that I may have eternal life?' Jesus answered, 'If thou wilt enter into life, keep the commandments.'" Bates interpreted that teaching to mean that "the only way, to enter life, was to keep the commandments." Furthermore, if Jesus did not mean what he said, "then he deceived the lawyer." Because of such statements, some Sundaykeeping Adventists called Bates a legalist.[26]

That he made legalistic claims related to the Sabbath is beyond question. On the other hand, he could also make gospel-oriented comments. In 1845, for example, he wrote that "God . . . pardoned my sins." Again about 1857 he observed that "all my poor services and a thousand times more could never pay the purchase of my redemption." Then in 1871 he could speak of God's "rich grace and pardoning mercy." And that is the language he had used regarding his experience at the time of his conversion, of which he had written that "God for Christ's sake did pardon my sins." He followed that statement with one noting that he had endeavored to walk according to God's will ever since then.[27]

The question is, what is the meaning of Bates' seemingly conflicting statements? Did he believe in salvation by law or salvation by grace? How can we harmonize the two perspectives?

One possible answer is rooted in Bates' understanding of where post-Millerite Adventism was in prophetic history. Between 1846 and 1847 he had come to believe that Revelation 14:6-12 represented a historical series of events. In that series, all Millerites had believed in the first angel of verses 6 and 7, the preaching of the judgment hour (Second Advent) message of Miller and his followers. Likewise, many Millerites had adopted the second message of verse 8 and had come out of Babylon by leaving their home denominations. He argued that if they had accepted the first two, it was only logical that they should receive the third message and the command to keep the commandments (including the Sabbath) of verse 12. It is also important to remember that Bates believed that the door of probation had closed in October 1844. Therefore it followed that he and his fellow believers had no special mission to the world at large, but *to those Adventists who had already accepted the first and second angels' messages and must incorporate the third and verse 12 before the Lord of the harvest of Revelation 14:14-20 could return.*

That picture of the times may help us resolve Bates' seemingly contradictory statements. From that historical perspective, he is appealing to people who had already been saved by grace and had accepted the Advent and even the first two angels' messages. But they needed, according to Bates' logic, to move forward into the third message and the observance of the Sabbath command. In that situation the necessity of accepting the full truth, including the need to obey all of God's commandments, begins to make sense.

Now let's listen to Bates, remembering that he equated God's covenant with the Ten Commandments. "Now all advent believers that have, and do, participate in the advent messages as given in Rev. xiv:6-13, will love and keep this covenant with God, and especially his Holy Sabbath, in this covenant; this is a part of the 144,000 now to be sealed. . . . All advent believers who despise, and reject this covenant, will just as certainly be burned and destroyed with the ungodly wicked at the desolation of this earth. . . . Every commandment in this covenant, must be kept to insure eternal life. Those that died before they heard the second advent message, never had this test. . . . Did you not know that Jesus taught eternal life through this same covenant also in Matt. xix:16, 17 [the rich young ruler]. . . . Finally, do you not know that God will reject you for despising his covenant in which is his holy Sabbath? . . . The present truth of which is the Sabbath, and the shut door [i.e., something happened on October 11, 1844]—It is impossible to keep one, and reject the other; whoever attempts it will fail."[28]

In that 1849 statement Bates is obviously speaking to Adventists who needed to take the final step in the chain of prophetic logic and begin to keep the seventh-day Sabbath. In that case the saving that comes with the observance of the Sabbath is not initial salvation but rather in faithfully following God in what Bates believed should have been clear to those who were familiar with the historic flow of Revelation 14. That logic shows up two years later when he writes that "all that are saved now, must keep the commandments of God, in accordance with the third angel's message.— Rev. xiv,12. No matter how much else we do, *if this third and last message is unheeded, we cannot be saved, any more than those who are now condemned for rejecting the first and second messages in verses 6-8.*"[29]

Such statements, deeply rooted in the post-Millerite shut door period of Sabbatarian Adventism, provide the most positive interpretation of Bates' seemingly legalistic statements. Unfortunately, they do not fully explain his language, since he continued to make legalistic statements after that historic period ended. In 1868 he again used the illustration of the rich young ruler and Christ's statement, "'if thou wilt enter into life, keep the commandments.'" "Thus," Bates concludes, "we have very carefully and prayerfully examined the testimony of prophets and apostles, and our Lord Jesus Christ, and the revelation of God, to the last promise in the prophecy, and find only one, and the very same, condition to inherit eternal life held forth to mortal man, and that is to keep the ten commandments of God. . . . Dear friends, if you really desire to have eternal life when Jesus comes, be sure, Oh! be sure, that you keep all the ten commandments of God."[30]

We need to couple that forthright statement with others that indicate in Bates a tendency toward legalism. Earlier we noted that by 1846 he would not eat fruit and vegetables, but only bread and water, because of some who ate fruit and vegetables between meals. Then in 1849 he argued that it was wrong to drive one's horse and buggy as little as three miles to church on Sabbath because that made a person responsible for forcing the horse to work. He claimed that the only solution was to either walk or travel to church before Sabbath and return home after the Sabbath hours. From his perspective, "we never need to fear of keeping the holy and sanctified Sabbath day too strict." Also he was quite certain that it was wrong for Adventists to be owning any property when the Lord returned. In a similar manner, according to Ellen White, Bates and others had made rebaptism a test "for others which the Lord has not bid them to make."[31]

Even the one recorded sermon we have from Bates on salvation is quite behavioristic and even perfectionistic. But it also provides the key for us to harmonize what in Bates appears to be a serious tension between legalism and the gospel of saving grace. "To be converted," he claimed in 1867, "is the beginning of our Christian experience. To overcome, is salvation and eternal life; the end of all our Christian experience. The requirement to overcome, we understand is addressed to all such as are converted, and their names written in the book of life. Some have supposed if they have once been converted and made just before God, that they should certainly be saved. Such are in a great error; for Solomon has said, 'There is not a just man upon earth, that doeth good and sinneth not.' Eccl. vii,20. *These sins then must all be overcome during our Christian experience.*"[32]

While his comment contains a great deal of truth, Bates' reasoning would take a strange course in Seventh-day Adventist history. By 1888, for example, Uriah Smith, George I. Butler, J. F. Ballenger, and others were teaching a belief in justification by faith built on the King James Version's misleading translation of Romans 3:25, which claims Christ's "righteousness for the remission of sins that are past." Thus Ballenger could write: "To make satisfaction for past sins, faith is *everything*. Precious indeed is that blood that blots out all sins, and makes a clean record of the past. Faith only can make the promises of God our own. But present duty is ours to perform. . . . Obey the voice of God and live, or disobey and die." That teaching put the emphasis on Christian living in terms of justification by works.[33]

Closely aligned was Smith's concept that "an enlightened obedience to all [God's] commandments" leads a person to Christ and is "the main point" of the third angel's message. Smith, like Bates, also used the rich young ruler of Matthew 19 to "prove" his position that those who wanted to enter eternal life must obey the commandments. Butler placed himself in the same camp when he argued that the whole point of the third angel's message is "the necessity of obedience to the law of God."[34]

It was just that line of legalistic logic that Ellen White, E. J. Waggoner, and A. T. Jones fought at the 1888 Minneapolis General Conference session. For her part, Ellen White, in looking back at the 1888 meetings, would claim that the essence of the third angel's message was "faith in the ability of Christ to save us amply and fully and entirely." On another occasion she would tie the third angel's message with "justification through faith" and "the gospel of His grace" that Adventism needed to preach so that "the world should no longer say that Seventh-day Adventists talk the law, the law, but do not teach or believe Christ." For her, obedience to the law was a fruitage of salvation in Christ rather than its foundation.[35]

Along that line, Ellen White's use of the story of the rich young ruler in Matthew 19 varied greatly from that of Bates, Smith, and Butler. Never did she quote Jesus in that context as saying that the way to gain heaven was to keep the commandments. Rather, invariably she pointed beyond what she called the "external and superficial" understanding of the young ruler (and Bates) to the deeper need of a total transformation that could only come through a personal relationship with Christ. To her the lesson of Matthew 19:16, 17 was not that one could gain salvation by the law, but that the rich young ruler had totally failed. While it was true, she pointed out, that he obeyed the external aspects of the Ten Commandments, he did not see that the law was rooted in the love of God. For her the rich young ruler had not been saved by keeping the commandments, but was totally lost.[36]

She and Bates stood worlds apart on the issue of salvation. While his approach to the rich young ruler's question was that one gained eternal life through obedience to the Ten Commandments, Ellen White wrote: "To every one inquiring, 'What must I do to be saved?' I answer, Believe on the Lord Jesus Christ," "all that is required of you is to take Jesus as your own precious Saviour." She was not, of course, against keeping the Ten Commandments and the Sabbath. But it was not the way to eternal

life. Rather, it was the way people who had already accepted eternal life
through faith in Christ now lived. Elsewhere, she could say that we can
"enter the goodly land if we keep the commandments," which could be
interpreted in a legalistic way. But, once again, she is not declaring, as did
Bates, that one gains salvation through commandment keeping, but rather
that those who are saved will walk with God in obedience.[37]

James White, the third founder of Seventh-day Adventism, was also
clear that obedience to the commandments could not save a person. "Let it
be distinctly understood," he wrote, "that there is no salvation in the law,
that is, there is no redeeming quality in the law." For White it was all important to have "living active faith in Jesus." Speaking of the Millerite message in 1850, he declared that it "led us to the feet of Jesus, to seek
forgiveness of all our sins, and a free and full salvation through the blood
of Christ." While James White appealed to people to "obey and honor
[God] by keeping his commandments," he also wrote that "we must seek a
full and free pardon of all our transgressions and errors, through the atonement of Jesus Christ, now while he pleads his blood before the Father."[38]

We will see in chapter 10 that the three founders of Sabbatarian
Adventism differed on several points. The topic of the law in salvation is
one of them. While the Whites could make what appear to be legalistic
statements, they definitely had a gospel orientation. And while Bates
could make what appear to be gospel statements, his basic approach was
legalistic—that salvation comes through keeping the law. Those two orientations have formed one of the ongoing tensions that the three founders
left to the movement they raised up.

In this chapter we have surveyed Bates' role in grasping the importance of the seventh-day Sabbath. That doctrinal teaching provided the
basis upon which he would begin to form a movement in 1846. Chapter
6 will take a look at his initiative in bringing together a core of like-
minded believers who would by 1847 and 1848 become an identifiable
Sabbatarian religious group.

---

[1] J. A. Begg, "Letter From Scotland," *Signs of the Times,* Apr. 1, 1841, p. 3.

[2] "To Correspondents," *Signs of the Times,* Apr. 6, 1842, p. 5.

[3] The best overall treatment of the interaction of the Seventh Day Baptists and the

Millerites on the Sabbath is found in Burt, "Historical Background," pp. 46-52.

[4] James Bradley, *Seventh-Day Baptist Register,* Nov. 17, 1841, p. 150, quoted in Burt, "Historical Background," p. 47; *An Apology for Introducing the Sabbath of the Fourth Commandment to the Consideration of the Christian Public,* Sabbath Tracts, vol. 1, no. 1 (New York: Sabbath Tract Society, James B. Swain, 1842), cited in Burt, p. 47; James Bailey, *History of the Seventh-Day Baptist General Conference* (Toledo, Ohio: S. Bailey, 1866), pp. 243, 244; see also *Seventh Day Baptists in Europe and America* (Plainfield, N.J.: American Sabbath Tract Society, 1910), vol. 1, pp. 185, 186.

[5] Bailey, *History of the Seventh-Day Baptist,* pp. 243, 244; George B. Ulter, "The Second Advent and the Sabbath," *Sabbath Recorder,* June 13, 1844, p. 2, quoted in Burt, "Historical Background," p. 48.

[6] "'The Lord's Day,'" Midnight Cry, Sept. 5, 1844, pp. 68, 69; "The 'Lord's Day,'" *Midnight Cry,* Sept. 12, 1844, pp. 76, 77; see also "The Lord's Day," *Midnight Cry,* Oct. 3, 1844, p. 100.

[7] George B. Ulter, "The Midnight Cry," *Sabbath Recorder,* October 10, 1844, p. 62; quoted in Burt, "Historical Background," p. 51.

[8] S. N. Haskell, "Our First Meeting-House," 1909 *General Conference Bulletin,* p. 290; Merlin D. Burt, "Rachel Preston—A Review of Her Life and Experience," unpub. ms, Nov. 1995.

[9] E. G. Farnsworth, "The First Seventh-day Adventist," *Review and Herald,* Feb. 21, 1918, p. 16; F. Wheeler, "A Message From Our Most Aged Minister," *Review and Herald,* Oct. 4, 1906, p. 9; F. W. Bartle to W. A. Spicer, undated letter (probably 1906), in William A. Spicer, *Pioneer Days of the Advent Movement: With Notes on Pioneer Workers and Early Experiences* (Washington, D.C.: Review and Herald Pub. Assn.), pp. 122, 123.

[10] Albert C. Johnson, *Advent Christian History* (Boston: Advent Christian Pub. Soc., 1918), p. 441; T. M. Preble, "The Sabbath," *Voice of Truth,* Aug. 27, 1845, p. 432.

[11] T. M. Preble, *Tract Showing that the Seventh Day Should Be Observed as the Sabbath, Instead of the First Day; "According to the Commandment"* (Nashua, N.H.: Murray & Kimball, 1845). The Feb. 28, 1845, issue of the *Hope of Israel* is not extant, but it was republished as T. M. Preble, "The Sabbath," *Review and Herald,* Aug. 23, 1870, pp. 73, 74.

[12] J. Bates, *Seventh Day Sabbath* (1846), p. 40; J. Bates, "Meetings in Michigan," *Review and Herald,* Feb. 8, 1870, p. 54.

[13] F. W. Bartle to W. A. Spicer, undated letter, in Spicer, *Pioneer Days,* p. 50 (report of an interview of George Wheeler by Bartle); H. S. Gurney, "Early Day Experiences Recounted by H. S. Gurney," unpub. ms, Apr. 12, 1896.

[14] J[oseph] B[ates] Hall to Melvin O. Bradford, Dec. 16, 1926; H. S. Gurney, "Early Day Experiences Recounted by H. S. Gurney," unpub. ms., Apr. 12, 1896. See also Joseph Bates Hall to W. A. Spicer, 1939, in Spicer, *Pioneer Days,* pp. 131, 132.

[15] H. S. Gurney, "Recollections of Early Advent Experience," *Review and Herald,* Jan. 3, 1888, p. 2.

[16] H. S. Gurney, "Early Day Experiences Recounted by H. S. Gurney," unpub. ms., Apr. 12, 1896; Charles H. Gurney to W. A. Spicer, undated letter, in W. A. Spicer, *Pioneer Days,* pp. 59, 60.

[17] Bates, *Seventh Day Sabbath* (1846), p. 40; J. Bates, "Letter From Bro. Bates," *Jubilee Standard,* June 12, 1845, p. 111.

[18] Burt, "Historical Background," pp. 271, 272, 256-260; cf. Clyde E. Hewitt, *Midnight and Morning* (Charlotte, N.C.: Venture Books, 1983), p. 186.

[19] H. S. Gurney, "Letter From Bro. Gurney," *Day-Star,* Oct. 11, 1845, p. 45; W. A. Spicer, *Pioneer Days,* p. 128; J. Bates, *Autobiography,* pp. 302, 303.

[20] [J. White], "Conferences," *Advent Review,* Nov. 1850, p. 72; Spalding, *Origin and History of Seventh-day Adventists,* vol. 1, p. 130, n. 15.

[21] T. M. Preble, "From Bro. T. M. Preble," *Harbinger and Advocate,* Oct. 6, 1849, p. 127; T. M. Preble, "Letter from T. M. Preble," *Advent Herald,* July 3, 1852, p. 214; The Western Advent Christian Publishing Association published Preble's book in Buchanan, Michigan, in 1867.

[22] [U. Smith], "Book Notice," *Review and Herald,* Aug. 6, 1867, p. 128; J. N. Loughborough, "Apostolic and Adventist Experience Compared," unpub. ms., n.d.

[23] Mrs. M. C. Stowell Crawford, "A Letter From a Veteran Worker," *Southern Watchman,* Apr. 25, 1905, p. 278.

[24] S. N. Haskell, obituary of Rachel Oaks Preston, *Review and Herald,* Mar. 3, 1868, p. 190.

[25] J. Bates, *Seventh Day Sabbath: A Perpetual Sign, From the Beginning, to the Entering into the Gates of the Holy City, According to the Commandment,* 2nd ed. rev. and enl. (New Bedford, Mass.: Benjamin Lindsey, 1847), pp. iii, 55, 56; J. Bates, *Second Advent Way Marks and High Heaps,* p. 79. See also, J. Bates, *Seventh Day Sabbath* (1847), p. 57; J. Bates, *Opening Heavens,* pp. 1, 36; J. Bates, *Vindication of the Seventh-day Sabbath,* p. 27; J. Bates in J. White, ed., *A Word to the "Little Flock,"* (n.p.: James White, 1847), p. 21; J. Bates, "New Testament Seventh Day Sabbath," *Review and Herald,* Jan. 1851, p. 32.

[26] J. Bates, "New Testament Testimony," *Review and Herald,* Dec. 1850, pp. 10-13; J. Bates, *Seventh Day Sabbath* (1846), p. 19, 26; H. C. R., "Bro Cole," *Bible Advocate,* July 29, 1847, p. 206. See also J. Bates, *Vindication of the Seventh-day Sabbath,* p. 5.

[27] J. Bates, "Letter From Bro. Joseph Bates," *Jubilee Standard,* May 29, 1845, p. 90; J. Bates to Church in Monterey and Allegan, cir. 1857; J. Bates, "Experience in Health Reform," *Health Reformer,* July 1871, p. 21; J. Bates to Parents, Sept. 26, 1827. See also J. Bates, *Autobiography,* pp. 43, 44; J. Bates, Logbook, Jan. 20, 1828; Jan. 28, 1828; Apr. 4, 1828.

[28] J. Bates, *Seal of the Living God,* pp. 61, 62, 64, 65.

[29] J. Bates, "Duty to Our Children," *Review and Herald,* Jan. 1851, p. 39 (italics supplied).

[30] J. Bates, "The Perpetuity of God's Commanded Covenant of Ten Commandments," *Review and Herald,* Oct. 27, 1868, p. 218.

[31] J. White, ed., *Early Life and Later Experience and Labors of Elder Joseph Bates,* pp. 311, 312; J. Bates, *Vindication of the Seventh-day Sabbath,* pp. 67, 77, 79; E. G. White to G. I. Butler, Dec. 13, 1886.

[32] J. Bates, "Experience of Repairers, and Restorers of Paths to Dwell In," *Review and Herald,* Dec. 10, 1867, p. 401 (italics supplied).

[33] J. F. Ballenger, "Justification by Works," *Review and Herald,* Oct. 20, 1891, p. 642.

[34] [U. Smith], "The Main Point," *Review and Herald,* Jan. 3, 1888, p. 8; [U. Smith], "Conditions of Everlasting Life," *Review and Herald,* Jan. 31, 1888, p. 72; G. I. Butler, "The Righteousness of the Law Fulfilled by Us," *Review and Herald,* May 14, 1889, pp. 313, 314. For a fuller discussion on the 1888 struggle over legalism, see George R. Knight, *Angry Saints: Tensions and Possibilities in the Adventist Struggle Over Righteousness by Faith* (Washington, D.C.: Review and Herald Pub. Assn., 1989), pp. 45-60.

[35] E. G. White, "Looking Back at Minneapolis," Ms 24, cir. Nov. or Dec. 1888; Ellen G. White, *Testimonies to Ministers* (Mountain View, Calif.: Pacific Press, 1962), pp. 91, 92.

[36] Ellen G. White, *Spiritual Gifts* (Battle Creek, Mich.: James White, 1860), vol. 2, pp. 239-243; Ellen G. White, *The Desire of Ages* (Mountain View, Calif.: Pacific Press Pub. Assn., 1940), pp. 518-523; Ellen G. White, *Christ's Object Lessons* (Washington, D.C.: Review and Herald Pub. Assn., 1941), pp. 390-392.

[37] E. G. White to Sister Lizzie, Feb. 21, 1891; E. G. White to Bro. and Sis. Hastings, Apr. 21, 1849.

[38] J. White, *Life Incidents,* p. 354; J. White, "Dear Brethren and Sisters," *Present Truth,* July 1849, p. 6; J. White, "The Third Angel's Message," *Present Truth,* Apr. 1850, pp. 66, 69.

CHAPTER VI

CATALYST FOR A MOVEMENT

BY 1845 the disappointed Adventists had only one passion: the delayed coming of Christ. They were convicted that it had to be soon. Some expected it in the spring of 1845, while others held to a fall date. H. S. Gurney took the latter position. Writing from New Bedford on September 29 he noted that "there is a little remnant in this vicinity who have not denied the *Name* of our King, and are determined not to return to Egypt. . . . We meet together, and Jesus meets with us: He loves us and we love to keep his commandments." "In a few days" he and his commandment-keeping group expected "the return of their King." Bates was a member of that anticipating congregation.[1]

In the same issue of the *Day-Star* in which we find Gurney's article appears another by a young Connexionist preacher as yet unknown to Gurney and Bates. He also was expecting Christ's return in October 1845. James White indicated that he was standing firm on the truth, but that some had tripped over "a wile of the Devil" by announcing their marriage. By doing so they had "denied their faith" in the soon-coming Second Advent. "The firm brethren in Maine who are waiting for Christ to come have no fellowship with such a move." That anti-marriage view, he later noted, was held in 1845 by "most of our brethren," since "such a step seemed to contemplate years of life in this world."[2]

Gurney, Bates, White, and the others who looked to an 1845 date would once again be frustrated. But they didn't give up their faith that God had guided the Adventist movement. Rather, as Bates points out, they continued to study their Bibles in an attempt to understand where they had gone wrong.[3] By early 1845, as we saw in chapter 5, some of them (including Bates) had already discovered the importance of the seventh-day Sabbath. But at the same time a second Bible teaching also began to unfold.

A NEW PERSPECTIVE ON DANIEL 8:14

That second teaching had to do with Daniel 8:14 ("Unto two thousand and three hundred days; then shall the sanctuary be cleansed"), a text that had led Miller to expect the return of Christ in 1844. But it became progressively clearer that the sanctuary of Daniel 8:14 could not be the earth as Miller had taught and that the cleansing was not the Second Advent. However, it was one thing to come to those negative conclusions, but quite another to determine the actual nature of the sanctuary and its cleansing.

Josiah Litch, one of the foremost Millerite preachers, had expressed doubts as to Miller's interpretation of the cleansing of the sanctuary after the spring 1844 disappointment. "It has not been proved," he observed in April 1844, "that the cleansing of the sanctuary, which was to take place at the end of the 2300 days, was the coming of Christ or the purification of the earth." Again he noted as he wrestled with the meaning of the recent disappointment, that they were most likely to be "in error relative to the event which marked the close."[4]

That line of thought arose again soon after the October 1844 disappointment. Thus Joseph Marsh could write in early November: "We cheerfully admit that we have been mistaken in the *nature* of the event we expected would occur on the tenth [day] of the seventh month, but we cannot yet admit that our great High Priest did not *on that very day,* accomplish *all* that the type would justify us to expect."[5]

Appolos Hale and Joseph Turner treated the issue in an article in January 1845. They equated the October 22 event with the coming of Christ to the Ancient of Days (God) in the judgment scene of Daniel 7. The two men concluded that "the coming of the bridegroom" indicated "some change of work or office, on the part of our Lord." Christ would return to earth to gather His elect *after* His work "within the veil—where he has gone to prepare a place for us" is completed. As a result, "some time must elapse" between the coming of the Bridegroom to the Ancient of Days and the coming in glory. Hale and Turner went on to indicate that *"the judgment is here!"*[6]

It would be some heretofore minor actors in the Advent drama who would develop the fullest exposition of the ideas suggested by Litch, Marsh, Hale, and Turner. One of those people would be O.R.L. Crosier, who periodically lived with an Adventist by the name of Hiram Edson in western New York. Edson would later claim that on the morning after the October disappointment he had had a vision that the sanctuary that needed to be cleansed was in heaven rather than on earth. That understanding, he claims, led him, Crosier, and a local physician by the name of F. B. Hahn into an extended Bible study on the topic.[7]

Crosier began to print his findings on the topic in March 1845 in the *Day-Dawn*. By that time he had concluded that the mediatorial work of Christ in the heavenly sanctuary consisted of two parts, "typified by the two apartments or services in the two apartments of the tabernacle." The first aspect involved "intercession for transgressors" while the second consisted of a work of "final atonement" that began in October 1844.[8]

Crosier wasn't the only shut door Adventist studying out the topic of Christ's ministry in the heavenly sanctuary in early 1845. Another was Emily Clemons, who published her findings in a periodical graphically entitled *Hope Within the Veil*. And a third was G. W. Peavey, who was teaching in April 1845 that Christ had "closed the work typified by the daily ministrations previous to the 10th day of the 7th month, and on that day went into the holiest of all." Peavey also saw an interrelationship between Daniel 8:14, Hebrews 9:23, and Leviticus 16 and concluded that the Most Holy Place of the heavenly sanctuary needed purification by Christ's blood on the antitypical day of atonement.[9]

On February 7, 1846, Crosier published his most significant article on the topic of Christ's ministry in the heavenly sanctuary. We can summarize his most important conclusions as follows: (1) A literal sanctuary exists in heaven. (2) The Hebrew sanctuary system offered a complete visual representation of the plan of salvation patterned after the heavenly sanctuary. (3) Just as the earthly priests had a two-phase ministry in the wilderness sanctuary, so Christ had a two-phase ministry in the heavenly. The first phase began in the holy place at His ascension, the second on October 22, 1844, when Christ moved from the first apartment of the heavenly sanctuary to the second. Thus the antitypical heavenly Day of Atonement started on that date. (4) The first phase of Christ's ministry dealt with forgiveness, while the second involves the blotting out of sins and the cleansing of both the sanctuary and individual believers. (5) The cleansing of Daniel 8:14 was a purification from sin and therefore was accomplished by blood rather than by fire. (6) Christ would not return to earth until He completed His second-apartment heavenly ministry.[10]

Joseph Bates, who was also looking for answers on the cleansing of the sanctuary of Daniel 8:14, read Crosier's article. "Allow me," he wrote in April or May 1846, "to recommend to your particular notice, O.R.L. Crosier's article in the Day Star Extra [sic], for the 7th of February, 1846, from the 37th to the 44th page. Read it again. In my humble opinion it is superior to any thing of the kind extant." Crosier's line of argument so impressed Bates that in May 1846 he secured the copyright to his first book in the name of "Him that sits upon the Throne in the . . . Heavenly Sanctuary."[11]

Nor was Bates the only shut door Adventist intrigued by Crosier's February 1846 article. Ellen White, writing in April 1847, noted that "the Lord shew me in vision, more than one year ago, that Brother Crosier had the true light, on the cleansing of the Sanctuary, &c; and that it was his will, that Brother C. should write out the view which he gave us in the Day-Star, Extra [sic], February 7, 1846."[12]

In early 1846 Bates had not yet met Crosier, Edson, or Hahn and most likely had not met James White or Ellen Harmon. But he would go out of his way to contact all of them before the end of 1846. Those encounters would not only change his life, they would prepare the way for the rise of the Sabbatarian Adventist movement in 1847 and 1848.

ENTER JAMES AND ELLEN WHITE

James White probably first met Bates in August 1846 when he and Miss Ellen Harmon visited New Bedford, Massachusetts. Bates, being his usual aggressive self, gave the young couple a Bible study on the topic of the Sabbath. But he apparently came on too forcefully. He "was keeping the Sabbath," Ellen wrote, "and urged its importance. I did not feel its importance, and thought that Bro. B. erred in dwelling upon the fourth commandment more than the other nine."[13] That Bible study was one of the most remarkable failures of Bates' entire career.

But the encounter with Bates wasn't the only significant event for the Whites that August. Another was the marriage of James White and Ellen Harmon on the thirtieth of the month in Portland, Maine. As we might expect, James was quite sensitive to the event, since less than a year before he had condemned others for marrying, claiming it was merely a sign of their disbelief in the soon-coming of the Lord. But time had not ended as soon as he had expected. "God had a work for both of us to do," he later explained in relationship to his marriage, "and he saw that we could greatly assist each other in that work." After all, 18-year-old Ellen needed a "lawful protector" if she was to travel the country bearing her "important . . . message to the world."[14] That adjustment would be one of several as those who were becoming Sabbatarians gradually realized that their work on earth wasn't finished yet.

Another significant event in August 1846 was the publication of Bates' first little book on the Sabbath—*The Seventh Day Sabbath, A Perpetual Sign, From the Beginning to the Entering Into the Gates of the Holy City, According to the Commandment*. That 48-page volume soon fell into the hands of the newly-married Whites. By reading that "little pamphlet," James writes, "I was established upon the Sabbath and began to teach it." Ellen White, while not mentioning Bates' book, recalls that "in the autumn of 1846 we began to observe the Bible Sabbath, and to teach and defend it."[15] Bates, ever the evangelist, had made converts of the two people who would be instrumental with him in the formation of Sabbatarian Adventism (and later Seventh-day Adventism).

But at that point the Sabbatarians were a small group indeed. Whereas many of the more fanatical elements among the shut door believers had observed the Sabbath earlier in 1845, by the autumn of 1846 that group had largely dissipated. As a result, few Sabbathkeepers remained among the Adventists. "When we received the light upon the fourth commandment," Ellen White wrote, "there were about twenty-five Adventists in Maine who observed the Sabbath; but these were so diverse in sentiment upon other points of doctrine, and so scattered in location, that their influence was very small. There was about the same number, in similar condition, in other parts of New England."[16] Truly confusion reigned. If anything was to come out of the efforts of Bates and his friends they would have to do a great amount of work.

Ellen White had a vision regarding the holiness of the Sabbath in April 1847. Later some apparently concluded that she had first accepted the Sabbath because of her vision. But she was quick to deny that perspective, writing that "I believed the truth upon the Sabbath question before I had seen anything in vision in reference to the Sabbath. It was months after I had commenced keeping the Sabbath before I was shown

JOSEPH BATES'
WORLD

Earliest known picture of Joseph
Bates, painted when he was
approximately 26 years old.

Abigail Hall, wife of James Madison Monroe Hall. Her husband met Bates on Fairhaven Bridge and became his first convert. She was converted soon after.

H. S. Gurney was Bate's evengelistic partner on many of his travels.

Joseph Bates is assumed to have attended Fairhaven Academy, an institution his father helped build in Fairhaven, Massachusetts.

Dartmoor Prison where the British government confined Bates as a prisoner of war.

Prudence Bates,
Joseph's wife of 52 years

Joseph Bates through the years

Above: Rachel Oaks, a widow, married Nathan Preston in 1843, the same year she moved to New Hampshire to be with her daughter. She brought the Sabbath to the Washington, New Hampshire, Millerites.

Left: Frederick Wheeler about 1860. He was the pastor of the Washington, New Hampshire, church in the spring of 1844 when Rachel Oaks arrived with her Sabbath message.

Bottom: Thomas Preble apparently received the seventh-day Sabbath from the Washington, New Hampshire, congregation. In 1845 he wrote the article and tract that convicted Bates of the importance of the Sabbath.

The Washington, New Hampshire, church

The Acushnet River
bridge connecting
Fairhaven and New
Bedford. It was on this
bridge that Bates met
James Madison Monroe
Hall with the message of
the Sabbath.

James and Ellen White, who with Bates became the cofounders of the Seventh-day Adventist Church.

Hiram Edison, who early on studied out the heavenly sanctuary idea with O.R.L. Crosier and accepted the Sabbath from Bates in late 1846.

M. E. Cornell, first-day Adventist brought into Sabbatarianism in Jackson, Michigan. He soon became one of the movement's most successful evangelists.

The Bates family home in Fairhaven. Joseph built it for Prudy after he left the sea, then sold it in February 1844.

its importance and its place in the third angel's message." [17]

The sharing between Bates and the Whites in the autumn of 1846 proved to be a two-way process. He may have provided them with an understanding of the importance of the seventh-day Sabbath, but they helped him to better understand spiritual gifts.

Ellen White had been having visionary experiences since December 1844. Bates after witnessing her in vision several times, declared himself to be a "'doubting Thomas.'" "'I do not believe in [her] visions,'" he said. "'But if I could believe that the testimony the sister has related to-night was indeed the voice of God to us, I should be the happiest man alive.'" He claimed to be deeply moved by her messages, believed she was sincere, and was somewhat mystified as to her experience. "Although I could see nothing in [the visions] that militated against the word," he later wrote, "yet I felt alarmed and tried exceedingly, and for a long time [was] unwilling to believe that it was any thing more than what was produced by a protracted debilitated state of her body." [18]

But even though he had his doubts, he did not just tune her out. Coming out of the Christian Connexion, he was at least open to the idea that the New Testament gifts of the Holy Spirit (including that of prophecy) would remain active in the church until the return of Christ. [19]

As a result, Bates decided to investigate what Ellen believed to be a divine gift of prophecy. "I therefore," he penned, "sought opportunities in presence of others, when her mind seemed freed from excitement, (out of meeting) to question, and cross question her, and her friends which accompanied her, especially her elder sister, to get if possible at the truth." When she was in vision, Bates added, "I listened to every word, and watched every move to detect deception, or mesmeric influences." [20]

The turning point came in November 1846 in Topsham, Maine, when Ellen White had a vision that included astronomical data. As an ex-seaman Bates was well acquainted with the topic. In fact, his first book, published earlier that year, was entitled *The Opening Heavens*. Much of the first 10 pages dealt with astronomic detail, indicating both his interest and grasp of the topic.

In November 1857 he told J. N. Loughborough of his experience that night in Topsham. "The account of how he," a person who had doubted the genuineness of her claim, "became convinced of the truthfulness of

Sr. White's visions, was of deep interest to me," Loughborough wrote. "One evening, in the presence of Bro. Bates, who as yet was an unbeliever in the visions, Sr. White had a vision, in which she soon began to talk about the stars. She gave a glowing description of the rosy-tinted belts which she saw across the surfce of some planet, and then added, 'I see four moons.' 'Oh,' said Bro. Bates, 'she is viewing *Jupiter.*' Then, as though having traveled farther through space, she commenced a description of belts and rings in their ever-varying beauty, and said, 'I see eight moons.' Bro. Bates exclaimed, 'She is describing Saturn.' Next came a description of Uranus, with his four moons; then a most wonderful description of the 'opening heavens,' with its glory, calling it an opening into a region more enlightened. Bro. Bates said that her description far eclipsed any account of the 'opening heavens' [probably Orion, which held an intense fascination for Bates and certain astronomers of the day] he had ever read."[21]

After Ellen White came out of vision, Bates asked her if she had ever studied astronomy. "I told him," she recalled, that "I had no recollection of ever looking into an astronomy." James White was of the same opinion regarding her total lack of knowledge on the topic. "It is well known," he wrote in describing the Topsham vision in early 1847, "that she knew nothing of astronomy, and could not answer one question in relation to the planets, before she had this vision." The evidence had been enough for the skeptical Bates. From that point on he firmly believed that she had a genuine gift of prophecy.[22]

He concluded by April 1847 that God had given her a special gift "to comfort and strengthen his 'scattered,' 'torn' and 'peeled people,' since the closing up of our work for the world in October, 1844." And in January 1848 Bates could heartily recommend "the simple, unadorned, scriptural, published visions of Ellen G. Harmon, now White." He urged his readers not to reject her work "because of her childhood and diseased bodily infirmities, and lack of worldly knowledge." After all, he pointed out, "God's manner has ever been to use the weak things of this world to confound the learned and mighty." God was employing her to "encourage the little flock" at the very time many of the previous leaders were deserting it.[23]

Bates, of course, was well aware that in the 1840s the ex-Millerite ranks included several false prophets. But, he declared, "that is no proof that God's word will fail and leave us without any true ones." "I was once slow," he added, "to believe that this sister's visions were of God. I did not oppose them," however, "for the word of the Lord is positively clear that spiritual visions will be given to his people in the last days." Bates' counsel to others, following the lead of Paul in 1 Thessalonians 5:19-21, was to "*try* the spirits" and "to *try* visions by proving all things and holding fast that which is good." Beyond Ellen White's visions, Bates believed on the basis of Acts 2:17, 19 that God was currently giving genuine dreams and visions to others of "his scattered children in many places, to prepare them for the coming scenes of this last coming conflict."[24]

Thus by late 1846 and early 1847 Bates had arrived at an appreciation of Ellen White's calling. The Whites in turn had come to value Bates as a "holy, humble servant of the Lord." "From my first acquaintance with him," James wrote, "I have loved him much. And the more I see of his devotedness to the holy advent cause, his caution, his holy life, his unfeigned love for the saints; the more I love and esteem him."[25]

Ellen also had positive feelings toward the man, noting that he was a "true Christian gentleman, courteous and kind." While still in her late teens she saw Bates (who was in his fifties) as one who treated her "tenderly as though I were his own child."[26]

With the uniting of the Whites and Bates on the concepts of the Sabbath, spiritual gifts, the two-apartment heavenly ministry of Christ, and the Advent, the core group that would soon raise up the Sabbatarian Adventist movement had formed. They would work together until Bates' death in 1872.

But Bates' did not limit his recruiting activity in late 1846 just to the Whites. Before the year ended he would also take his Sabbath message to Crosier, Hahn, and Edson (who had unitedly studied out the heavenly ministry of Christ) in western New York.

TAKING THE SABBATH TO THE "SANCTUARY PEOPLE"

A periodical that brought the Whites, Bates, Edson, and Crosier into at least name recognition of each other was the *Day-Star,* published by Enoch Jacobs in Cincinnati, Ohio. All of them had written for that periodical, and all of them, presumably, had read each other's articles.

Late in 1846 Hiram Edson hosted a meeting at his house. Those invited included not only Crosier and Hahn and others in western New

York, but also special guests from New England—Bates and James White. It is impossible to be conclusive from extant evidence, but it is quite possible that the meeting originated as a response to Bates' *Seventh Day Sabbath* booklet published a few months before, which may have reached as far as western New York. What we do know is that Bates attended the meetings without White, who found himself detained in the east.[27]

One point on the agenda was the seventh-day Sabbath, which Edson claims he had been favorable toward for some months, but without any definite conviction. But during the meetings we are told that "Bates stood and drew from his pocket his Sabbath tract and began to read. Brother Edson was so interested in it, and delighted with it, that he could scarcely keep his seat till [Bates] had finished. . . . As soon as he had finished reading Brother Edson was on his feet and said, 'Brother Bates, that is light and truth. The seventh day is the Sabbath, and I am with you to keep it."[28]

The positive response of the sanctuary group to Bates' Sabbath message seems to have been unanimous. Although Crosier may have hesitated a short time before fully accepting that new doctrine, he soon began featuring articles on the Sabbath in the *Day-Dawn*. In April 1847 we find the *Day-Dawn,* with Crosier as editor, advertising and marketing the revised edition of Bates' *Seventh Day Sabbath,* noting that "it is faithfully written, and presents in a conclusive manner the scriptural reasons for keeping the Sabbath of the Lord our God, which is the 7th day."[29]

In the same issue Hahn proclaims that "THE 7TH DAY IS THE SABBATH OF THE LORD OUR GOD." He closes his article with an appeal: "As Bro. Joseph Bates has written somewhat extensively and given the scriptural evidence on the subject, I do hope the brethren will procure a copy and examine the subject in the fear of God, and keep *one* sabbath of the Lord our God, before entering upon the sabbath of rest which remains for the people of God." Edson also reports on March 1, 1847, that he has been reading "Bates's 2nd edition on the sabbath, and would recommend the careful reading of it to all such as are willing to *do* the commandments of God 'That they may have right to the tree of life and enter in through the gates into the city.'"[30]

Bates' visit to Hiram Edson's home in Port Gibson, New York, led to important additions to the small core of Sabbathkeepers. It was there that the proponent of the Sabbath doctrine first met with the developers of the heavenly sanctuary understanding. Thus it is almost certain that those present discussed the heavenly sanctuary idea and its implications for Adventist theology along with the importance of the seventh-day Sabbath, both doctrines being explored within the context of the end-time prophecies that made all of those men Adventists. Bates undoubtedly gleaned many insights on the interrelatedness of the Sabbath, the heavenly ministry, and the prophecies during the New York meetings. Those insights would do much to enrich the January 1847 revision of *The Seventh Day Sabbath: A Perpetual Sign*. And that book, as we shall see in chapter 7, would be instrumental in forming a Sabbatarian Adventist identity.

Unfortunately, Crosier and Hahn did not stick with the developing Sabbatarian believers. In August 1848 James White wrote of Crosier that he had "given up the Sabbath and does not expect the Lord until 1877. Poor soul, he is shut up in gross darkness."[31] Crosier would later become one of the most active in writing against the views of Bates and the other Sabbatarians. Hahn would slip away more quietly but just as certainly.

THE BEGINNING OF TEAMWORK

Early 1847 was a crucial time for the developing group of Sabbatarians. With the January 1847 publication of the second edition of the *Seventh Day Sabbath* they for the first time had a major document that linked together the Sabbath, the heavenly ministry of Christ, and the Second Advent into a theological package tied especially to Revelation 11:19 and Revelation 12:17 through the end of chapter 14. That document focused on the role of those key doctrines in relation to what Bates had come to see as the progressive chain of events arising from the successive messages of the three angels of Revelation 14. The theological structure set forth in his January 1847 book furnished them with an outline of a Sabbatarian Adventist theology. Also it provided them a theological base for further Biblical understanding that was helpful in explaining both their past experience and their future direction.

By early 1847, we should note, such individuals as Bates, Edson, and James and Ellen White had united not only on their understanding of the Sabbath, the Second Advent, and the two-phase ministry of Christ, but also on the fact that individuals were not immortal and that they would not burn perpetually in hell. James had brought the teachings related to immortality with him from the Christian Connexion and Ellen had gotten them indirectly from the Connexion in 1843 through her mother. Bates, as we noted earlier, during the 1820s had believed that people were born immortal and that they burned perpetually, but by the mid-1840s he also had changed his mind on those topics—probably through his relationship with the Christian Connexion. At any rate, by the late forties he was no longer describing dead believers as being in heaven, but as awaiting their blessing "at the resurrection." Likewise, he referred to unbelievers and the wicked as those who would "be burned and destroyed . . . at the desolation of this earth."[32]

Thus by early 1847 those who were coming together as Sabbatarians were already united in what they would come to think of as their pillar doctrines—(1) the premillennial Second Advent, (2) Christ's two-phase ministry in the heavenly sanctuary, (3) the perpetuity of the seventh-day Sabbath, and (4) the nonimmortality of the soul. But even though they were in basic agreement on the main points, they still had much study and discussion before them as they sought to fill out the meaning of their theology and its implications for them in their current historical position.

Ellen White probably has in mind discussions that began in 1847 when she wrote that "my husband, Elder Joseph Bates, Father Pierce, Elder Edson, and others . . . were among those who, after the passing of the time in 1844, searched for truth. . . . These men would meet together, and search for the truth as for hidden treasure. I met with them, and we studied and prayed earnestly; for we felt that we must learn God's truth. Often we remained together until late at night, and sometimes through the entire night, praying for light and studying the word." "After earnest prayer," she noted in referring to the same experience, "if any point was not understood, it was discussed and each one expressed his opinion freely; then we would again bow in prayer, and earnest supplications went up to heaven that God would help us to see eye to eye, that we might be one, as Christ and the Father are one. Many tears were shed."[33]

"As we fasted and prayed, great power came upon us. But I could not understand the reasoning of the brethren. My mind was locked, as it were, and I could not comprehend what we were studying. Then the Spirit of God would come upon me, I would be taken off in vision, and a clear explanation of the passages we had been studying would be given me, with instruction as to the position we were to take regarding truth and duty. Again and again this happened." She went on to say that her mind "continued to be locked to the Scriptures" "for two or three years." That condition prevailed in her mind until "some time after my second son was born [July 1849]. . . . Ever since, the Scriptures have been an open book to me."[34]

About the only time frame that statement fits into in Ellen White's life was the period from mid-1847 to late 1849. Apparently the discussions took place subsequent to the autumn 1846 meetings when a core group of Sabbatarians had already united on the cardinal doctrines that would form the theological groundwork for their movement.

If they had crystalized their doctrines before the discussions and Ellen White's experience described above, then what contributions did her visions make "regarding truth and duty"? Since it was obviously not the central doctrines, her contribution must have involved points of clarification in regard to certain biblical ideas and duties. Two such contributions that we will examine in future chapters come to mind. One concerned the meaning of the "angel ascending from the east, having the seal of God"— a point that Bates and the others had been struggling with (see chapter 8). A second item had to do with her November 1848 publishing vision in which she told her husband of his responsibility to print a little paper whose influence would eventually go clear around the world (see chapter 10). Bates would be deeply involved with both issues. Those were the types of controversial issues that Ellen White's visions brought to closure in the period running from mid-1847 to late 1849.

By April 1847 we find Bates and the Whites working more closely together. On April 7 we find her writing to Joseph regarding a vision she had had confirming the importance of the Sabbath, the mark of the beast, and other topics that he had already set forth in his January 1847 revision of the *Seventh Day Sabbath*. James White requested Bates to have 1,000 copies of Ellen's vision and Bates' letter of response to it printed as a broadside (i.e., a single sheet of paper). White reimbursed Bates the $7.50 for the printing bill, trusting "in the Lord for money to be sent in" to him from those, such as Leonard and Elvira Hastings, who had some funds and were sympathetic to the developing Sabbatarian ideas.[35]

The most substantial result of the cooperation between Bates and the Whites up through May 1847 was the publication of *A Word to the "Little*

Flock" that month, a 24-page booklet in which all three presented articles. James White, who had the collection printed, points out in the booklet's preface that the articles had been written for Crosier's *Day-Dawn,* but since that periodical was no longer being published he had no choice but to release them in pamphlet form. As Merlin Burt indicates, between late 1844 and May 1847 the periodicals that Bates and the Whites had earlier published in (e.g., the *Day-Star,* the *Day-Dawn,* and the *Jubilee Standard*) had either gone out of existence or had turned against their position. As a result, they were forced to go their own way. Beyond that, Burt points out, through the publication of *A Word to the "Little Flock"* James White took a more direct leadership in the young Sabbatarian movement.[36]

Up to that point the initiative had generally resided with Bates. However, by the end of the decade, as we shall see in chapter 10, White would be in control. But in between May 1847 and that time the two would experience some tension over the issue of leadership—a struggle that almost brought Sabbatarian Adventism to an early end.

The six months between November 1846 and May 1847 were of crucial importance to both Bates and the developing Sabbatarian movement. Not only did Bates create links with the Whites but also with Edson, Crosier, and Hahn. Those relationships enriched Bates' understanding of both the sanctuary and the Sabbath in relation to the Second Advent and the apocalyptic message of revelation. The early months of 1847 would see the beginning of a lasting teamwork between the Whites, Bates, Edson, and others. That period witnessed the publication of Bates' second edition of the *Seventh Day Sabbath,* the beginning of enriching discussions among the Sabbatarians on themes related to that book, and the May publication of *A Word to the "Little Flock,"* a work that largely featured the fruit of those discussions and demonstrated a rising self-consciousness among the leading Sabbatarians.

Central to all of those developments was a series of books by Bates that highlighted both a distinct Sabbatarian theological perspective and a unique Sabbatarian historical perspective. It is to those two topics that we turn to in the next three chapters.

---

[1] H. S. Gurney, "Letter From Bro. Gurney," *Day-Star,* Oct. 11, 1845, p. 45.

[2] J. White, "Letter From Bro. White," *Day-Star,* Oct. 11, 1845, p. 47; J. White, "Watchman, What of the Night?" *Day-Star,* Sept. 20, 1845, pp. 25, 26; J. White and E. G. White, *Life Sketches: Ancestry, Early Life, Christian Experience, and Extensive Labors, of Elder James White, and His Wife, Mrs. Ellen G. White* (Battle Creek, Mich.: Seventh-day Adventist Pub. Assn., 1888), p. 126.

[3] J. Bates, *Autobiography,* p. 300. J. White gave up his 1845 expectation "a few days before the time passed" due to an E. Harmon vision on the topic. See J. White, in *A Word to the "Little Flock,"* p. 22.

[4] [J. Litch], "The Rise and Progress of Adventism," *Advent Shield,* May 1844, pp. 75, 80.

[5] [J. Marsh], "Our Position," *Voice of Truth,* Nov. 7, 1844, p. 166.

[6] Apollos Hale and Joseph Turner, "Has Not the Savior Come as the Bridegroom?" *Advent Mirror,* Jan. 1845, p. 3.

[7] Hiram Edson, unpub. ms, n.d. Reprinted in George R. Knight, comp. and ed. *1844 and the Rise of Sabbatarian Adventism* (Hagerstown, Md.: Review and Herald Pub. Assn., 1994), pp. 123-126.

[8] O.R.L. Crosier, "To All Who Are Waiting for Redemption. The Following Is Addressed," *Ontario Messenger,* Mar. 26, 1845, last page. The editors note that this article had been printed as part of the *Day-Dawn* the week before. I am indebted to Merlin D. Burt for recently discovering this document.

[9] G. W. Peavey, "Letter From Bro. G. W. Peavey," *Jubilee Standard,* Apr. 24, 1845, p. 55; G. W. Peavey, "'Unto Two Thousand and Three Hundred Days: Then Shall the Sanctuary Be Cleansed,'" *Jubilee Standard,* Aug. 7, 1845, p. 166; for Emily Clemons' contribution to sanctuary theology, see Burt, "The Historical Background," pp. 179-185.

[10] O.R.L. Crosier, "The Law of Moses," *Day-Star,* Extra, Feb. 7, 1846, pp. 37-44.

[11] J. Bates, *Opening Heavens,* pp. 25, 1.

[12] E. G. White to Eli Curtis, Apr. 21, 1847.

[13] J. White and E. G. White, *Life Sketches* (1888), p. 236; E. G. White, *Spiritual Gifts,* vol. 2, p. 82. Bates several times places his meeting with the Whites in early 1845 (see, e.g., J. Bates, "Testimonial," *Review and Herald,* Mar. 26, 1861, p. 152), but appears from other evidence to be relying upon faulty memory.

[14] J. White and E. G. White, *Life Sketches* (1888), pp. 126, 238; cf. J. White to Bro. Collins, Aug. 26, 1846.

[15] J. White, *Life Incidents,* p. 269; E. G. White, *Testimonies for the Church* (Mountain View, Calif.: Pacific Press Pub. Assn., 1948), vol. 1, p. 75.

[16] E. G. White, *Testimonies for the Church,* vol. 1, p. 77.

[17] E. G. White to J. Bates, Apr. 7, 1847; E. G. White to J. N. Loughborough, Aug. 24, 1874.

[18] J. White and E. G. White, *Life Sketches* (1888), p. 236; J. Bates, "Remarks," in J. White, ed., *A Word to the "Little Flock,"* p. 21.

[19] Kinkade, *The Bible Doctrine,* pp. 332, 333.

[20] J. Bates, "Remarks," in J. White, ed., *A Word to the "Little Flock",* p. 21.

[21] J. Bates, *Autobiography,* p. 151; J. Bates, *Opening Heavens,* pp. 6-12; J. N. Loughborough, "Recollections of the Past—No. 16," *Review and Herald,* Nov. 30, 1886, p. 745.

[22] E. G. White, *Spiritual Gifts*, vol. 2, p. 83; J. White, *A Word to the "Little Flock,"* p. 22.

[23] J. Bates, "Remarks," in J. White, ed., *A Word to the "Little Flock,"* p. 21; J. Bates, *Vindication of the Seventh-day Sabbath*, pp. 96, 97.

[24] J. Bates, *Seal of the Living God*, pp. 27, 30-32; for a discussion of visionary excesses in post-disappointment Adventism, see Knight, *Millennial Fever*, pp. 254-256.

[25] J. White to Sis. Hastings, Aug. 22, 1847.

[26] J. White and E. G. White, *Life Sketches* (1888), p. 236.

[27] H. Edson, unpub. ms, in Knight, *1844*, p. 126; P. Z. Kinne, "Hiram Edson's Experience as Related to P. Z. Kinne," unpub. ms., n.d. (Kinne, who had become a Seventh-day Adventist in 1860, was a neighbor of Edson's and claims that Edson had related his story to him several times.); J. White, *Life Incidents*, p. 269.

[28] P. Z. Kinne, "Hiram Edson's Experience as Related to P. Z. Kinne," unpub. ms., n.d.; A. W. Spaulding, "Light on the Sanctuary: Adapted From the Manuscript of Hiram Edson," *Youth's Instructor*, Mar. 8, 1910, p. 6. (Spaulding had access to a larger portion of the Edson manuscript than is now extant. L. E. Froom in his *Finding the Lost Prophetic Witnesses* [Washington, D.C.: Review and Herald Pub. Assn., 1946], p. 47, states that the Edson manuscript contained 30 pages when it was acquired for the Advent Source Collection, as opposed to its present 12 pages.)

[29] Spaulding, "Light on the Sanctuary: Adapted From the Manuscript of Hiram Edson," *Youth's Instructor*, Mar. 8, 1910, p. 6; "Notice," *Day-Dawn*, Apr. 2, 1847, p. 6; cf. "Notice," *Day-Dawn*, Mar. 19, 1847, p. 4.

[30] F. B. Hahn, "The Time Is at Hand," *Day-Dawn*, Apr. 2, 1847, p. 6; H. Edson, "Letter From Bro. Edson," *Day-Dawn*, Apr. 2, 1847, pp. 7-8.

[31] J. White to Bro. and Sis. Hastings, Aug. 26, 1848.

[32] J. Bates, *Vindication of the Seventh-day Sabbath*, pp. 109, 110; J. Bates, *Seal of the Living God*, p. 62. For the early development of Adventism's understanding of conditional immortality, see G. R. Knight, *A Search for Identity: The Development of Seventh-day Adventist Beliefs* (Hagerstown, Md.: Review and Herald Pub. Assn., 2000), pp. 72-74.

[33] E. G. White to J. H. Kellogg, Nov. 20, 1903; E. G. White, *Christian Experience and Teachings* (Mountain View, Calif.: Pacific Press Pub. Assn., 1940), pp. 192, 193.

[34] E. G. White to J. H. Kellogg, Nov. 20, 1903; E. G. White, "Establishing the Foundation of Our Faith," Ms 135, Nov. 4, 1903.

[35] "A Vision," a broadside published by Joseph Bates, probably in May 1847; J. White to Sis. Hastings, May 21, 1847.

[36] J. White, in *A Word to the "Little Flock,"* p. 1. Burt, "Historical Background," p. 308.

CHAPTER VII

SABBATARIAN ADVENTISM'S FIRST THEOLOGIAN: THEOLOGY AS HISTORY (Part I)

A S a result of the disappointment of October 1844, Bates wrote that "hope sunk and courage died." We noted near the end of chapter 4 that Millerism split into several factions in early 1845, with some believing that something had really happened on October 22, 1844 (the shut door Adventists) and others holding that the date involved no fulfillment of prophecy (the open door Adventists). Concerning some among the shut door group, Bates later wrote that "those who believed that the time was right, and had really passed, now turned their attention to the examination of their position. It soon became apparent that the mistake was not in the time, but in the event to take place at the end of the period. . . . We had been teaching that the sanctuary was the earth, and that its cleansing was its purification by fire at the second advent of Christ. In this was our mistake, for, upon a careful examination, we were unable to discover anything in the Bible to sustain such a position." [1]

Their Bible study eventually led them, as we saw in chapter 6, to see the cleansing in relation to Christ's high priestly ministry in the heavenly sanctuary. They also, as we noted in the last two chapters, came to a fuller understanding of the seventh-day Sabbath.

Bates became a leading advocate of those new ideas and served as a catalyst in developing a core of like-minded believers. Between August 1846 and January 1849 he would publish four books indicating an increasing understanding of the place of the Sabbath in prophetic history and two books setting forth his understanding of the historic progress of Adventism across time. The arguments in those two sets of books are intertwined, but for purposes of clarity we will examine the contribution of the Sabbath volumes in chapters 7 and 8 and the historical books in chapter 9.

SABBATH BOOK NUMBER 1: THE ENTERING WEDGE

Bates published his *Seventh Day Sabbath, A Perpetual Sign* in August 1846. In his earlier book *The Opening Heavens* (May 1846) he had briefly mentioned the seventh-day Sabbath and the fact that the Papacy had sought to change the worship day to the first day of the week,[2] but he devoted his August book entirely to the topic, making the 48-page document the most extensive treatment of the Sabbath to date by an Adventist.

Bates was quite clear as to his purpose in writing his little book. "Brother J. B. Cook," he noted, "has written a short piece in his excellent paper, the ADVENT TESTIMONY." But Cook's piece was too short and not broad enough. "And as brother Preble's [1845] Tract now before me, did not embrace the arguments which have been presented since he published it, it appeared to me that something was called for in this time of falling back from this great subject. I therefore present this book, hoping at least, that it will help to strengthen and save all honest souls seeking after truth."[3]

We need to note three important points in the above quotation. First, that truth is progressive, that a better grasp of the importance of the Sabbath had been gained since the publication of Preble's 12-page *Tract* some 15 months previously. Bates proposed to highlight that fuller understanding.

Second, there had been a "time of falling back from this great subject" of the seventh-day Sabbath among those Adventists who had previously observed it. Merlin Burt helps us make sense of that "falling back" when he writes that "during the summer and fall of 1845 the Sabbath had been taken captive by Bridegroom spiritualizers" who had associated it with certain of their excesses and fanaticisms, while neglecting Preble's emphasis on the Sabbath's connection to creation and the Ten Commandments. Those problems had not only caused many Adventists to abandon the seventh-day Sabbath but even shook Bates himself on its validity shortly after he accepted it in mid-1845.[4]

But, Burt demonstrates, "by the summer of 1846 the fanaticism had burned itself out." That left "only a few Sabbath adherents," such as Bates.[5]

The resulting situation brings us to the third and major reason that Bates decided to pen his first book on the Sabbath. He needed to "help to strengthen and save all honest souls seeking after truth." Burt correctly argues that Bates desired to move the Sabbath away from its fanatical association and to "re-establish the Sabbath on a biblical creation and Ten Commandment basis."[6]

In short, Bates' 1846 book on the Sabbath was an evangelistic tool to reignite, balance out, and inform interest in the Sabbath among the still bewildered Adventists. In order to accomplish his purpose, he "circulated gratuitously" his *Seventh Day Sabbath*. And the book accomplished its purpose, convicting the Whites; Edson, Crosier, and their colleagues; and others on the importance of the seventh-day Sabbath.[7] Thus in the fullest sense the 1846 edition of the *Seventh Day Sabbath* was an entering wedge on the topic.

The book itself largely presents a Seventh Day Baptist concept of the Sabbath. Bates divided it into four parts. The first (pp. 3-9) rooted the Sabbath historically in the Genesis creation. That meant, he argued, "that the weekly Sabbath was not made for the Jews only, (but as Jesus says, for 'man') for the Jews had no existence until more than two thousand years after it was established."[8]

The second section (pp. 9-16) argues that the Bible nowhere abolishes the Sabbath or transfers it to Sunday. Bates concludes with an allusion to the new covenant, asking "of what use [are] the ten commandments written on our hearts, if it was not to render perfect obedience to them."[9]

The third section (pp. 16-27) examines texts that purportedly support the view that the Sabbath has been abolished. It included a discussion of the distinction between the moral and the ceremonial laws. Bates concludes the section by quoting an authority who supports the concept that there are only "two ways in which any law can cease to be binding upon the people. It may expire by its own limitations, or it may be repealed by the same authority which exacted it." He points out that since neither of those conditions exist for the Sabbath, it is therefore still binding.[10]

Bates' final section (pp. 27-47) touches on several topics, including the alleged change of the Sabbath. Examining the pertinent New Testament passages, he finds no biblical warrant for such a shift in days and concludes that it was done by the Pope who fulfilled Daniel 7:25 with its prophecy about the little horn thinking to change times and laws. That was a point he had earlier made in his *Opening Heavens*. Other topics treated in part four include the time to begin and end the Sabbath (6:00 p.m. Friday to 6:00 p.m. Saturday) and the fact that Christians are a part of true Israel and are thus obligated to keep God's covenant, including the Ten Commandments.[11]

Two points of special interest in the 1846 edition of the *Seventh Day Sabbath* indicate that Bates was beginning to interpret the Sabbath in the light of an Adventist theological framework rather than a merely Seventh Day Baptist one. The first is the thought in the "Preface" that "the *seventh day Sabbath*" is "to be restored before the second advent of Jesus Christ." That idea derived from the restorationist platform that Bates had brought with him from the Christian Connexion. According to that understanding, the Reformation was not complete and would not be until all the great Bible truths neglected or perverted down through history found their rightful place in God's church.[12]

The second very Adventist tilt in the 1846 edition is Bates' interpretation of the Sabbath within the context of the book of Revelation. He tied the Sabbath to the three angels' messages of Revelation 14. "In the xiv ch. Rev. 6-11, [John] saw three angels following each other in succession: first one preaching the everlasting gospel (second advent doctrine); 2d, announcing the fall of Babylon; 3d, calling God's people out of her by showing the awful destruction that awaited all such as did not obey." Then, "he sees the separation and cries out, 'Here is the patients [sic] of the Saints, here are they that keep the commandments of God and the faith of Jesus.' . . . Now it seems to me that the seventh day Sabbath is more clearly included in these commandments, than thou shalt not steal, not kill, nor commit adultery, for it is the only one that was written at the creation or in the *beginning*."[13]

The linking of the seventh-day Sabbath to the three angels of Revelation 14 was a crucial step in "adventizing" Bates' understanding of its importance. He would build extensively upon that connection in his 1847 revision of the *Seventh Day Sabbath*.

SABBATH BOOK NUMBER 2: THE INTERPRETIVE WEDGE

Whereas we can see the 1846 edition of his book on the Sabbath as an entering wedge into the minds and hearts of the Whites, Edson, and others who read it, the 1847 edition of *The Seventh Day Sabbath* should be viewed as an interpretive wedge. As such, the 1847 edition not only presented the Sabbath as the correct day, but it developed significant arguments that presented the importance of the Sabbath from a uniquely Adventist perspective. The new edition demonstrates that Bates' understanding of the end-time importance of the Sabbath had grown greatly between August 1846 and January 1847. Some of that development undoubtedly resulted from his dialogs with Crosier, Edson, and Hahn in western New York late in 1846.

The 1847 edition of the *Seventh Day Sabbath* saw the book expand from 48 to 63 pages. The core 48 pages remained essentially the same. The additions were a two-page preface to the new edition (pp. iii, iv) and an 11-page added section near the end of the book (pp. 49-60). It is into those 13 pages that Bates poured the new interpretive data that would move the book from being a largely Seventh Day Baptist perspective to presenting a Sabbatarian Adventist understanding.

Bates' 1847 preface lists two reasons for the new edition. The first was an increasing demand for the book. The second was that it afforded him "an opportunity of spreading additional light from the Word on this important subject of present truth."[14] That new light would form around five new themes—four of them being helpful and one problematic.

The first theme would be "present truth" itself. Bates did not originate the term but he did fill it with new content. The Millerites earlier had employed "present truth" to refer to the imminent return of Jesus, meaning that that event was a special truth for their time. Later, they applied it to the seventh-month movement (i.e., the proclamation in 1844 that the Second Advent would take place on October 22 of that year). Thus the Millerites not only used the term "present truth," but they saw it as progressive and dynamic.[15]

Bates employed "present truth" in the 1847 edition of his Sabbath book to refer especially to the seventh-day Sabbath as it related to the opening of the heavenly temple and the Second Advent. Present truth for him referred to those special concepts discovered since October 1844 and that were necessary for enabling the Sabbatarian Adventist believers to understand their place in history. Rolf Pöhler notes that "Joseph Bates was the first to apply the expression [present truth] to the newly discovered Sabbath truth."[16]

James White agreed with Bates on the content of present truth. In 1849, after quoting 2 Peter 1:12, which speaks of being "established in the

PRESENT TRUTH," White wrote that "in Peter's time there was present truth, or truth applicable to that present time. The Church [has] ever had a present truth. The present truth now, is that which shows present duty, and the right position for us who are about to witness the time of trouble." To both Bates and White present truth, as we shall see below, was intimately related to the message of Revelation 14:12. White was so taken up with the phrase that he titled the periodical he founded in July 1849 (the first Sabbatarian Adventist periodical) as *The Present Truth.*[17]

A second new theme introduced in the 1847 edition of the *Seventh Day Sabbath* was the opening up of the temple in heaven, revealing the ark of the testament (Rev. 11:19). And the ark, of course, contained the Ten Commandments. Bates reasoned that "this Temple has been opened for some purpose," but that it was not so that humans could enter it. Rather, it implied "a space of time in which the commandments will be fully kept."[18]

John Nevins Andrews summarized Bates' insight by noting that "he was one of the first [the very first Sabbatarian] to see that the central object of the sanctuary is the ark of God, and that under the mercy-seat [covering the ark] is God's holy law, containing the Sabbath."[19] Through that insight Bates united an end-time understanding of the Sabbath with an end-time perspective of the heavenly sanctuary.

At this early date Bates may not have come to the conclusion that the opening up of the Most Holy Place of the heavenly temple (the part containing the ark) in Revelation 11:19 was tied to his and Crosier's new understanding of the cleansing of the second apartment of the heavenly sanctuary in Daniel 8:14. At least he does not make the connection explicit in his 1847 book.

A third important theme connected to the Sabbath in his 1847 revision related to God's covenants with human beings. This is the problematic contribution of the revision in that he gave salvific power to the law by more than once asserting such thoughts as "the keeping of GOD'S SABBATH" and the other nine commandments "SAVES THE SOUL!"[20] We discussed that topic quite fully in chapter 5 and will not repeat it here. It is important to recall, however, that the other two founders of Sabbatarian Adventism (James and Ellen White) were not in harmony with Bates in his legalism. Thus from the very beginning of Sabbatarian Adventism there has existed two diverse strands related to salvation—

one legalistic and the other with a gospel-centered orientation.

But embedded in the section in which Bates deals with the covenants is his fourth contribution to Adventist theology in his 1847 edition. That one stands at the very center of Sabbatarian Adventist theology and helped Bates and those who read him place their movement in the flow of eschatological or apocalyptic history.

Bates had touched upon the relationship of the Sabbath to the three angels' messages of Revelation 14 in the 1846 edition, but by 1847 he had developed his thoughts much more fully. With this topic we have come to the most significant interpretive contribution of Bates' 1847 revision of the *Seventh Day Sabbath*.

In this section he roots Sabbatarian Adventism in the flow of Millerite history when he asserts that "the history of God's people for the last seven years [i.e., 1840-1847], or more, is described by John in Rev. xiv:6-13."[21] At that point Bates begins to present his understanding of the three angels' messages as a sequential series. His approach will set the model for all subsequent Sabbatarian interpretations of the passage. Note the sequence:

1. The first angel (verses 6, 7) announces "the everlasting gospel at the hour of God's judgment. This without any doubt represents all those who were preaching the second Advent doctrine since 1840." Thus the first angel symbolizes the Millerite movement.

2. The second angel's message (verse 8) was preached by "some of the same Advent lecturers" and had to do with the fall of Babylon.

3. The third angel's message for Bates at this stage of his understanding included only verses 9-11. He equated its meaning with that of Revelation 18:4 with its call to come out of Babylon. All who did not respond received a curse and the mark of the beast. The cry of the third angel of Revelation 14:9-11 and 18:4 took place "at Midnight in the fall of 1844." And, Bates adds, many came out. Thus for him in 1847 the preaching of the three angels' messages had all been accomplished before the great disappointment of October 22, 1844.

4. That conclusion brought him to the post-disappointment period and Revelation 14:12. That verse ("Here is the patience of the saints: here are they that keep the commandments of God, and the

faith of Jesus."), which would become the central text in Seventh-day Adventist self understanding, Bates interpreted as *following* the three angels' messages. That is, *in his 1847 understanding, the preaching of Revelation 14:12 did not begin until after October 1844.* Proclaimed by "the very same [people] that came out of Babylon," that group would be faithful to God by keeping all of His commandments, including the seventh-day Sabbath.[22]

Thus, in summary, we can diagram Bates' 1847 interpretation of Revelation 14:6-12 as follows:

October
1844

verses 6, 7	verse 8	verses 9-11	verse 12
1st angel	2nd angel	3rd angel	The preaching of the Sabbath beginning after the disappointment

As we will see in chapter 9, James White would vigorously disagree with some of the details of Bates' interpretation of this all important passage, even though he accepted the essence of Bates' interpretive framework. That framework in many ways stands at the very foundation of what would become Sabbatarian and later Seventh-day Adventist theology.

Then Bates went on in his 1847 presentation to note "that such a people can be found on the earth as described in the 12v. and have been uniting in companies for the last two years, on the commandments of God and faith or testimony of Jesus."[23] With that stroke of his pen Bates not only placed the incipient Sabbatarians in the flow of prophetic history, but he also rooted them in historic time. Those identifications became absolutely foundational in the development of a Sabbatarian Adventist self-identity.

His interpretations not only helped those who were becoming part of a movement see themselves in terms of their place in past history, but it also set the stage for an understanding of the movement's future history as described in the book of Revelation. It is in the outlining of that future history that he set forth what has now become known as "great controversy theology."

Bates' beginning point for great controversy theology is his assertion that the Sabbathkeeping group that had been uniting in companies on the basis of Revelation 14:12 was also the remnant (or "last end") of God's church that would at the conclusion of time be "'keeping the commandments of God and the testimony of Jesus Christ.' xii:17." But that faithfulness, he pointed out, means that they would be "made war with" for obeying all of God's commandments.[24]

And why, he asked, would the remnant endure persecution for keeping the commandments when other Christians also professed to obey them? Because, he argues, they are truly practicing what they profess to believe by "living 'by every word which proceedeth out of the mouth of God'" through "keeping the Sabbath holy, just as God has told them in the commandments."[25]

Again, he asked, what about the tens of thousands of Adventists who don't observe the seventh day, "what will become of them?" "Consult John," Bates replied, "he knows better than we do; he has only described two companies" in Revelation 14:9-12 at the end of time. "One is keeping the commandments and faith of Jesus. The other has the mark of the beast. How? . . . Is it not clear that the first day of the week for the Sabbath or holy day is a mark of the beast [which changed the Sabbath according to Daniel 7:25]. It surely will be admitted that the Devil was and is the father of all the wicked deeds of Imperial and papal Rome. It is clear then from this history that Sunday, or first day, is his Sabbath throughout christendom."[26]

The beast "will be very careful . . . not to make *war* on any but those who keep God's Sabbath holy." But in the end, everyone will "be judged according to their works." It is only "them that do (that practice) his commandments" who "enter in through the gates into the city."[27] As noted in chapter 5, it is possible to conclude in the flow of his argument that Bates might not have been as legalistic as his words sometimes imply since he was speaking to people who were already Christians and who were merely following the dictates of their consciences as they lived for God by obeying His commands. But on the other hand, as also noted previously, Bates' legalistic statements throughout his ministry transcended that specific context.

The two pages in which Bates developed the great controversy theology in his 1847 edition of the *Seventh Day Sabbath* are two of the most influential in Sabbatarian Adventist history. In them he:

1. Outlined the interpretive framework of the three angels' messages.

2. Placed Sabbatarian Adventism in the flow of prophetic and actual history.
3. Set forth the remnant concept of Revelation 12:17.
4. Sketched the great end-time struggle over the commandments of God that dominates Revelation 12:17–14:14.
5. Made an identification of the mark of the beast.

The thoughts on those two pages would do much to shape Adventist thinking in the years and decades to come.

Most people have assumed that Ellen White developed the great controversy theology. The idea that it came through Bates' Bible study disturbs some. But his publication of his understanding of great controversy theology preceded Ellen White's vision on the topic by three months.

It was on April 7, 1847, that Ellen White wrote Bates, informing him that she had had an important vision the previous Sabbath (April 3). In it she entered the second apartment of the heavenly sanctuary where she saw the ark of the covenant. In the ark were the Ten Commandments, with the first four shining brighter than the second table of the law, and with the fourth glowing even more than all the rest.[28]

After noting the perpetuity of the Sabbath and its historic change, she wrote that "I saw that the holy Sabbath is, and will be, the separating wall between the true Israel of God and unbelievers; and that the Sabbath is the great question, to unite the hearts of God's dear waiting saints." At that point she described the time of trouble, the opportunity to preach the Sabbath to the "nominal Adventists," and the end-time conflict over the Sabbath between those who had the mark of the beast and those who had it not.[29]

It is obvious that her vision did not initiate the great controversy theology. Rather, it confirmed points already developed by Bates in Bible study. And it is the vision reported in the April 7 letter that Bates published at James White's request as a broadside entitled *A Vision*. Then in May it would appear as a part of *A Word to the "Little Flock."*[30]

A fifth important theological issue promoted by Bates' 1847 revision of the *Seventh Day Sabbath* is his expansion of the concept that the Sabbath needed to be restored before the end of time. He had alluded to that idea briefly in the 1846 edition, but in 1847 he greatly expanded his thoughts on the topic. In the process he tied the Sabbath's restoration to his great controversy theology.

"Now that the keeping of the seventh day Sabbath," he writes, "has been made void by the working of satan [sic], and is to be restored as one of the *all* things spoken of by the holy prophets since the world began, before Jesus can come, is evident." At that point he cites Acts 3:20, 21 and Isaiah 58:12, the latter text dealing with restoration of the Sabbath. He then adds "that there will yet be a mighty struggle about the restoring and keeping [of] the seventh day Sabbath, that will test every living soul that enters the gates of the city." That truth, he asserts, "cannot be disputed. It is evident that the Devil is making war on all such. See Rev. xii:17."[31]

The added 13 pages to Bates' 1846 tract as found in the 1847 edition represent a milestone in Bates' theological development and in the growth of the movement that his traveling and writing was bringing into being. It presented the interpretive framework within which all future Sabbatarian theological thinking would take place. The 1847 book would not only be a catalyst to those who agreed with Bates, but it also engendered a vigorous response from those who disagreed with him. After all, he had tied Sundaykeeping to the mark of the beast and uplifted faithfulness to the Sabbath as essential to salvation. He had thrown down the gauntlet of war. And those Adventists who rejected his viewpoint would not be tardy in picking it up.

---

[1] J. Bates, *Autobiography,* pp. 300, 301.

[2] J. Bates, *Opening Heavens,* pp. 35, 36.

[3] J. Bates, *Seventh Day Sabbath* (1846), p. 41.

[4] Burt, "Historical Background," p. 278; J. Bates, *Seventh Day Sabbath* (1846), p. 40.

[5] Burt, "Historical Background," p. 278.

[6] *Ibid.;* J. Bates, *Seventh Day Sabbath* (1846), p. 41.

[7] J. White, *Life Incidents,* p. 269.

[8] J. Bates, *Seventh Day Sabbath* (1846), p. 7.

[9] *Ibid.,* p. 15.

[10] *Ibid.,* p. 26.

[11] *Ibid.,* pp. 41, 42, 43, 47, 48; J. Bates, *Opening Heavens,* p. 35.

[12] J. Bates, *Seventh Day Sabbath* (1846), p. 1; cf. Kinkade, *The Bible Doctrine,* p. 331.

[13] J. Bates, *Seventh Day Sabbath* (1846), p. 24.

[14] J. Bates, *Seventh Day Sabbath* (1847), p. iii.

[15] R. Hutchinson, "Letter From R. Hutchinson," *Midnight Cry,* Aug. 24, 1843, p. 8; "Present Truth," *Voice of Truth,* Oct. 2, 1844, p. 144. For a discussion of the dynamic na-

ture of present truth in Adventism, see Knight, *A Search for Identity,* pp. 19-21.

[16] J. Bates, *Seventh Day Sabbath* (1847), pp. iii, iv; Rolf J. Pöhler, *Continuity and Change in Adventist Teaching: A Case Study in Doctrinal Development* (Frankfurt am Main: Peter Lang, 2000), p. 181.

[17] [J. White, editorial], *Present Truth,* July 1849, p. 1.

[18] J. Bates, *Seventh Day Sabbath* (1847), pp. iii, iv.

[19] J. N. Andrews and L. R. Conradi, *History of the Sabbath and First Day of the Week,* 4th ed. rev. and enl. (Washington, D.C.: Review and Herald Pub. Assn., 1912), p. 774.

[20] See, e.g., J. Bates, *Seventh Day Sabbath* (1847), pp. 55, 56.

[21] *Ibid.,* p. 58.

[22] *Ibid.;* see also J. Bates, *Second Advent Way Marks and High Heaps,* p. 27 for the third angel's message ending in October 1844.

[23] J. Bates, *Seventh Day Sabbath* (1847), pp. 58, 59.

[24] *Ibid.,* p. 59.

[25] *Ibid.*

[26] *Ibid.,* pp. 59, 45.

[27] *Ibid.,* pp. 59, 60.

[28] E. G. White to J. Bates, Apr. 7, 1847, published in J. White, ed., *A Word to the "Little Flock,"* pp. 18, 19.

[29] *Ibid.*

[30] J. White to Sis. Hastings, May 21, 1847.

[31] J. Bates, *Seventh Day Sabbath* (1847), p. 60.

CHAPTER VIII

SABBATARIAN ADVENTISM'S FIRST THEOLOGIAN: THEOLOGY AS HISTORY (Part II)

CHAPTER 7 began the discussion of Joseph Bates' role as Sabbatarian Adventism's first theologian. In particular, it discussed the 1846 edition of the *Seventh Day Sabbath* as an entering wedge that led several significant shut door Adventists to accept the Sabbath.

That chapter also highlighted the 1847 revision of his book as an interpretive wedge. If the significance of the first edition was that it functioned as an evangelistic tool in opening minds to the Sabbath, the second edition's added function was to place the Sabbath in an Adventist, prophetic framework. The present chapter will pick up where the previous one left off and discuss Bates' third and fourth books on the Sabbath.

SABBATH BOOK NUMBER 3: A PROJECT OF AGGRESSION

Bates' 1847 revision of the *Seventh Day Sabbath* triggered a number of varied reactions. We noted in chapter 6 the enthusiastic and positive responses of Hiram Edson, O.R.L. Crosier, and F. B. Hahn in the *Day-Dawn* during March and April 1847. All three accepted it and seemed to be placing the *Day-Dawn* in position to be an advocate of the seventh-day Sabbath along with the shut door and the heavenly sanctuary understandings.

The 1847 book had put the Sabbath on the agenda, and the editors of several Adventist periodicals had to face the topic that year. Thus Joseph Marsh of the *Voice of Truth* reported that "we have had repeated calls from different parts of the country, for our views on the Seventh Day or Jewish Sabbath." As a result, he decided to republish an extensive article against the Sabbath. "The arguments in favor of the abolishing of the Jewish sabbath," he noted, "we deem unaswerable." Two months later Marsh asserted that "we think we are justified by Scripture and the best church history in observing the first day of the week as a day of worship."[1]

The most vigorous response to the excitement Bates stirred up over the seventh-day Sabbath took place in *The Bible Advocate*. But unlike the other periodicals, which took one side or the other on the topic, the discussion in the *Advocate* had extensive presentations from both viewpoints. Merlin Burt, the chronicler of that exchange, notes that "the *Bible Advocate* became the medium for the final serious discussion on the Sabbath in a non-Shut-Door Millerite publication." The arguments for each perspective show up in the pages of the *Advocate* between July 1847 and February 1848. Bates, however, felt that he was being "excluded from that paper," even though it was his publication that had done so much to stimulate the *Advocate*'s discussion in the first place. Burt points out that the *Advocate* printed neither Bates nor James White because they both belonged to the shut-door camp of Adventism.[2]

But just because the discussion didn't include Bates doesn't mean that people ignored him. On July 29, 1847, near the opening of the extended debate, one writer to the *Advocate* commented that "I see that the brethren in the 'Day Dawn' [sic], make the keeping of the seventh day, indispensible to full salvation. And Bro. J. Bates in a pamphlet sent out some time since, argued the subject at full length, and I see he thinks his arguments unanswerable. And in a pamphlet recently published by J. W[hite] he [Bates] has taken the visions of a sister down east to help support the argument. I want to ask Bro. Bates, and all the brethren through the Advocate [sic], if it will not be safe to look for our rule of duty, in the New Testament."[3]

The fact that Bates' little book had fueled the debate is also evident in the issues of the *Advocate* for August 27 and September 23, 1847, and January 13, 1848. And some believed that "Bro. Bates" and the other proponents of the seventh-day Sabbath "must stand condemned at the dread tribunal of God" for their legalism and for seeking to place the yoke of the Pharisees on others.[4]

The most forceful articles on behalf of the seventh-day Sabbath in the *Advocate* in late 1847 and early 1848 came from the pen of J. B. Cook. But, unfortunately for Bates and his seventh-day colleagues, by September of 1848 Cook had reversed his position and had begun writing articles on "why the Sabbath is *not now enforced*" even though every other precept of the decalogue was still in force. Thus Cook joined the ranks of T. M.

Preble, Crosier, and others who had abandoned their belief in the importance of the seventh-day Sabbath. Burt points out that "the abandonment of the Sabbath by these three men severed the final link that Sabbatarian Adventism held with 'nominal' or 'non-Shut-Door' Adventism. From 1848 onward, Adventist seventh-day Sabbath advocacy was the unique possession of those joined with James and Ellen White and Joseph Bates."[5]

That brings us to Bates' third book on the Sabbath. Since he had not been a part of the debate in the *Advocate*, Bates now set forth his position in January 1848 in a book entitled *A Vindication of the Seventh-day Sabbath and the Commandments of God: With a Further History of God's Peculiar People, From 1847 to 1848*.

Writing it was the easy part of the book's production. Finding money to pay for its printing was more difficult. James White reports that "in the autumn of 1847, Bro. Bates sat down to write a work of more than one hundred pages, with only a York shilling [about 12½ cents] at his command."[6]

It is apparently in connection with the publication of *A Vindication of the Seventh-day Sabbath* that Bates' "grocery crisis" took place. Just before he went into print his wife asked him to buy some flour. But only having 12½ cents, he was able to buy only four pounds. His wife, not knowing his circumstances, asked how it was that he, a man who had sailed ships around the world, had come home with only a little flour. At that point he told her two things. First, that he had used all his savings. And, second, that he was writing a book on the Sabbath. That really flustered her. After all, she hadn't even accepted the Sabbath. As Bates put it, "she does not comprehend my duty." As usual, he told Prudy that God would take care of them.[7]

Soon after that, J. N. Loughborough tells us, Bates felt impressed to go to the post office, where he found he had a check in the mail for $10.00. With that he was able to buy sufficient groceries and at least think about printing his book. But when he took it to the printer he still didn't have sufficient funds. So H. S. Gurney secretly paid the bill. Gurney's son recalls that "my father went to the printer and paid the account. When Elder Bates went for his books and asked for his bill, the printer told him the account had been paid in full. 'But,' said Elder Bates, 'I have not paid it.' 'Well,' replied the printer, 'someone else did. I do not know who it was, or where he came from—but a man came into my office, paid for the printing, and went out.'"[8]

That was good news to the trusting Bates, who to the day of his death did not know who had taken care of his printing bill. But he could still rejoice in God's care. "Since 1st day of Jan. 1848," he penned in April of that year, "God has wonderfully provided me money to sustain myself and family. $15.40 was due for rent. The day your letter came," he told Brother and Sister Hastings, ". . . $15 came from one quarter and your dollar finished the balance. Praise the Lord. I wondered but it was in answer to prayer. No one had been told of it and my wife does not now know that I have paid my rent. She does not comprehend my duty. In this way I am sustained, and have been for three months. God knows all my wants. My neighbors do not. Thus God retains me in his vineyard." He closed his letter, "Yours waiting for God to speak, Amen."[9]

But just because Bates had been provided with what he saw as special blessings from God did not mean that he did not endure periods of discomfort. Some months after the "grocery crisis," James White reports that Mrs. Bates had again asked her husband to buy some flour. "Brother Bates," White reported, "had only money enough to buy two pounds of flour so off he went and soon he came in with two pounds of flour. His wife asked, what have you been doing? What will you do next? She declared that she would not bake it."[10] Prudy was apparently just as stubborn as her husband, whom she undoubtedly believed had gone overboard on the Sabbath issue.

The two stories about Bates' finances, even though they are similar, should not be confused. The first is definitely set in the autumn of 1847 during the writing of *Vindication,* while the second is contemporarily dated to the Bristol Conference in mid-1848. What the stories point to is the nearly constant financial difficulties that Bates would experience for the rest of his life. He was a man who had given all for what he believed to be the cause of God, and who would continue to live on the edge of financial solvency so that he could work in ministry despite no regular pay.

The preface of *A Vindication of the Seventh-day Sabbath* sets an aggressive tone. Bates warns his readers not to "forget, while seeking to understand the Scriptures with a simple and honest desire to live *here* by every word of God, to read again and again the warning that God" gave to His people in Revelation 12 and 14. None, he continued, will fully realize God's blessings "but those who are keeping *all* of the Commandments of

God, especially his Holy Seventh-day Sabbath."[11]

He then gets down to his real burden: "I tell you there is not an Advent paper (that I have heard of) published in the land, that is leading to the kingdom. I do not say but what they publish many truths, but their heretical doctrines will, if followed, never, no never, lead you to God!"[12]

With that sentiment Bates lays out his challenge to other Adventists and alerts his readers that his book deals with the attacks that the Sabbath had sustained in the *Advocate* and other periodicals. He makes that purpose explicit again near the end of *Vindication* when he writes that "the very object in sending forth this work, has been to expose these deceivers, who for the last five months more especially, have been bearing down upon this remnant in a paper war, with all the power they could wield."[13]

With that paragraph Bates had put all his cards on the table. Not only were the Sabbath observers the remnant of Revelation 12:17, but the Sundaykeepers were on the devil's side in their warfare on the Sabbath observers. Thus both sides were, as Bates saw it, a fulfillment of eschatological prophecy.

Here Bates' aggressive nature comes through at its strongest. He set out in *Vindication* to "expose these deceivers" who had attacked the Sabbath, and expose them he would. The book's first paragraph addresses the "Sabbath haters" who had written in the *Bible Advocate* and the *Advent Harbinger*. His special targets were Joseph Marsh (editor of the *Harbinger*), Timothy Cole (editor of the *Advocate*), Joseph Turner, and an author who signed himself as "Barnabas." For 60 pages Bates attacks their position. So blunt were his words that Cole would later describe them as being slanderous and as expressing "dark insinuations."[14]

And Bates' accusations had been strong. He had not only refuted the arguments against the Sabbath, but, Burt points out, he had, among other things, alluded to Turner's mesmeric influence on "some of the dear sisters"; accused Cole of a cover-up in not printing all of the material he had on the positive side of the seventh-day argument; and exposed "Barnabas" as Jacob Weston, whom "Bates charged . . . with deceptively trying to get money from C. Stowe through forgery and dissimulation and of other shady financial activities."[15]

With those charges the lid flew off what may have appeared to outsiders to be a somewhat peaceful Adventist community. James White reported that on March 13 "Turner wrote Brother Bates a threatening letter and gave him three weeks to make an acknowledgment of what he had stated in his pamphlet or he should bring him to proper justice." "Well," White added, "his three weeks were out nearly three months ago and Brother Bates is not yet brought to justice."[16]

Weston, meanwhile, had gone through a church trial because of "the charges brought against him by Brother Bates" and "has confessed his forgery." White surmised that the reason that Turner hadn't done anything was that he feared he would "also be exposed." Bates held the same opinion, claiming that "these wolves are too guilty to make much stir about the subject." As to Weston, Bates felt that justice had taken place. "I am glad," he penned, that "the arrow hit him on the head" and that "he has found that he could not long carry on his dark insinuations and open violation of God's holy law under a masked name."[17]

For his own self, Bates had no special concerns. "I have no fear of them," he wrote on April 7. "I know that God is on the side with them who honestly keep His commandments. . . . 'Though an host should encamp against me, I will not fear.' One will yet chase a thousand and two put 10,000 to flight. God be praised that day is dawning, its clear, its certain."[18]

"The only reason then," he added, "that I can see for his [Weston] calling me the Devil . . . is for what I have dared to say against his ungodly conduct. Its not possible for him to impeach my Christian character where I have been known. . . . I fear no search warrants, no scrutiny. My moral character where my home has been for the last 55 years, is beyond the reach of my neighbors; therefore I have nothing to fear from strangers. Indeed, I have no trouble about it. I am satisfied that I am about my Master's business. *And all such characters that I see prowling among the scattered flock of God, if they don't flee, they will hear my voice.*" He would "cry against them."[19]

Beyond the 60 pages in *A Vindication of the Seventh-day Sabbath* taken up in refuting and exposing the "Sabbath haters," Bates published a 15-page letter he had written to William Miller, faulting him for having given up the logic of his earlier position on the shut door (that October 22 had fulfilled prophecy) and for siding with Himes and Marsh (pp. 62-76). The next seven pages (pp. 76-82) focused on the time to begin the Sabbath and proper Sabbath observance, with some of his suggestions being quite rigid. Pages 82 to 91 recapitulate his beliefs regarding Daniel's 2300 days being fulfilled in 1844, the uselessness of setting other dates on the basis of Daniel 8:14, the high priestly ministry of Christ since October 1844, and the rise of the Sabbatarian movement as prophesied in Revelation 14:12. *Vindication's* final 21 pages (92-112) retrace his understanding of the flow of prophetic history (a topic we will treat more fully in chapter 9) and include a lengthy section on the sealing of God's end-time people (see pp. 92-102). That latter topic would become the focal point of his fourth Sabbath book.

Meanwhile, the publication of *Vindication* in January 1848 had definitely set the Shut-Door Sabbatarian Adventists apart as a distinct movement. He and James White, who considered *Vindication* to be "right in the main,"[20] were now the sole leaders among the Sabbathkeeping Adventists. Bates' aggressiveness had resulted in further separation from other Adventist groups.

THE SABBATARIAN CONFERENCES AND THE GATHERING TIME

By mid-1847 the leaders of what was becoming Sabbatarian Adventism were largely united in their beliefs. The next step would be to share their beliefs with others. Their preliminary tactic was to organize a series of conferences. The first Sabbatarian conference convened in the spring of 1848 in Rocky Hill, Connecticut. At least five more took place that year, along with several more in 1849 and 1850. Bates and the Whites were the driving force behind the conferences. And whenever possible all three attended them.

The purpose of the conferences, according to James White, was the "uniting [of] the brethren on the great truths connected with the message of the third angel."[21] By 1848 many Adventists in New England and western New York had become convinced of the truth of one or more of the Sabbatarian doctrines, but they lacked a common consensus.

We need to keep in mind that the conferences sought not to determine doctrine but to spread it evangelistically. The audience, of course, since the Sabbatarians believed that probation had closed for all who had rejected Millerism, was limited to other Adventists—those who had already accepted the first and hopefully the second angels' messages. The task of the evangelists was to present the third angel's message, including the importance of Christ's heavenly ministry, as a part of the answer to what took place at the end of the 2300 days.

James White's report of the first Sabbatarian conference illustrates both the intent of the conferences and some of the dynamics involved. "We had a meeting that evening [Thursday, April 20, 1848] of about fifteen in all," White wrote. "Friday morning the brethren came in until we numbered about fifty. They were not all fully in the truth. Our meeting that day was very interesting. Bro. Bates presented the commandments in a clear light, and their importance was urged home by powerful testimonies. The word had effect to establish those already in the truth, and to awaken those who were not fully decided." [22]

The goal and forces at work in the conferences come out even more clearly in Ellen White's report of the second one, which took place in "Bro. Arnold's barn" in Volney, New York, in August 1848. "There were about thirty-five present [including Bates and Gurney]," she penned, "all that could be collected in that part of the State. There were hardly two agreed. Each was strenuous for his views, declaring that they were according to the Bible. All were anxious for an opportunity to advance their sentiments, or to preach to us. They were told that we had not come so great a distance to hear them, but had come to teach them the truth." After a strenuous meeting in which many of them advocated the various confused ideas of shut-door adventism, she noted that many yielded their errors and united "upon the third angel's message. Our meeting ended victoriously. Truth gained the victory." [23]

Note in the above recollections that Bates and the Whites assumed a strong leadership role. They invariably report Bates as preaching on topics related to the Sabbath and the third angel.

The conferences were successful. "By the spring of 1849," James White observed, "the subject of the Sabbath began to attract considerable notice from Advent believers." [24] In November of that year he could claim that "by the proclamation of the Sabbath truth in . . . connection with the Advent movement, God is making known those that are His. In western N.Y. the number of Sabbath keepers is increasing fast. There are more than twice the number now than six months ago. So it is [also] more or less in Maine, Mass., N.H., Vermont, and Conn. . . .

"The scattering time [as a result of the October disappointment] we have had; it is in the past, and now the time for the saints to be gathered into the unity of the faith, and be sealed by one holy, uniting truth has come. . . . It is true that the work moves slowly, but it moves sure, and it gathers strength at every step. . . .

"Our past Advent experience, and present position and future work is marked out in Rev. 14 Chap. as plain as the prophetic pencil could write it. Thank God that we see it. . . . I believe that the Sabbath truth is yet to ring through the land, as the Advent never has. . . .

". . . I am sick of all our Advent papers, and all our Advent editors, poor creatures. Lamps gone out, still trying to light their blind brethren to the Kingdom of God."[25]

The conference held in Dorchester, Massachusetts, on November 17 and 18, 1848, would hold special interest for Bates. It would make a major impact on his life in at least two ways—one positive and one he viewed as a negative.

SABBATH BOOK NUMBER 4: A PROJECT OF EXTENSION

Both aspects resulted from a vision Ellen White had at Dorchester. The first is that "we were taught to publish the sealing message and God's blessing would follow."[26]

Bates had been interested in the sealing of the 144,000 of Revelation 7:1-4 and 14:1 since at least early 1846. And even though he wrote of the sealing in the general context of the Sabbath at that time, he did not explicitly indicate what relationship (if any) they might have.[27]

His interest in the seal didn't go away with the passage of time. How could it? After all, Bates found it discussed in the book of Revelation, which contrasts those who have the seal of God in their forehead with those who have the mark of the beast in their forehead or on their hand. Beyond that, it is obvious from Revelation that the sealing had to take place before the Second Advent. But unlike the spiritualizers, who "taught that the 144,000 were all 'sealed and safe' since October 1844," Bates saw the sealing as an ongoing experience.[28]

He extensively set forth his understanding of the seal of God in January 1848 in *A Vindication of the Seventh-day Sabbath* (pp. 92-102). In that work he taught that the "angel ascending from the east" was those who were preaching the three angels' messages. Unlike Miller, whose work had started in the west and moved toward the Atlantic coast, the message of the three angels and Revelation 14:12 had begun on the eastern coast and then spread west.[29]

Bates in January 1848 was not very specific about the seal. He did, however, believe that the sealing process had already begun, that those in the process of being sealed would be those who were to be translated or delivered from the earth at the Second Advent without seeing death, and that they would be "the same ones that had come out of the churches" in response to the second angel's message to flee Babylon or the false churches.[30]

At that time he did not identify the seal with the Sabbath, but he came extremely close to doing so when he wrote of those who had left Babylon that "their second advent profession, as in Rev. xiv:12, if adhered to, will bind them to Jesus and seal, or mark, them for the city." He then referred his readers to Revelation 22:14, which reads in the King James Version: "Blessed are they that do his commandments, that they may have right to the tree of life, and may enter in through the gates into the city." Such allusions make it almost certain that Bates had equated the Sabbath and the seal by January 1848. A letter that Bates wrote in August adds probability to that conclusion when he explicitly states, while discussing his argument in *Vindication*, that the seal of God is the Sabbath. He noted in his August letter that the sealing of God's people could not be completed until they were united on the Sabbath. The issue of the sealing was coming more and more to the forefront of his thinking.[31]

But unity on the sealing message was easier to talk about than to achieve, even though the believers held the Sabbatarian conferences to gain that very unity. On November 19, 1848, James White, in describing the recently completed Dorchester conference, noted that during the meeting they had been "arguing some points" which "we did not see alike, in relation to the sealing angel. Its rising from the east, etc. etc. etc."[32]

Bates, he reports, had been struggling with his responsibility to publish the sealing message. "We all felt like uniting to ask wisdom from God on the points in dispute [and] Bro. Bates['] duty in writing. We had an exceeding powerful meeting. Ellen was again taken off in vision."[33]

"She then began to describe the Sabbath light which was the sealing truth." "It arose," she said, "from the rising of the sun." The Sabbath message, she told them, had begun in weakness but it would grow stronger and stronger.[34]

At that point, White indicated that his wife's vision had "corrected Bro. Bates' error on the ascending from the east which was one point of dispute amongst us. You know his view was that the ascending was our going to" western New York up the Erie Canal last August. "This has ever tried me much. Ellen saw that that was erroneous and that the ascending was not to go from one place up to another, but it was this Sabbath seal rising in light, strength, and glory, and power."

"She told Bro. Bates," White added, "to write the things he had seen and heard and the blessing of God would attend it." That is, "he was to write the sealing message as it was corrected by her vision."[35]

In response, Bates published his fourth and final book on the Sabbath in January 1849. *A Seal of the Living God* is best seen as an extension and expansion of the theology of the Sabbath that he had set forth in his two editions of *The Seventh Day Sabbath: A Perpetual Sign* and *A Vindication of the Seventh-day Sabbath*.

In *A Seal of the Living God* Bates once again hammers home the crucial role of the Sabbath in end-time events. The book also discusses how Ellen White's prophetic gift had not only supported his sealing message but had corrected it in terms of the angel ascending from the east. *A Seal* also linked the time of trouble to the sealing. On that latter point, the year 1848 saw several revolutions erupt in Europe. Both James White and Bates tied those disturbances to the beginning of the time of trouble of Daniel 12:2 and the sealing of God's people. Because of the events taking place in the world, Bates felt a great urgency to proclaim the sealing message. He believed that the end was extremely near.[36]

The book also included another discussion on the covenants. As usual, he identified the everlasting covenant as the Ten Commandments. Beyond that, he was quite explicit that only those advent believers who kept the covenant "and especially his Holy Sabbath" would be sealed, while "all advent believers who despise, and reject this covenant, will just as certainly be burned and destroyed with the ungodly wicked at the desolation of this earth. . . . Every commandment in this covenant, must be kept to insure eternal life." But those who "died before they heard the second advent message, never had this test." He regarded decisions on such issues as vital because the judgment had already begun.[37]

Bates concludes the book with a discussion of those lifestyle practices that will characterize God's end-time, sealed people, including abstinence from tobacco and alcohol, the partaking of "good wholesome food," and the duty to sell everything they owned except enough to sustain their families. Given the world crisis of 1848, he (and both of the Whites) were quite certain that the end was upon them. The faithful ones must be ready for their Lord.[38]

In line with his counsel to others, it is significant that Bates, who had sold all his property and given all he had to the Advent movement, had no money to pay for the printing of *A Seal of the Living God.* "A young widow," J. N. Loughborough tells us, "learning of the situation, sold a small home which she possessed in the country, and gave to Elder Bates half of the amount she received for it."[39]

The second impact of the Dorchester vision on Bates had to do with a message Ellen White had for her husband after she came out of vision. "At a meeting held in Dorchester, Mass., [in] November, 1848," she later recalled, "I had been given a view of the proclamation of the sealing message, and of the duty of the brethren to publish the light that was shining upon our pathway." Sometime after the vision ended, she continued, "I said to my husband: 'I have a message for you. You must begin to print a little paper and send it out to the people. Let it be small at first; but as the people read, they will send you means with which to print, and it will be a success from the first. From this small beginning it was shown me to be like streams of light that went clear round the world."[40]

That straightforward message, apparently given to James in private, would soon be the source of a great deal of tension between him and Bates. We will return to that topic in chapter 10. But before examining that conflict we need to look at the changing views of the Sabbatarian leaders on the shut door concept and examine Bates as Sabbatarian Adventism's first historian.

DOORS: OPEN AND SHUT

As you will recall from our earlier discussion, the Sabbatarians had arisen from among the shut door sector of post-disappointment Adventism. Up into 1849 the shut door had had two meanings for the

Sabbatarians. The first, explicitly taught by Miller, stated that probation for sinners would close at the end of the 2300 days when the door was shut on the foolish virgins. The second meaning was that something had happened in October 1844.

Bates held firmly to both of those positions. In fact, he had been one of the most adamant of the shut door advocates. During May 1845, for example, he had written that "the door is shut—not half or three-quarters of the way—but effectually. And our fallen brethren [the Albany Adventists] will soon see their sad mistake!" Even as late as 1850 he was still condemning the Albany Adventists for believing that they could make converts. As Arthur Spalding observes, the "most strenuous" of Sabbatarian Adventism's three founders "in maintaining the 'shut door' was Joseph Bates."[41]

Yet as Merlin Burt points out, even Bates by the time of the publishing of *A Seal of the Living God* in January 1849 realized that Sabbatarian Adventism had a message beyond the ranks of the ex-Millerites. The issue apparently arose in Bates' mind when he began to think about where the 144,000 individuals who needed to be sealed before the end of time would come from. He claimed that two classes would make up that number. First, those advent believers who would accept the Sabbath. And second, "the other part are those who do not yet, so well understand the advent doctrine; but are endeavoring to serve God with their whole hearts, and are willing, and will receive this covenant and Sabbath as soon as they hear it explained." These two groups "will constitute the 144,000, now to be sealed."[42]

And how were those non-adventist types to be reached? His answer was quite explicit—through religious publications being sent around the world, just as they had been circulated during the Millerite period. Bates may have picked up that idea from Ellen White's November 1848 Dorchester vision that stated that Adventist publications would be like "streams of light that went clear round the world."[43]

Thus by early 1849 Bates held to a partially open door for people in other parts of the world, who had not had enough contact with the earlier Millerite message to have been able to firmly reject it. On the other hand, he seems to have remained quite convinced in the late forties that probation had closed for those in North America—a population already adequately evangelized. Thus his continued denunciation of the Albany Adventists and their attempts to convert people when it was already too late.

Bates would hold onto his hardline shut door views for those in North America who had not responded to the Millerite message up into the early 1850s. But by 1852 James White and even Bates had changed their position from a shut evangelistic door to an open evangelistic door. That very year Bates made his first convert in Battle Creek—David Hewitt, who had never been a Millerite. It was a new day for Adventist evangelism. Bates apparently had gone to Michigan seeking stray Adventists to convince on the message of the third angel and managed to convert Hewitt in the process.[44]

Thus between 1849 and 1852 the shut door of evangelism had opened in the minds of Bates and his colleagues. But that opened evangelistic door had a counterpart related to a different allusion to the door metaphor. The new understanding directly related to a vision Ellen White experienced on March 24, 1849. "I saw," she wrote, that "the commandments of God and shut door could not be separated. I saw the time for the commandments of God to shine out to His people was when the door was opened in the inner apartment of the heavenly sanctuary in 1844. Then Jesus rose up and shut the door in the outer apartment and opened the door in the inner apartment and passed into the Most Holy Place, and the faith of Israel now reaches within the second veil where Jesus now stands by the ark. I saw that Jesus had shut the door in the Holy Place and no man can open it, and that he had opened the door in the Most Holy Place and no man can shut it; and that since Jesus had opened the door in the Most Holy Place the commandments have been shining out and God has been testing His people on the holy Sabbath."[45]

In effect, Ellen White had linked the opening of the second apartment of the heavenly sanctuary to the preaching of the Sabbath and the sealing message. Thus she connected the open door of evangelism to the open door of a new message that Sabbatarian Adventists must preach before Jesus could come. Bates would make that same linkage in November 1850.[46]

In the last two chapters we have seen that Joseph Bates was Sabbatarian Adventism's first theologian. In the next chapter we will view him as the movement's first historian. We will also discover that in the mind of Bates history and theology were two sides of the same coin.

---

[1] [J. Marsh], "Seventh-Day Sabbath Abolished," *Voice of Truth*, Apr. 28, 1847, p. 37;

"Questions and Answers," *Voice of Truth*, June 23, 1847, p. 101.

[2] Burt, "Historical Background," pp. 326, 327 (see pp. 326-352 for an extensive treatment of the *Bible Advocate* discussions and Bates' response to them); J. Bates, *Vindication of the Seventh-Day Sabbath*, p. 8; the *Advocate* discussions were originally documented by C. Mervyn Maxwell, "Joseph Bates and Seventh-day Adventist Sabbath Theology," in K. A. Strand, ed., *The Sabbath in Scripture and History* (Washington, D.C.: Review and Herald Pub. Assn., 1982), p. 357, but he never developed the material.

[3] H.C.R., "Bro. Cole," *Bible Advocate,* July 29, 1847, p. 206.

[4] Nath'l Jones, "Bro. Cole," *Bible Advocate,* Aug. 26, 1847, p. 30; John Gibson, "Bro. Cole," *Bible Advocate,* Sept. 23, 1847, p. 63; J. Turner, "The Sabbath—Not Changed," *Bible Advocate,* Jan. 13, 1848, pp. 170, 171; C. Stowe, "Bro. Cole," *Bible Advocate,* Nov. 4, 1847, p. 98; Barnabas, "Dear Bro. Cole," *Bible Advocate,* Sept. 16, 1847, p. 52.

[5] J. B. Cook, "The Sabbath, No. II," *Advent Harbinger*, Sept. 30, 1848, p. 113; J. B. Cook, "The Sabbath, No. III," *Advent Harbinger,* Oct. 21, 1848, p. 138; Burt, "Historical Background," pp. 345, 346.

[6] J. White, *Life Incidents*, p. 269.

[7] J. Bates to Bro. and Sis. Hastings, Apr. 7, 1848; J. N. Loughborough, "Second Advent Experience—No. 4," *Review and Herald,* June 28, 1923, p. 9.

[8] J. N. Loughborough, "Second Advent Experience—No. 4," *Review and Herald,* June 28, 1923, pp. 9, 10; G. H. Gurney to W. A. Spicer, undated letter, in Spicer, *Pioneer Days,* pp. 59, 60.

[9] J. Bates to Bro. and Sis. Hastings, Apr. 7, 1848.

[10] J. White to Bro. [Howland], July 2, 1848.

[11] J. Bates, *Vindication of the Seventh-day Sabbath,* p. 1.

[12] *Ibid.*

[13] *Ibid.,* p. 106.

[14] *Ibid.,* pp. 106, 3; T. Cole, "We Spent the Sabbath. . . . ," *Bible Advocate,* Mar. 2, 1848, pp. 22, 23; cited in Burt, "Historical Background," p. 348.

[15] Burt, "Historical Background," pp. 349-351; J. Bates, *Vindication of the Seventh-day Sabbath,* pp. 16, 17, 47, 48, 29-31.

[16] J. White to Bro. [Howland], July 2, 1848.

[17] *Ibid.;* J. Bates to Bro. and Sis. Hastings, Apr. 7, 1848.

[18] J. Bates to Bro. and Sis. Hastings, Apr. 7, 1848.

[19] *Ibid.* (italics supplied).

[20] J. White to Bro. [Howland], July 2, 1848.

[21] J. White, "A Brief Sketch of the Past," *Review and Herald,* May 6, 1852, p. 5.

[22] J. White to Bro. Howland, undated letter, in E. G. White, *Spiritual Gifts,* vol. 2, p. 93.

[23] E. G. White, *ibid.,* pp. 97-99.

[24] J. White, *Life Incidents,* p. 275.

[25] J. White to Bro. Bowles, Nov, 8, 1849.

[26] J. Bates, *Seal of the Living God,* p. 26.

[27] J. Bates, *Opening Heavens,* p. 37.

[28] Pöhler, *Continuity and Change in Adventist Teaching,* p. 72.

[29] J. Bates, *Vindication of the Seventh-day Sabbath,* pp. 94, 95.

[30] *Ibid.,* pp. 96, 99.

[31] *Ibid.,* p. 95; J. Bates to Bro. and Sis. Hastings, Aug. 7, 1848.

[32] J. White to Bro. and Sis. Howland, Nov, 19, 1848.

[33] *Ibid.*

[34] *Ibid.*

[35] *Ibid.*

[36] J. Bates, *Seal of the Living God,* pp. 24-32, 15, 48, 50.

[37] *Ibid.,* pp. 60-62, 38, 39.

[38] *Ibid.,* pp. 66-69; J. White, [editorial], *Present Truth,* July 1849, p. 1; E. G. White to Bro. and Sis. Hastings, Mar. 23, 1849; cf. J. Bates, *Vindication of the Seventh-day Sabbath,* p. 67.

[39] J. N. Loughborough, *The Great Second Advent Movement: Its Rise and Progress* (Washington, D.C.: Review and Herald Pub. Assn., 1905), p. 312.

[40] E. G. White, *Life Sketches of Ellen G. White* (Mountain View, Calif.: Pacific Press Pub. Assn., 1915), p. 125.

[41] J. Bates, "Letter From Bro. Joseph Bates," *Jubilee Standard,* May 29, 1845, p. 90; J. Bates, "Midnight Cry in the Past," *Review and Herald,* Dec. 1850, p. 23; J. Bates, "The Laodicean Church," *Review and Herald,* Nov. 1850, pp. 7, 8; Arthur W. Spalding, *Origin and History of Seventh-day Adventists,* vol. 1, p. 163.

[42] Burt, "Historical Background," p. 368; J. Bates, *Seal of the Living God,* pp. 61, 62. See also, Damsteegt, *Foundations of the Seventh-day Adventist Message and Mission,* pp. 158-160.

[43] J. Bates, *Seal of the Living God,* p. 34; E. G. White, *Life Sketches* (1915), p. 125.

[44] J. White, "The Work of the Lord," *Review and Herald,* May 6, 1852, pp. 4, 5; Spalding, *Origin and History of Seventh-day Adventists,* vol. 1, pp. 255, 257, 258; "Open and Shut Door," *Seventh-day Adventist Encyclopedia,* 2d rev. ed. (Hagerstown, Md.: Review and Herald Pub. Assn., 1996), vol. 2, pp. 249-252.

[45] E. G. White to Bro. and Sis. Hastings, Apr. 21, 1849.

[46] J. Bates, "The Laodicean Church," *Review and Herald,* Nov. 1850, p. 8; see also, Burt, "Historical Background," pp. 373-384.

Chapter IX

SABBATARIAN ADVENTISM'S FIRST
HISTORIAN: HISTORY AS THEOLOGY

JOSEPH Bates was not only Sabbatarian Adventism's first theologian, he was also the movement's first historian. But as indicated by the subtitles to chapters 7-9, Bates never quite separated history and theology in his mind. Rather, they were two aspects of the same topic.

Nearly every one of his book titles reflects that interrelatedness of theology and history. That is true of even his two editions of *The Seventh Day Sabbath, A Perpetual Sign* (1846, 1847), which carry the subtitle of *From the Beginning to the Entering Into the Gates of the Holy City, According to the Commandment.* That same historical bent appears in his *Opening Heavens* (1846) and most explicitly in his 1847 *Second Advent Way Marks and High Heaps: Or a Connected View, of the Fulfillment of Prophecy, by God's Peculiar People, From the Year 1840 to 1847.* He extends that history in A *Vindication of the Seventh-day Sabbath* (1848), which has *With a Further History of God's Peculiar People, From 1847 to 1848* as part of its subtitle. There is even a sense in which his *Seal of the Living God* (1849) moves his history into 1849, since Bates saw the sealing as the big event of the year and accordingly supplied *A Hundred Fourty-Four Thousand, of the Servants of God Being Sealed, in 1849* as the subtitle.

For Bates Sabbatarian Adventism was a movement and a message anchored in history. More than that, he equated the flow of history with prophecy both fulfilled and being fulfilled. Whereas in chapters 7 and 8, we examined those of Bates' books that focused on the theological aspect of his message, the present chapter will emphasize those of his works that take history as their primary orientation.

HISTORY BOOK NUMBER 1:
ANALYZING THE SPIRITUALIZERS

We noted in chapter 4 that Millerism split into several parts after the

October 1844 disappointment. One of those sections came to believe that Christ had arrived on October 22, 1844, but that He had come spiritually into the hearts of men and women rather than visibly in the clouds of heaven.

That sector of Adventism witnessed a great deal of fanaticism during 1845 and early 1846. On one level, a significant number held that it was wrong to work, since they were now in the seventh millennium and God's eternal Sabbath had begun. To work would "result in their final destruction."[1]

Other extremists, in order to demonstrate that they were spiritually in heaven, sought to follow Christ's injunction to humble themselves and become as little children. Thus, recalls Sylvester Bliss, some sat on the floor as an act of humility, while others shaved their heads or acted like children in understanding. Even more impressive (or humbling) must have been those who crept around their houses on all fours. Not only was such humility practiced at home and in church, but some found it necessary to witness to the world around them by crawling through the busy streets of town.[2]

While the non-Adventist community might smile at the sight of their neighbors crawling to the local store, they did not find some of the actual and supposed sexual aberrations of the Spiritualizers nearly so humorous. Topping the list of complaints in this area were beliefs regarding holy kissing and spiritual wifery. J. D. Pickands, for example, defended a man and a woman who had deserted their spouses and families and had lived together for several months as a "spiritual pair" as they traveled from place to place. Pickands said that such conduct "was consistent with their doctrine, which would permit a 'spiritual matrimony without sexual connexion.'" A local judge, having less exalted views of the relationship, ordered the couple to post bail at "'$200 each, on the charge of adultery.'"[3]

On the other end of the sexual morality spectrum was Enoch Jacobs, who led a large number of spiritualizing Adventists into Shakerism beginning in early 1846. The celebate Shakers believed that the second coming of Christ's spirit had taken place in their prophetess Ann Lee in 1770. Many disappointed Adventists, feeling the need to escape the sneers of a hostile world, eventually concluded that the Shakers had had the truth all along—that Christ had indeed come in spirit.[4] The fact that Jacobs was one of the spearheads of the move toward Shakerism was problematic for

Bates, since Jacobs' *Day-Star* had been one of the shut door periodicals in which he published articles. In fact, one of the earliest contacts between Bates and James White and Ellen Harmon was undoubtedly through the pages of the *Day-Star,* for which all three had written.

The spiritualizing confusion, including the drift toward Shakerism, deeply disturbed Bates. It was in that context that he penned his first little book in early May 1846: *The Opening Heavens, or a Connected View of the Testimony of the Prophets and Apostles, Concerning the Opening Heavens, Compared With Astronomical Observations, and of the Present and Future Location of the New Jerusalem, the Paradise of God.*

His purpose for writing was "to correct, or 'rebuke' the spiritual views . . . in respect to the appearing and kingdom of our Lord and Saviour Jesus Christ." "Thousands," he noted, "who have been looking for the personal appearing of the Lord Jesus from heaven in these last days, have, in their disappointment about his coming, given up the only Scriptural view, and are now teaching that he has come in spirit."[5]

As its title page indicates, Bates based his 39-page tract partly on scriptural evidence and partly on the astronomical facts of the day. On the scriptural side of his argument, he amasses the biblical data that indicates a literal Second Advent and a literal New Jerusalem that would eventually descend from heaven. He left no doubt that the Bible taught that people would "'SEE *the Son of man coming in the clouds of heaven.*'" Beyond that, Bates emphasized the fact that the "great error" of the Spiritualizers "has arisen in consequence of taking the symbolical meaning" of the Bible, "and rejecting the true."[6]

It is in that context that he first raises the issue of the heavenly sanctuary. In particular, he recommended the article O.R.L. Crosier had published on the topic in the February 7, 1846, issue of the *Day-Star* Extra. "In my humble opinion," Bates exuded, "it is superior to any thing of the kind extant." He went on to emphasize the literalness of the heavenly sanctuary, in the process equating the sanctuary with the New Jerusalem. That sanctuary, he argued, must be cleansed along with the saints. And it would be accomplished by blood, just as in the earthly sanctuary. In his argument Bates went out of his way to note that neither the earth nor any thing or any group of people on the earth was the sanctuary.[7]

On the astronomical side of the argument in *The Opening Heavens*

Bates' main point was to describe the great "gap" in the sky known as Orion's Sword . . . through which one may see (as it were) part of a much brighter region," which he equated with the third heaven or the realm of God. He concluded his treatment by noting that the New Jerusalem or heavenly sanctuary or "our coming Lord's EVERLASTING kingdom" was "about to descend from the 'third heaven' by the way of the open door, down by the 'flaming sword' of Orion." His appeal was for God's people to be ready.[8]

Bates claimed that the Spiritualizers' interpretation of Scripture was as deceptive as sailing into Boston Harbor at night during a severe storm. To do that could put both ship and passengers on the rocks without warning. "Good God," he exclaimed, "help us steer clear of these spiritual interpretations of Thy word, where it is made so clear that the second coming and kingdom of Christ will be as literal and real, as the events that transpired at the first Advent, now recorded in history."[9]

It is interesting to note that Bates raised the issue of the seventh-day Sabbath in his May 1846 book. After quoting Revelation 22:14 to the effect that it would be commandment keepers who would "'enter in through the gates into the [heavenly] city,'" he asked his readers to cite "chapter and verse" to show where God had abolished the fourth commandment. "I say it cannot be found within the lids of the bible [sic]."[10]

A gift from a "poor sister" who had sold "a fine stripped rag carpet" that she had just completed for her home made the publication of *The Opening Heavens* possible for the financially destitute Bates. But like Bates himself, she had a firm belief that she would soon be in a heavenly sphere that would pale into insignificance the sacrifice of the only carpet she had ever owned.[11]

In that little book Bates took one of his first steps toward placing what would eventually become Sabbatarian Adventism into the flow of prophetic history. Prophetic history was a topic that had interested him ever since the October 1844 disappointment. As early as December 4 of that year he had been exploring the implications of Revelation 10 and noted that the Revelator was providing "a history of the events which were to transpire" before the sounding of the seventh trumpet. Bates concluded a letter to the periodical *Voice of Truth* by asking the Lord to "help us to obtain our true position on this stormy sea, and again spread all our sails for the gale that shall waft us into the harbor of glory." [12]

Historical positioning within the prophetic framework was crucial to him. While he had begun to work out its details in *The Opening Heavens,* his most significant contribution would come with the publication of *Second Advent Way Marks and High Heaps, or a Connected View, of the Fulfillment of Prophecy, by God's Peculiar People, From the Year 1840 to 1847.*

HISTORY BOOK NUMBER 2:
ANALYZING THE ALBANY ADVENTISTS

Like so many of Bates' books, the publication of *Second Advent Way Marks* was made possible by someone else sacrificially paying for it. In this case a young woman sold her house and provided Bates with the funds to pay the printing costs.[13]

Some have found the book's title to be interesting if not downright peculiar. Bates got the idea from Jeremiah 31:21: "'Set thee up *waymarks,* make thee high *heaps;* set thine heart toward the highway, even the way which thou wentest.'"[14] The idea behind both Bates' title and the biblical text is that in a land that did not have regular roads, people across time have marked trees to show the pathway. Or, in terrain without trees, individuals leave little piles (heaps) of stones to designate a route. Beyond that symbolism, the Old Testament uses piles of stones to help Israel remember how God had led in its past history (see, e.g., Joshua 4:1-7, 21, 22).

Bates employed those symbols to indicate how God had led His Adventist people in their recent past, especially from 1840 to 1847. As Bates put it, "The design of the author of the following pages is to strengthen and encourage the honest hearted, humble people of God, that have been, and still are, willing to keep the COMMANDMENTS of God and the testimony of Jesus, to hold on to their past experience, in the connected chain of wonderful events and fulfilment of prophecy, which have been developed during the last seven years. . . . While we are in the fiery furnace, being shaped for the building that is in the heaven of heavens, we are exhorted to look back to these WAYMARKS and HIGH HEAPS in our pathway, that our confidence may be unshaken in our glorious commander, who has brought us off victorious thus far" and has promised victory if we trust in Him.[15]

In short, *Way Marks* is a tracing of God's providential leading of

Adventism from its beginning up through 1847. Part of Bates' purpose, C. Mervyn Maxwell points out, was to restore confidence in the 1844 movement by reviewing the evidence of how God had led them in the past.[16]

The first landmark centers on the work of William Miller and his preaching of the judgment hour message of the first angel of Revelation 14:6, 7. After tracing Miller's religious movement, Bates remarks that *"all"* advent believers were "agreed down to this point."[17]

Subsequent landmarks built upon the Millerite platform. Especially important were the second angel's message of Revelation 14:8 regarding the fall of Babylon and the third angel's message of verses 9-11 that indicated the punishment of those who refused to leave Babylon. As noted in chapter 7, at this early date Bates did not include verse 12 in the third angel's message. Beyond that, he had the third message ending in October 1844.[18] James White, as we will see later, would soon challenge both positions.

Bates' fifth waymark was the midnight cry message of S. S. Snow that Christ would come on the Jewish Day of Atonement (October 22) in 1844. Bates had not the slightest doubt in the validity of that movement. Nor did he in 1847 have any question about probation having forever closed for all but Adventists on that date. As far as he was concerned "our work ended here for the world."[19]

That conclusion brought Bates to waymarks six through eight, in which those Millerites following Himes rejected the fulfillment of prophecy in October 1844 along with the close of probation at that time. Those holding such "heresies" formed a new church organization at Albany, New York, in May 1845 and thereby became the lukewarm or nominal Laodicean church, while Bates saw those Adventists who remained faithful to God's leading in their past and to the Sabbath as now comprising the church of Philadelphia or church of brotherly love.[20]

Bates firmly believed that he knew the intended evangelistic audience of the Philadelphia Sabbatarians. It is the backsliders of the Laodicean Albany Adventists "that we are after; we want to get them out to our meetings, that they may hear us preach the doctrine of the kingdom, and be converted, and become good and substantial adventists."[21]

The ninth waymark was the call of Revelation 14:12 to keep all the commandments of God (including the Sabbath), which had begun to be preached soon after the October 1844 disappointment. "God's children," Bates expounded, "are to be saved, if at all, by doing or keeping the commandments." [22]

The final waymark was the perilous situations the Sabbathkeepers would have to face as they approached the end of time. The very next sign, he claimed, was for "the voice of God to shake the heavens and the earth." Believers needed to remember the waymarks of God's leading so that they might be ready for their Lord. [23]

The message of Bates' two historical books is quite clear. In short, the Spiritualizers had fallen off the pathway of faith through spiritualizing away (regarding as non-literal) the obvious meaning of the Bible, while the Albany Adventists had gone astray by denying Miller's understanding of prophecy and forgetting how God had led His people in their past history. The moral of that history was clear to Bates: God was forming an Adventist people who were obeying the commandments of God. From his perspective, the Sabbatarians were the only group of Adventists that had remained faithful to divine leading.

VARIATIONS ON A THEME

The general flow of events set forth by Bates in *Second Advent Waymarks* became an anchor point for him throughout his post-disappointment experience. Thus in 1848 he could write that "you will also see that the *Waymarks* and high heaps in your pathway, *past and present*, are the only sure earthly guides to the peaceful haven of eternal rest." [24]

In that context he could never excuse Himes, Litch, and Miller for leading so many Adventists astray at the Albany meetings in May 1845. That same month he wrote that he saw no need for "organizations and a creed . . . for God's waiting people at this last moment of time. . . . It does appear plain to me that the next organization for God's people, after leaving Babylon, will be in the air with our glorious King." [25] Of course, at the center of Bates' criticism of the Albany Adventists was their rejection of some of the waymarks, including the October fulfillment of prophecy. In the years to come he would repeatedly stigmatize the Albany movement as being the Laodicean church of Revelation 3. [26]

In particular, he became quite aggressive against the leaders of the Albany Adventists—Miller, Himes, and Litch. In June 1845 he confronted Litch, who "thinks we ran off the track last fall [October 1844]." To the contrary, Bates asserted, it was Litch who was off the track. Joseph was quite convinced that God would lead them if they held onto their prophetic history.[27]

An old associate, J. V. Himes, also came under Bates' guns. Himes had written to him on October 30, 1844, indicating that he believed that God had guided in the recent movement and that they had *"condemned the world"* through their faith. But, Bates claimed in later years, it was Himes himself, having changed his position on that crucial waymark, who now stood condemned.[28]

While Bates targeted Litch and Himes, Miller received the brunt of his ire. In an extensive letter[29] that Bates eventually published, he claims that the Adventist pioneer had lost the affection of the Sabbatarians because he had called them "Fanatics, Door-Shutters, and almost any thing but honest people" and had made them feel "that they are worse than the heathen." The Sabbatarians had originally followed Miller's message, Bates told him, because "you began with a strait-forward bible [sic] course, and it cut like a sword with two edges." But now Miller had rejected his own logic and "our track has been made dark by your opposition." Telling Miller that if he should meet the Sabbatarians in the kingdom of God he would have some confessing to do, Bates noted that "our course is onward [i.e., along the path of the waymarks]; we leave you to say what you please of us." [30]

Bates particularly lamented that "thousands on thousands" had followed their Adventist leaders and had "turned into the enemy's ranks, leaving the remnant to finish up the work" of preaching God's truth and gathering in the 144,000.[31]

Central to his thinking was the fact that the fulfillment of Bible prophecy was a "harmonious chain of events" that had both sequence and direction. And at the focal point of that chain of Bible prophecy were the messages of the three angels that proceeded from Miller's hour of God's judgment message up through the time that the Sabbath message would be given right before the second advent of Christ (Rev. 14:6-20).[32]

Soon after the disappointment Bates began to utilize the chain-of-prophetic-events approach to history. He brought the concept to its maturity between 1846 and 1848. But he would continue to focus on that interpretive model for both history and theology for the rest of his life. Bates would stick by the general outline of his earlier understanding of the progress of prophetic history even though he would vary the details as time passed.[33]

J. N. Loughborough recalled that when he was working with Bates as a young preacher in 1853 and 1854 the older man's "favorite subject" was way marks and high heaps.[34] In that interpretation of history Bates bequeathed a legacy to Sabbatarianism that would shape both its theological self-understanding and its mission.

A THEOLOGICAL/HISTORICAL LEGACY
FOR JAMES WHITE AND HIS PROTÉGÉS

James White was excited about Bates' *Second Advent Way Marks and High Heaps*. He praised it to a friend a month after its publication, noting that "Brother Bates is out with a book on our past experience. I think it will do good." Three months later James wrote that Bates' "works on the Lord's Sabbath, and our past experience are very precious to us in this time of trial." He went on to "thank God for qualifying our Brother Bates so that he has so clearly harmonized our past experience with the Bible, and also so clearly defended the Sabbath question." At that point in his letter, though, White ominously added that he fully agreed with Bates "in the main."[35]

Without the slightest doubt White greatly appreciated Bates' harmonization of Adventist history with prophecy. Nor can we have any doubt that for White the high point of that harmonization had to do with the ongoing flow of the messages of the three angels of Revelation 14. Both men regarded the fulfillment of that prophecy as a successive chain of events. But they viewed its flow somewhat differently.

Bates, as we saw in chapter 7, held that the first angel's message of Revelation 14:6, 7 had begun with Miller's preaching of the message of the hour of God's judgment. The second angel (verse 8) with its proclamation of the fall of Babylon followed the first. And the third (verses 9-11), which specified the punishment of those who refused to come out of the fallen churches, succeeded the second and took the flow of history up to the October 1844 disappointment. It was after that, according to Bates, that the Sabbath message of Revelation 14 had begun.[36] Chapter 7 diagramed Bates' understanding of the three angels' messages as follows:

October
1844

verses 6, 7	verse 8	verses 9-11	verse 12
1st angel	2nd angel	3rd angel	The preaching of the Sabbath beginning after the disappointment

While White generally concurred with Bates on the three angels' messages, in May 1847 he publicly took issue with the older man on the historic timing of the sequence of the three messages, claiming that he could not agree with him. For James "the second angel brought us to the 7th month, 1844," while the third (in which he included verses 9-12 as opposed to Bates' 9-11) had begun at that time.[37] White's revised understanding appears as follows:

October
1844

verses 6, 7	verse 8	verses 9-12
1st angel	2nd angel	3rd angel

Bates soon accepted White's perspective of the three angel's sequence, but eventually both of them would see the messages as not only being sequential but also simultaneous, an understanding that we can diagram in the following manner:

October
1844

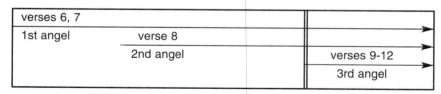

Here the messages began at different times but each continues to the end of time. As a result, the Sabbatarian Adventists would eventually come to refer to their mission as either the preaching of the message of the three angels or the preaching of the message of the third angel.

Speaking of his developing grasp of the three angels of Revelation 14, Bates could look back from 1868 and claim that "although at first the light on this subject was not one-tenth part as clear as it is at the present time, the humble children of God were ready to receive [it] and walk in it."[38]

Even though White had refined Bates' early understanding of the sequence of Revelation 14, he was still indebted to the older man for the perspective itself. That viewpoint would form the central core of his and his wife's interpretation of prophetic history for the rest of their extended ministries.

Enthused by Bates' understanding of prophetic history, James wrote that "our past Advent experience, and present position and future work is marked out in Rev. 14 Chap. as plain as the prophetic pencil could write it."[39]

It was that progressive message that White would preach as a "chain of events" extending from the time of Miller "down to the time when 'the vine of the earth' will be cast 'into the great wine-press of the wrath of God'" (see Rev. 14:14-20). The first angel's message had brought the Adventists the Second Advent truth and eventually caused conflict with the denominations in which they held their membership. At that point, White argued, "the second angel's message called us out from the fallen churches where we are now free to think, and act for ourselves in the fear of God." At that very time, he pointed out, they had discovered the Sabbath truth. "It is an exceedingly interesting fact," White penned, "that the Sabbath question began to be agitated among second advent believers immediately after they were called out of the churches by the second angel's message. God's work moves in order. The Sabbath truth came up in just the right time to fulfil prophecy," especially the prophecy of the third angel's message.[40]

God "called us from the bondage of the churches in 1844," White proclaimed in an echo of Bates' message to the disappointed Millerites, "and there humbled us, and has been proving us, and has been developing the hearts of his people, and seeing whether they would keep his commandments. . . . Many stopped at the first angel's message, and others at the second, and many will refuse the third; but a few will 'follow the Lamb withersoever he goeth,' and go up and possess the land."[41]

Bates in his theological and historical works had pioneered James

White's understanding of Adventism. That framework would shape White's thinking and ministry for the rest of his life. Not only would he be guided by Bates' historical/theological perspective of Adventism's place in prophetic history, but so would White's protégés. James would promote such younger men as John Nevins Andrews and Uriah Smith in the 1850s and 1860s as they filled out the prophetic outline first set forth by Bates in 1847 and 1848.

White's wife would also find Bates' chain-of-events prophetic understanding to be forceful. "In reviewing our past history," Ellen White would later write, "having traveled over every step of advance to our present standing, I can say, Praise God! As I see what the Lord has wrought, I am filled with astonishment, and with confidence in Christ as leader. We have nothing to fear for the future, except as we shall forget the way the Lord has led us, and His teaching in our past history."[42] She would spend a great deal of her energy in a lifetime of writing in developing the great controversy theme of Revelation 12:17–14:20 first highlighted by Bates in his January 1847 book on the Sabbath.

Because of the work of Bates, Sabbatarians and then Seventh-day Adventists would see themselves as a people of prophecy. That understanding would not only shape their theology but it would eventually empower their sense of mission.

A MISSIOLOGICAL LEGACY
FOR A WORLDWIDE MOVEMENT

Bates' understanding of prophetic history not only left the Sabbatarians with a theological/historical legacy but also a missiological one.

One of the most remarkable aspects of Sabbatarian Adventism and the Seventh-day Adventist Church has been its continuing growth across time. In 1845 when there were an estimated 50,000 Albany or first day Adventists, there existed almost no Sabbatarians. As we noted above, the Sabbatarian movement really didn't get under way until about 1848.

D. T. Taylor published the first Adventist census in 1860. He counted 584 ministers, with 365 advocating Sunday and 57 the seventh day. Beyond that, he estimated some 54,000 laymembers, but did not attempt to break them down according to belief. However, other sources indicate that more than 3,000 were Sabbatarians.[43]

Taylor's census also gathered estimates regarding the subscription lists of the various Adventist journals. The Advent Christian *World's Crisis* and the Evangelical Adventist *Advent Herald* (movements representing nearly all of the Sundaykeeping Adventists) had circulations respectively of 2,900 and 2,100 subscribers, while the much smaller Sabbatarian group supported 2,300 subscriptions to the *Review and Herald* and 2,000 to the *Youth's Instructor.* Taylor went out of his way to note that the promoters of the Sabbatarian *Review and Herald,* "though a decided minority, are very devoted, zealous, and active in the promulgation of their peculiar views of Sunday and Sabbath."[44]

A century and a half later the Evangelical Adventist denomination would be gone and the Advent Christians would claim a United States membership of 26,264, while the Seventh-day Adventist Church recorded 880,921 members in the United States and approximately 13,000,000 worldwide. As Clyde Hewitt, an Advent Christian historian, put it, "the tiniest of the Millerite offshoot groups was the one which would become by far the largest."[45]

The same sort of picture emerges when we compare the statistics of the Seventh Day Baptists with the Seventh-day Adventists. Their 4,800 members in the United States in 1995 was less than their estimated 6,000 in the 1840s. As one Seventh Day Baptist preacher told Bates, "there was a power attending" the Sabbatarian message "that waked up, and brought people to keep the Sabbath, which [the Seventh Day Baptist] preaching could not do." He claimed that the Baptists had been able to convince people on the correctness of the Sabbath, but that they could not get them motivated as the Sabbatarians did.[46]

In the face of such statistics it is obvious that merely preaching the correct doctrine of the Advent or the Sabbath was not sufficient in itself to create a mission mentality that would lead to serious growth. What, we need to ask, did the Sabbatarians have that the Sundaykeeping Adventists and the Seventh Day Baptists lacked? That question takes us back to Bates and his chain-of-events understanding of prophetic history.

Bates' perspective finds its roots in Millerism. It was a state of prophetic urgency that made Millerism a mission-driven movement. And that arose from a specific interpretation of the prophecies of Daniel and Revelation. The Millerites gave of their time and means because they believed with all their hearts that they had a message people *must* hear.

That same impetus entered Sabbatarian Adventism through Bates' extension of the chain-of-prophecy view of history beyond the first and second angels' messages to the third. In other words, Bates' historical/theological understanding not only maintained Miller's prophetic scheme of interpretation but extended it in such a way as to give meaning to both the 1844 disappointment and the remaining time before Christ's advent. Central to that expanded interpretation was not only the progressive nature of the three angels' messages of Revelation 14, but his placing of the second apartment ministry of Christ (Rev. 11:19) and the seventh-day Sabbath (Rev. 12:17; 14:12) in an apocalyptic, great controversy context. The Sabbatarians through Bates began to see themselves as a prophetic movement rather than merely as another church.

That self understanding would eventually drive the Sabbatarians to mission. By the beginning of the twenty-first century the conviction that they were a movement of prophecy had resulted in Seventh-day Adventism sponsoring one of the most widespread mission-outreach programs in the history of Christianity. By 2002 it had established work in 203 of the 228 countries then recognized by the United Nations.[47]

That kind of dedication did not come by accident—it was the direct result of Bates' chain-of-events prophetic understanding of mission responsibility. Motivating that prophetic conviction was the imperative of the first angel of Revelation 14:6, 7 to preach "to every nation, and kindred, and tongue, and people" and the teaching of Revelation 10:11 that the disappointed ones "must prophesy again before many peoples, and nations, and tongues, and kings."[48] While the full extent of that commission was not apparent to Bates in the 1840s (he still held largely to his shut door convictions), it progressively became clearer to the denomination that would follow him in its understanding of prophecy.

Hewitt, in seeking in 1983 to explain the success of the Seventh-day Adventists as opposed to the attrition faced by his Advent Christians, touched upon an essential element when he noted that "Seventh-day Adventists are convinced that they have been divinely ordained to carry on the prophetic work started by William Miller. They are dedicated to the task."[49] Both the conviction and the earliest dedication to the task of spreading the third angel's message find their roots in the thought and life of Joseph Bates, who would become not only Adventism's first theologian but also its first "missionary."

In contrast to the prophetically-based Sabbatarian conviction, Hewitt's father wrote to F. D. Nichol in 1944 that the Advent Christians had given up Miller's interpretation of Daniel 8:14 and the 2300 days and had no unanimity on the meaning of the text. Another leading Advent Christian scholar interviewed in 1984 noted that his denomination no longer even had any agreed-upon interpretation of the millennium—a teaching at the very heart of Miller's contribution.[50]

The other post-Millerite Adventist bodies all stepped off of Miller's prophetic platform. That abandonment eventually led to missiological aimlessness. By way of contrast, Joseph Bates not only stayed on the platform but strengthened and extended it in such a way that the logic of his prophetic chain-of-events impelled the Sabbatarians to become an aggressive mission-oriented movement.

In 1869 the Seventh Day Baptist General Conference sent a message to the Seventh-day Adventist General Conference, rejoicing "that in God's good providence he has, in you, so largely increased the number of those who observe His holy Sabbath." It is strange to the Seventh Day Baptist leadership, the message continued, "that after the apparently fruitless toil of the long night which has been upon us, this gratifying change [in the number of Sabbathkeepers] should come so suddenly." The letter went on to reject any eschatological implications of the Sabbath.[51]

But it was just those eschatological, prophetic implications that stood at the center of Bates' understanding of both history and theology. It was what he did with them that would make the Sabbatarians an aggressive, mission-oriented people from 1848 onward.[52] Thus he was not only Sabbatarian Adventism's first theologian and first historian, but also its first mission theorist. The combined understanding of those three fields, as we will see in chapter 11, would become a driving force as he becomes the movement's first missionary.

---

[1] J. V. Himes, "Visit to Portland With Brother Miller," *Morning Watch*, June 12, 1845, p. 192. For a more extensive treatment of post-disappointment Millerite fanaticism, see Knight, *Millennial Fever*, pp. 245-266.

[2] Sylvester Bliss, *Memoirs of William Miller* (Boston: Joshua V. Himes, 1853), p. 309; "Mutual Conference of Adventists at Albany," *Morning Watch,* May 8, 1845, p. 151; E. G. White, *Life Sketches* (1915), pp. 85, 86.

[3] "Spiritual Wifery," *Advent Herald,* Apr. 8, 1846, p. 72.

[4] On Adventism and Shakerism, see Knight, *Millennial Fever,* pp. 257-263. See also, Lawrence Foster, "Had Prophecy Failed? Contrasting Perspectives of the Millerites and Shakers," in Numbers and Butler, eds., *The Disappointed,* pp. 173-188; Stephen J. Stein, *The Shaker Experience in America* (New Haven, Conn.: Yale University Press, 1992), pp. 208-210.

[5] J. Bates, *Opening Heavens,* p. 1.

[6] *Ibid.,* pp. 17, 20.

[7] *Ibid.,* pp. 25, 28, 29, 31, 32, 21.

[8] *Ibid.,* pp. 6-12, 39.

[9] *Ibid.,* p. 27.

[10] *Ibid.,* p. 36.

[11] J. N. Loughborough, "Second Advent Experience—No. 5," *Review and Herald,* July 5, 1923, p. 5; J. N. Loughborough, "Early Experiences in the Publishing Work—No. 4," *Review and Herald,* June 4, 1908, pp. 19, 20.

[12] J. Bates, "Dear Brother," *Voice of Truth,* Dec. 18, 1844, pp. 187, 188.

[13] J. N. Loughborough, "Early Experiences in the Publishing Work—No. 5," *Review and Herald,* June 18, 1908, p. 19.

[14] J. Bates, *Second Advent Way Marks and High Heaps,* p. 3.

[15] *Ibid.,* p. 1.

[16] C. Mervyn Maxwell, "The Investigative Judgment: Its Early Development," in Frank B. Holbrook, ed. *Doctrine of the Sanctuary: A Historical Survey (1845-1863)* (Silver Spring, Md.: Biblical Research Institute, 1989), p. 137.

[17] J. Bates, *Second Advent Way Marks,* pp. 6-16.

[18] *Ibid.,* pp. 16-29.

[19] *Ibid.,* pp. 30-33.

[20] *Ibid.,* pp. 33-68.

[21] *Ibid.,* p. 53.

[22] *Ibid.,* pp. 68, 77, 79.

[23] *Ibid.,* pp. 79, 80.

[24] J. Bates, *Vindication of the Seventh-day Sabbath,* p. 1.

[25] J. Bates, "Letter From Bro. Joseph Bates," *Jubilee Standard,* May 29, 1845, p. 90.

[26] See, e.g., J. Bates, "The Laodicean Church," *Review and Herald,* Nov. 1850, pp. 7, 8; J. Bates, "Our Labor in the Philadelphia and Laodicean Churches," *Review and Herald,* Aug. 19, 1851, pp. 13, 14.

[27] J. Bates, "Letter From Bro. Bates," *Jubilee Standard,* June 12, 1845, p. 111.

[28] J. V. Himes to J. Bates, Oct. 30, 1844, in J. Bates, "Midnight Cry in the Past," *Review and Herald,* Dec. 1850, p. 23; J. Bates, *Second Advent Waymarks and High Heaps,* pp. 45, 46.

[29] J. Bates, *Vindication of the Seventh-day Sabbath,* pp. 62-76.

[30] *Ibid.,* pp. 62, 66-71.

[31] *Ibid.,* pp. 97, 98.

[32] *Ibid.,* pp. 110, 102-104.

[33] See, e.g., *The Advent Review,* Sept. 1850, pp. 51-56; Nov. 1850, pp. 65-70.

[34] J. N. Loughborough, "Some Individual Experience, A Companion to the Book, 'The Great Second Advent Movement,'" unpub. ms., n.d., preface, p. 1.

[35] J. White to Sis. Hastings, May 21, 1847; J. White to Sis. Hastings, Aug. 22, 1847.

[36] J. Bates, *Seventh Day Sabbath* (1847), pp. 58, 59.

[37] J. White, in *A Word to the "Little Flock,"* p. 11.

[38] J. Bates, *Autobiography,* p. 304.

[39] J. White to Bro. Bowles, Nov. 8, 1849; cf. J. White to Bro. and Sis. Hastings, Aug. 26, 1848.

[40] J. White, "The Third Angel's Message," *Present Truth,* Apr. 1850, pp. 65, 68.

[41] *Ibid.,* p. 68.

[42] E. G. White, *Life Sketches* (1915), p. 196.

[43] Daniel T. Taylor, "Our Statistical Report," *World's Crisis,* Jan. 25, 1860, p. 81; "Seventh-day Adventist Church," in *Seventh-day Adventist Encyclopedia* (2d rev. ed., 1996), vol. 2, p. 577.

[44] Daniel T. Taylor, "Our Statistical Report," *World's Crisis,* Feb. 15, 1860, p. 96; Daniel T. Taylor, "Our Statistical Report," *World's Crisis,* Feb. 8, 1860, p. 89.

[45] Eileen W. Linder, ed., *Year Book of American and Canadian Churches 2002* (Nashville, Tenn.: Abingdon Press, 2002), pp. 347, 358; Clyde E. Hewitt, *Midnight and Morning* (Charlotte, N.C.: Venture Books, 1983), p. 275.

[46] Linder, ed., *Year Book of American and Canadian Churches 2002,* p. 358; O. P. Hull, cited by J. Bates, "From Bro. Bates," *Review and Herald,* Sept. 2, 1852, p. 69; Russel J. Thomsen, *Seventh-day [sic] Baptists: Their Legacy to Adventists* (Mountain View, Calif.: Pacific Press Pub. Assn., 1971), p. 93.

[47] *139th Annual Statistical Report—2001* (Silver Spring, Md.: General Conference of Seventh-day Adventists, 2001), p. 69.

[48] For historical treatments of the prophetic root of Adventist mission, see Damsteegt, *Foundations of the Seventh-day Adventist Message and Mission;* Knight, *Millennial Fever,* pp. 327-342; George R. Knight, *The Fat Lady and the Kingdom: Adventist Mission Confronts the Challenges of Institutionalism and Secularization* (Boise, Idaho: Pacific Press Pub. Assn., 1995), pp. 129-145.

[49] C. E. Hewitt, *Midnight and Morning,* p. 277.

[50] C. H. Hewitt to F. D. Nichol, May 24, 1944, in Nichol, *The Midnight Cry,* pp. 476, 477; Interview of Moses C. Crouse by George R. Knight, Aurora College, Aurora, Ill., Oct. 18, 1984.

[51] "Response From the Seventh-day Baptists," *Review and Herald,* Nov. 23, 1869, p. 176.

[52] For a treatment of the ever widening Seventh-day Adventist concept of mission, see Knight, *Fat Lady,* pp. 57-80.

ChAPTER X

PATRIARCHS IN CONFLICT
AND THE TRANSFER OF LEADERSHIP

JAMES White and Bates had the highest regard for one another. "We esteem Brother Bates very highly," White noted in 1847. "From my first acquaintance with him I have loved him much. And the more I see of his devotedness to the holy advent cause, his caution, his holy life, his unfeigned love for the saints; the more I love and esteem him."[1] In his turn, Bates reciprocated those sentiments.

SHORT-TERM DISAGREEMENTS

But just because the two men loved and respected one another does not mean that they always agreed or that their relationship was tension free. We saw in the last chapter that White agreed with Bates' published interpretation of Adventism's place in prophetic history "in the main," but not totally.[2] The point of difference, we noted, was over the time to begin the third angel's message and its exact content. The two men eventually came to harmonize on White's position, but we can imagine a few earnest and perhaps lively discussions before they reached agreement.

They had still other points of difference between them that they eventually resolved in one way or another. One was that Bates thought the heavenly temple *was* the New Jerusalem, while White taught that it was *"in"* the New Jerusalem.[3]

Another issue that set the two men to "arguing" in November 1848 centered on their respective interpretations of the sealing "angel ascending from the east." White had been very much "tried" regarding Bates' view that the ascending from the east "was our going to N.Y. up the canal last Aug."[4] The two men and their colleagues in study had undoubtedly gone as far as they could in clarifying this detail through Bible study but were still at an impasse.

At that point Ellen White had a vision that helped them work through their difference. According to the vision, "it was this Sabbath seal rising in light, strength, and glory, and power." James held that the vision "corrected Bro. Bates' error" on the topic. "This was an extremely interesting time to me and to us all," White wrote, "for God was correcting errors in the view Bro. Bates had taken of the ascending."[5]

Ellen White's role is of interest as they began to refine the *details* of the doctrinal understandings the Whites, Bates, and others had agreed on by early 1847. It is apparently during the time period surrounding the November 1848 vision regarding the identity of the angel ascending from the east that Ellen White could not follow the reasoning of her "husband, Elder Joseph Bates, Father Pierce, Elder Edson, and others" as they searched "for the truth as for hidden treasure . . . sometimes through the entire night." She claimed that her "mind was locked, as it were" and that she "could not comprehend what we were studying." But when they could not come to a resolution, she noted, "then the Spirit of God would come upon me, I would be taken off in vision, and a clear explanation of the passages we had been studying would be given me. . . . Again and again this happened."[6]

Some earlier interpreters of Adventist history have tied that visionary experience to the formation of Adventist doctrine. But as I have to some extent demonstrated earlier in this book and more exhaustively in *A Search for Identity*, people who never became Sabbatarians studied out each of the distinctive doctrines and then Joseph Bates welded them together by early 1847 into a coherent Sabbatarian Adventist theology. The period surrounding Ellen White's November 1848 sealing vision, extending from perhaps mid-1847 to late 1849, matches the picture better, especially since she notes that it was "for two or three years" that her "mind continued to be locked to the Scriptures" and that it was "some time after [her] second son was born" in late July 1849 that her mind was freed "and ever since, the Scriptures [had] been an open book" to her.[7]

The time period extending from mid-1847 to late 1849 provides a more probable situation for that experience than any other. If that is the case, then it was the details of the developing Sabbatarian understanding of apocalyptic and doctrine that Ellen White's visions explicated rather than the apocalyptic framework or the basic doctrines themselves. Such an interpretation fits what we know about both the development of the basic Sabbatarian understandings between 1845 and early 1847 and such explanatory visions as the one in November 1848 regarding the sealing angel ascending from the east.

If we think of such disagreements as the exact definition of the third angel's message, the relationship of the heavenly temple to the New Jerusalem, and the identity of the sealing angel as short-term disputes, the relationship between Bates and James White also suffered from controversies that simmered over a longer period of time. It is to some of those long-term disagreements that we now turn.

THE CASE OF THE PRE-ADVENT JUDGMENT

One long-standing contention between the two patriarchs of Adventism had to do with the pre-Advent judgment. Josiah Litch, who argued that a pre-Advent or trial judgment would have to take place before the resurrection could occur, had raised that topic as early as 1841 and 1842.[8]

Certain leading shut door Adventists picked up aspects of that concept soon after the 1844 disappointment. Enoch Jacobs, for example, after discussing the breastplate of judgment worn by the high priest on the Day of Atonement, concluded a month after the disappointment that "unless something as decisive as the setting of the judgment took place on the tenth day [Oct. 22, 1844], the antitype is not yet given," prophecy is not fulfilled, and Adventists were still in darkness. Again, in January 1845 Apollos Hale and Joseph Turner called for a deeper understanding of the wedding parables. In particular, they pointed out that the wedding parable of Luke 12 claims that people needed to wait until Christ returned from the wedding. The two men went on to note that the wedding parable of Matthew 22 has a judgment scene in which the king examines his guests to determine whether they are wearing a wedding garment. Turner and Hale compared these wedding parables to Christ's reception of His kingdom in the judgment scene of Daniel 7. They concluded that beginning on October 22 Christ had a work to perform "in the invisible world." Accordingly, they proclaimed, *"the judgment is here!"*[9]

It was along such lines of reasoning that some post-disappointment Adventists began to argue that such favorite Millerite passages as the judgment of Daniel 7 and the arrival of the bridegroom at the wedding actually meant the coming of Christ to the pre-Advent judgment rather than His return in the clouds of heaven. They applied that same rationale to the cleansing of the sanctuary of Daniel 8:14 and the judgment hour of Revelation 14:7. William Miller took that position in March 1845 when he noted that since 1844 God was "in his last Judicial character deciding the cases of all the righteous, so that Christ . . . will know whom to collect at his coming."[10]

Bates also accepted that line of argument. He was probably the first of the Sabbatarian leaders to teach the pre-Advent judgment. "Respecting 'the hour of God's judgment is come,'" he wrote in early 1847, "there must be order and time, for God in his judicial character to decide the cases of all the righteous, that their names may be registered in the Lamb's Book of Life, and they be fully prepared for that eventful moment of their change from mortal to immortality." And in late 1848 he claimed that "the dead saints are now being judged."[11]

It appears that by January 5, 1849, Ellen White agreed with Bates on the pre-Advent judgment. Commenting about a vision she received on that date, she wrote that she "saw that Jesus would not leave the most holy place until every case was decided either for salvation or destruction."[12]

By way of contrast, the third founder of Sabbatarian Adventism, James White, disagreed with Bates on the pre-Advent judgment as late as September 1850. In that month he wrote that "many minds have been confused by the conflicting views that have been published on" the subject of the judgment. "Some have contended that the day of judgment was prior to the second advent. This view is certainly without foundation in the word of God." Undoubtedly he aimed his remarks at Bates, the foremost Sabbatarian who had gone into print on the topic by that time. James believed that "the great day of judgment will be one thousand years long" and would "be introduced by the second advent." As to a pre-Advent judgment, White had observed that "it is not necessary that the final sentence should be given before the first resurrection, as some have taught; for the names of the saints are written in heaven, and Jesus, and the angels will certainly know who to raise, and gather to the New Jerusalem." White obviously was still holding that position in late 1850.[13]

But as early as June 1851 it appears that his view had begun to shift somewhat, as he began to write of the examination of the wedding guests in the same way that Bates did. But it would not be until January 1857 that James White came out clearly for the teaching of the pre-Advent judgment—a concept that earlier that month had for the first time received the title of the "investigative judgment."[14] At that point it can be safely claimed that all of the leading Sabbatarians were teaching the pre-Advent judgment.

We should note that we find no particular pattern in the way the founders worked out their disagreements. James White's conclusions on the definition of the third angel's message eventually won out. On the judgment, Bates' position would become the accepted one, while it was a vision from Ellen White that finally brought harmony on the issue of the angel rising from the east. We will see more variations as we examine some of their other differences.

THE CASE OF DATE SETTING

After the failure of the prediction that Christ would return in October 1844, it was only natural for the disappointed Adventists to continue to establish dates for that event on the basis of the various prophecies. Thus William Miller and Josiah Litch came to expect that Jesus would appear before the end of the Jewish year 1844 (that is, by the spring of 1845). H. H. Gross, Joseph Marsh, and others set dates in 1846, and when that year passed Gross discovered reasons to look for Christ in 1847.[15]

The early Sabbatarians had not been adverse to date setting. In September 1845 James White firmly believed that Jesus would arrive in October of that year. At that time he held that an Adventist couple who had announced their marriage had fallen for a "wile of the Devil," and had "denied their faith" in the Second Advent, since "such a step seemed to contemplate years of life in this world."[16]

Yet "a few days before the time passed," James recalled, the young Ellen Harmon "saw in vision, that we should be disappointed, and that the saints must pass through the 'time of Jacob's trouble,' which was future."[17]

That experience apparently cured James White of speculating on the date of the Second Advent, but not Bates. In 1850 he wrote that "the seven spots of blood on the Golden Altar and before the Mercy Seat, I fully believe represents the duration of the judicial proceedings on the living saints in the Most Holy."[18] In other words, Bates had concluded that the pre-Advent judgment would last seven years and would conclude in

October 1851, at which time Christ would return.

Given his stature in Sabbatarian Adventism, Bates soon gathered a following for his new time scheme. But both of the Whites would vigorously resist him. In November 1850 Ellen White publicly claimed that "the Lord showed me that time had not been a test since 1844, and that time will never again be a test." Then in July 1851, as excitement on the topic mounted, she wrote in the *Review and Herald* that "the Lord has shown me that the message of the third angel must go, and be proclaimed to the scattered children of the Lord, and that it should not be hung on time; for time will never be a test again. I saw that some were getting a false excitement arising from preaching time. . . . I saw that some were making every thing bend to the time of this next fall—that is, making their calculations in reference to that time." [19]

The next month James cut loose on Bates, claiming that he had been against his time teaching from its inception a year earlier. Referring specifically to Bates' theory, White wrote that "some who have thus taught we esteem very highly, and love 'fervently' as brethren, and we feel that it becomes us to be slow to say anything to hurt their feelings; yet we cannot refrain from giving some reasons why we do not receive *the time*." He then launched into six reasons why he believed Bates was wrong. [20]

The combined confrontation by the Whites apparently convinced Bates (who believed Ellen to be a prophet) that he had been wrong on the time issue. Soon he and most of those who had followed him dropped the emphasis. As a result, James could report in early September that the "seven years time" was a non-issue in his recent tour among the churches. But some, Ellen reported in November, had held onto the time expectation and were very "low and dark," confused, and distracted. [21]

The "seven spots" crisis cured Bates of time setting. After that, although he would see the end as near, he never again set a date for the Second Advent. The closest he would come was his "this generation" teaching. Citing the words of Jesus that "this generation will not pass away till all these things are fulfilled" (Matt. 24:34), Bates defined "this generation" as the one that had witnessed the dark day of 1780 and the falling of the stars in 1833. According to that theory, the Lord would have to come soon since those who had witnessed the earlier of those events had become quite aged. He preached that message for the rest of his life. [22]

THE CASE OF THE TIME TO BEGIN THE SABBATH

Unlike the other issues treated in this chapter, the three central leaders of early Adventism had no dispute with each other on when to begin and end the Sabbath, except for a very short period in late 1855.

In spite of the fact that the Seventh Day Baptists, from whom Bates indirectly got the Sabbath, observed it from sunset to sunset, Bates himself argued that it should be kept from 6:00 p.m. Friday to 6:00 p.m. Saturday. He put forth that position in his 1846 book on the Sabbath, claiming that "history shows that the Jews . . . commenced their days at 6 o'clock in the evening."[23]

Bates had three main pillars for his argument. First, from the Genesis creation story he concluded that the day began in the evening ("'the evening and the morning were the first day'" [Gen. 1:5]). Second, he argued that time needed to be established "from the centre of the earth, the equator, where, at the beginning of the sacred year, the sun rises and sets at 6 o'clock." Third, if people were "to keep the Sabbath in *time,* just as Jesus did," then they needed to follow the equatorial time just as He had in Palestine. And if people observes Sabbath from 6:00 p.m. to 6:00 p.m. then everyone around the globe would be keeping the same Sabbath, a coordination that would be impossible if people of different latitudes relied on the variableness of sunset in their location. The 6:00 p.m. time was important, Bates asserted, because God "is an exact time keeper."[24]

In 1848 Bates would enrich his argument by taking the parable of the laborers in Matthew 20:1-12 and showing that the day had 12 hours, and that the twelfth hour ended at 6:00 p.m. in the evening for the Jews. The matter of the time was significant to Bates. In 1849 he claimed that "it is just as sinful in the sight of God to wilfully reject the Bible light on the commencing of the Sabbath . . . as it would be not to keep it at all."[25]

Not everyone was happy with Bates' solution. James White later noted that "the six o'clock time was called in question by a portion of believers as early as 1847, some maintaining that the Sabbath commenced at sunrise, while others claimed Bible evidence in favor of sunset."[26]

The sunrise group must have been especially aggressive. Ellen White received a vision during the late 1840s showing "that to commence the Sabbath at sunrise was wrong. She then heard an angel repeat these words, 'From even unto even shall ye celebrate your Sabbaths.'" Bates was present and soon persuaded all present that "even" was 6:00 p.m. The vision, James White later pointed out, "did not teach the six o'clock time. It only corrected the sunrise time." But that insight became clearer only later.[27] Ellen White apparently thought in her own mind that it pointed to 6:00 p.m., since she would hold that position for years to come.

James White claims that he was never fully satisfied with the 6:00 p.m. time, even though he kept his Sabbaths on that basis for nearly 10 years. That may have been partly due to a misunderstanding of his wife's 1847 or 1848 vision combating the sunrise interpretation. But he was definitely influenced in that direction by another charismatic experience in July 1848.

He reported at that time that a serious disagreement had arisen among the Sabbatarians on when to begin the Sabbath, with some pushing for sundown and others for 6:00 p.m. "A week ago Sabbath," he wrote, "we made this a subject of prayer. The Holy Ghost came down, Brother Chamberlain was filled with the power. In this state he cried out in an unknown tongue. The interpretation followed which was this: 'Give me the chalk, Give me the chalk.' Well, thought I, if there is none in the house then I shall doubt this, but in a moment a brother took down a good piece of chalk. Brother Chamberlain took it and in the power he drew this figure on the floor:"[28]

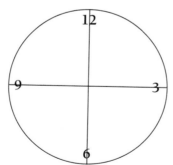

Chamberlain apparently taught that "this represents Jesus' words. Are there not twelve hours in the day. This figure represents the day or the last half of the day. Daylight is half gone when the sun is south or half way from each horizon, at 12 o'clock. Now go each way six hours and you will get the twelve hour day. At any time [of] year the day ends at 6 P.M. Here is where the Sabbath begins at 6 P.M. Satan would get us from this time."[29]

James' interpretation of that experience was that "Satan would get us from this [6:00 p.m.] time," that we should keep the Sabbath as it was given to Bates. "God has raised up Brother Bates to give this truth. I should have more faith in his opinion that any other man's."[30]

But even with the Sabbatarian leadership fairly well agreed on the 6:00 p.m. time, the sunset issue kept intruding itself and creating disharmony. As a result, Bates wrote a further article defending his position in April 1851. The young J. N. Andrews produced one taking the same position in June of that year. Then James White reprinted Bates' 1851 article in May 1853 because of the several "inquiries respecting the time to commence the Sabbath" that had come to him as *Review* editor.[31]

By 1854 the matter had become so troublesome that James feared "division unless the question could be settled by good testimony." White claimed that he never had been completely satisfied on the 6:00 p.m. time and that Sabbatarians had never fully investigated it from the Bible. He would later note that Bates' "decided [i.e., stubborn] stand upon the question, and respect for his years, and his godly life" were undoubtedly reasons why they had "not sooner investigated" this point from the Bible "as thoroughly as some other points."[32]

In June 1854 he urged D. P. Hall to prepare a study on the topic of the time to begin Sabbath, but nothing came of the request even though James repeated it six months later. Then in the summer of 1855 White made the same request of J. N. Andrews, who undertook the task with his usual thoroughness.[33]

Andrews, who reversed his earlier position on the topic, demonstrated from nine texts in the Old Testament and two from the new that "even" and the "evening" of the Sabbath were identical with sunset. He presented his Bible study (later published in the *Review and Herald* of December 4) before a conference of believers on November 17, 1855, in Battle Creek, Michigan.[34]

James White reported that Andrews' Bible study settled the minds of nearly all of those present that the sunset time was correct. He undoubtedly included himself in that group. But not everyone was in harmony with Andrews' conclusions. As White put it, "Bates, and a few others" were at that point out of harmony with the body of believers. Bates had taught the 6:00 p.m. position for a decade, and he dug in to defend his position.

White doesn't indicate who the others were who disagreed with Andrews' conclusions, but Uriah Smith tells us that one of them was Ellen White.[35]

The tension over the issue, with two of the three founders of the movement being out of harmony with the majority, must have been both serious and apparent to all. Two days after Andrews presented his study, James later recalled, they "had a special season of prayer" during which "Mrs. W. had a vision, one item of which was that [the] sunset time was correct. That settled the matter with Bro. Bates and others, and general harmony has since prevailed among us upon this point."[36]

Those present would draw two conclusions from that series of events. The first, pointed out by Uriah Smith, was that even though some accused Ellen White of seeking to manipulate the body of believers through her visions, it was far from the case, since in this instance the vision "was contrary to her own sentiment at the time the vision was given."[37]

James White drew out a second important lesson. "The question naturally arises," he pointed out, "If the visions are given to correct the erring, why did she not sooner see the error of the six o'clock time? For one," he noted, "I have ever been thankful that God corrected the error in his own good time, and did not suffer an unhappy division to exist among us upon the point. . . .

"It does not appear to be the desire of the Lord to teach his people by the gifts of the Spirit on the Bible questions until his servants have diligently searched his word. When this was done upon the subject of [the] time to commence the Sabbath, and most were established, and some were in danger of being out of harmony with the body on this subject, then, yes, *then*, was the very time for God to magnify his goodness in the manifestation of the gift of his Spirit in the accomplishment of its proper work. The sacred Scriptures are given us as the rule of faith and duty, and we are commanded to search them. . . .

"Let the gifts have their proper place in the church. God has never set them in the very front, and commanded us to look to them to lead us in the path of truth, and the way to Heaven. His word he has magnified. The Scriptures of the Old and New Testament are man's lamp to light up his path to the kingdom. Follow that. But if you err from Bible truth, and are in danger of being lost, it may be that God will in the time of his choice correct you, and bring you back to the Bible, and save you."[38]

Even in their differences, Bates and the Whites agreed on the relationship of the Bible and spiritual gifts. Basic truths were to be discovered through Bible study, with the gifts, when necessary, providing confirmation of the conclusions reached through that study. In the case of the time to begin the Sabbath, Ellen White's vision cleared Bates' eyes, encouraged him to look at the evidence twice, and helped him gain control of his stubbornness. He considered the experience a "rich blessing from the Most Holy Place in the heaven of heavens."[39]

FLASHPOINT: THE PUBLISHING CRISIS

A major turning point in Sabbatarian Adventism came in November 1848 at Dorchester, Massachusetts. The leaders of the movement had earnestly prayed at a conference held at Topsham, Maine, between October 20 and 22 that a way might open to publish the truths that they had discovered. The next month at Dorchester their prayer received an answer. Bates notes that at that meeting Ellen White asked him to write a little book on the sealing message, published two months later as *A Seal of the Living God.*[40]

James White's recollections were essentially the same. He writes that he and Bates had been "arguing some points" on which they "did not see alike, in relation to the sealing angel." At that point, Ellen White had a vision showing where Joseph had been wrong in his interpretation (see discussion in chapter 8). The next day James wrote to friends noting that his wife had "told Bro. Bates to write the things he had seen and heard and the blessing of God would attend it." That is, "he was to write the sealing message as it was corrected by her vision."[41]

The participants on both sides of what would in time become a controversy agreed that Ellen White requested Bates, in relationship to the Dorchester vision, to write a pamphlet. What is less clear is how many people heard Ellen White telling her husband to begin publishing, as she later put it, a "little paper" that would eventually become "like streams of light that went clear round the world."[42] She says that she told him "after" the vision, but we have no indication how long afterward or whether Bates or others were present when she mentioned it to him.

At any rate, James took his wife's request to heart. In July 1849 he published the initial number of *Present Truth,* the first Sabbatarian periodical. He indicated to his readers that his desire had been to publish the material in pamphlet form, but that would have taken weeks, so he put his material out in periodical form with the idea that he would later be able to stitch together a number of such issues to create a pamphlet.[43]

The periodical format, however, seemed to be what the Sabbatarian Adventist movement needed. August found James publishing notices of forthcoming meetings of believers and soon thereafter he began to include letters from believers. As a result, *Present Truth* quickly became an organ of communication that tied the developing movement together, giving its editor a prominence he had not had before.

Bates, however, was quite upset with the new development, so upset that he refused to cooperate with James White in the paper. White, looking back from the perspective of 1860, wrote that "the oldest preacher among us [Bates], and almost the only fellow-laborer we then had in this cause, refused for one year to write for our little paper, because to publish a paper was to do as others had done who had backslidden. It was hard tugging alone with such an influence to meet."[44]

It appears that Joseph didn't become incensed over the paper until he realized that it was becoming a permanent periodical. In October 1849 he and James seemed to be working harmoniously together, with White writing that Bates "is a tried friend, and a bold Christian."[45] But about that time it must have dawned on the older man that White had indeed begun a periodical, thereby copying the methods of the "Laodicean" Adventists.

Relations between the two men took a definite turn for the worse in December when James wrote to Bates that money was being squandered that could have been used to support the publication of the paper. Bates responded with what must have been a fiery letter, apparently indicating that the periodical was consuming too much money and time that should have gone directly into evangelism, thus in effect delaying the Lord's coming.[46]

White penned that "Brother Bates wrote me a letter than threw me down as low as I ever was." "I had [already] been in a hot furnace for some time on account of the burden I felt for the little paper." But Bates' letter made it even worse—"the burden grew heavier and heavier on me" and "I gave it up forever." "I think" the paper "will die. . . . I think I shall hang all up for the present."[47]

It was while in that "depressed, miserable state of mind" that on

January 9, 1850, the Whites attended a prayer meeting with some other believers. "The power came down more and more," James wrote in his description of the meeting, "and we all shouted and praised the Lord. . . . In this state of feelings among us Ellen was taken off in vision."[48]

"'I saw the paper,'" she reported of the vision, "'and that it was needed. That souls were hungry for the truth that must be written in the paper. I saw that if the paper stopped for want of means, and those hungry sheep died for want of the paper, it would not be James' fault, but it would be the fault of those to whom God had lent his money, to be faithful stewards over, and they let it lie idle; and the blood of souls would be upon their garments. I saw that the paper should go; and if they let it die they would weep in anguish soon. I saw that God did not want James to stop yet; but he must *write, write, write, write,* and speed the message and let it go. I saw that it would go where God's servants cannot go.'"[49]

James, as we might expect, felt elated. "I shall write him [Bates] this vision," he penned the next day, "which will, no doubt, make him see a little differently on some things."[50]

Arthur White observes that James' letter did indeed change Bates' mind. But what he doesn't tell us is that the transformation wasn't deep enough. Round two of the publishing crisis opened up 10 months later. Early October 1850 found Ellen White writing stronger things about Bates than at any other time in their long association. According to her, Bates was teaching "'sell all ye have'" in a wrong light, he had erred repeatedly in praying for the sick before unbelievers, he was wrong in "attending the washing of [the] saints' feet and the communion among unbelievers," he had been "quick to receive error" and "slow to receive truth," he had applied Revelation 18:4 on coming out of Babylon incorrectly and caused confusion, he had been stubborn and not "ready to yield up a dear point when clear light shines," and he had not the gift of discernment and needed to be careful lest what he did and said should harm the flock of believers.[51]

Tucked away in the midst of that catalogue of problems was a note on James' periodical. Ellen White claimed that Bates was at fault in not supporting her husband in the publication of the paper. Whereas he had written for the dying shut door papers in the scattering time in 1845 and 1846, "now in the gathering time when precious souls that have been hid beneath the rubbish and have not had the privilege of hearing the truth, need light from different ones, his testimony has been withheld. . . . God wanted the papers to cease in the scattering time, but now the truth [of the third angel's message] should be sung, preached, prayed, and published."[52]

The fault in the tension between Bates and James White, however, was not all on one side. While it was true, Ellen White pointed out, that the "above named errors of Brother Bates and others more dangerous brought confusion and had destroyed James' confidence in Brother Bates," her husband himself harbored a share of the fault. Even though "James at first had godly jealousy for the truth," eventually "other jealousy crept in until he was jealous of most every move Brother Bates would make."[53]

The Sabbatarian movement had reached a crisis point. The leaders finally had a message to preach and had finally arrived at the gathering time of evangelization, only to have the movement founder on the stubborn personalities of its two leaders. The crisis had reached a seriousness where it was not merely between Bates and White, but "the disunion between the shepherds," Ellen White claimed, "had affected the flock." She cautioned Bates and her husband to "'Press together, press together, press together, press together . . . , lest the sheep be scattered.'"[54]

The existing records of that period indicate that the issue of the "little paper" lay at the root of the problem between Bates and White. "I saw," wrote Ellen White later in October 1850, "that a paper was needed and that all should be interested in it. I saw that the burden of the paper was laid on James, and that it is as important to publish the truth as to preach it. I saw that James should not be discouraged if all did not feel the interest in the paper that he did. I saw that Bro. Bates had not the interest in the paper that he should have, and that his lack of interest had discouraged James. I saw that James should set his face as a flint, and go forward. I saw the flock looking for the paper, and were ready like hungry children to eat the truth published in it." She went on to note that "Bro. Bates must be careful and be willing to receive the light that comes in other ways besides through visions. I saw that he was too slow to receive light from his brethren."[55]

The next month Ellen White penned that it was "necessary for the paper to be published" because it "would go where the messengers could not go." December found her claiming that the publication would bring "souls to a knowledge of the truth," and that Bates "must buckle on the armor."[56]

Ellen White's strong words finally broke through to the rather hard-

headed Bates. From that point on his articles would appear in the periodicals
edited by James White, and when James established the *Review and Herald* as
the flagship magazine of the Sabbatarians, Bates' name was listed along with
White's and two others on the masthead as the Publishing Committee.

The year 1851 finds Bates taking subscriptions for the *Review,* finding
"hungry starving sheep" who "wanted the paper sent to them," and praising God in the rapid increase in the number of believers as "the paper and
the Messengers go forth." By 1852 he had joined White in raising funds
to establish a "Printing Office" so that the Sabbatarians could print their
own papers.[57]

The crisis had been breached. White and Bates were once again working in harmony. Ellen White, as we might expect, was overjoyed. "We
have received letters from some that we have never before heard from,"
she wrote in April 1851. "There is a great call for publications. The work
of the Lord is moving onward." That year would be one of rapid growth
as the Sabbatarian movement went into high gear in what its leaders called
the "gathering time." By the end of the year the number of adherents stood
close to 2,500.[58]

THE LARGER ISSUE: THE TRANSFER OF LEADERSHIP

How is it, we might ask, that Bates and White could get so crosswise
with each other in 1849 and 1850 that they came near destroying the
Sabbatarian Adventist movement that they both had given so much to establish? In other words, what brought the movement to its crisis point in
October 1850?

Possible answers are plentiful. For one, they disagreed on publishing
policy. And not only was James upsetting Bates with the regular publication of *Present Truth,* but he had added the *Advent Review* to his editorial
task in August 1850 and was planning on a larger paper that would com-
bine the other two. He intended to begin publishing the *Review and Herald*
in November. With that in mind, October was a natural time for difficulty
to arise on the topic.

From Bates' perspective the difference in publishing modes may have
taken on added importance since he was quite certain that Ellen White
had told him at Dorchester in November 1848 that the way to go was with
a continuation of his production of pamphlets. On the other hand, he may

have been quite unaware at the time that she had shortly after that encouraged her husband to begin a periodical ministry. Any misunderstanding or even partial understandings along those lines could have generated problems in his mind.

Other dynamics were also operating during 1849 and 1850 that help explain the suspicions between the two men. After all, at the very same time as the publishing crisis Bates and White were also at loggerheads on date setting for the Second Advent and on the nature of the judgment, with White publicly disagreeing with Bates in his periodicals on the pre-Advent judgment.

And then there was the question of authority. A snippet from White's September 1849 correspondence enables us to get a glimpse into that dynamic. Speaking of a Sister Lawrence, James wrote that "Brother Bates encouraged her to go and I wrote to stop her from going, but it did not stop her. And when she got to Connecticut [sic], I had the whole trouble of her, and Brother Bates and Gurney did not seem to care a straw to take care of her." [59] Even without understanding the details of that problem, it is clear that by 1849 the topic of authority was becoming important between the two rather stubborn leaders of the Sabbatarian movement.

That issue may provide the key to the disharmony between Bates and White that climaxed in 1850. Up to 1849 Bates had been the acknowledged leader of the movement. He had developed the Sabbatarian theology, had called the initial meetings that brought the Sabbatarians together, and had, with the exception of *A Word to the "Little Flock,"* been their publisher.

But by 1850 Bates had taken the religious movement as far as he could. We might say that he had run out of steam by 1849-1850. His strength, as Ellen White put it at the height of the crisis, was the "gift to talk the Word," but he didn't have "the gift of discernment." [60] Nor did he have extensive organizational abilities. Beyond that, he had run out of ideas. His publications after 1849 would nearly all be rehashes of his earlier ideas.

On the other side of the energy/creativity fence was the younger James White, who was bursting with ideas on how to take Sabbatarian Adventism into the future. If Bates had been the man for the hour in the mid-1840s, it was James who had the vision needed to lead Adventism in the 1850s and 1860s. He not only had vision, but he had the creative ability to make it into a reality.

In short, we should see the publishing crisis as a surface manifestation of what was in actuality a generational transference of leadership from Bates to White. Bates as a leader had provided essential functions in the 1840s, but new challenges called for new talents and a new leader. White's publishing of periodicals and Sabbatarian Adventism's first hymnal (*Hymns for God's Peculiar People That Keep the Commandments of God and the Faith of Jesus*) in 1849 were in one sense a flexing of his leadership. From 1850 onward White would be the undisputed head of the Sabbatarian movement. His editorship of the *Review and Herald,* a periodical that literally tied the Sabbatarians together as a movement in the 1850s, established him as its guiding voice.

It is impossible to know if Bates or even White was conscious of the administrative struggle taking place between them, but the outcome is historically clear. Sabbatarian Adventism went into the 1850s with a new and younger leader. Adventism had successfully survived its first crisis in the transference of authority from one generation to another. Looking back from the end of the 1850s, Ellen White would write that "I saw that God had chosen James to fill an important place, and has made him His agent to forward His work. I was pointed back to the commencement of the work and was shown that God thrust him out that he might obtain an experience to fill the place He designed for him to occupy as one to manage in His cause, to forward the work, to take responsibilities, and to risk something on the success of this message."[61]

AFTERMATH

If by late 1850 Bates had come over to support James White and his publication of the *Review and Herald,* that doesn't mean that no subsequent problems developed between the two men or that they lived happily ever after. Bates apparently more than once got involved in "whispering campaigns" against White because he had "too good a horse" and thus must be making too much money, and again because of the way James at times dealt with people.[62]

But those differences were relatively minor after 1850. For two such strong and independent men, the record demonstrates that they got on remarkably well. Bates seems to have come to terms with the fact that it was best for the younger man to lead the development and spread of the movement. Their relationship, in fact, could at times even be rather play-ful. In 1864, for example, White published what he considered to be a rather far-fetched prophetic interpretation from Bates, adding in an edito-rial note that "we are always glad to hear from our venerable Bro. Bates. It is evident that he loves the Advent doctrine, and all connected with it that has been good. His application of the prophecy of Isaiah to the chart seems to us to be apocryphal, but it will do no harm unless others make such doubtful exposition of equal importance with plainly revealed, vital points of doctrine."[63]

The two men would sustain a generally supportive relationship with each other between 1851 and 1872, when Bates died. Three years before his death he wrote that James White "is still and ever has been, the man of my choice, called of God (as I firmly believe) to the place he has so long and faithfully filled." As to the extent of Bates' having come to grips with his need to support White's publishing ventures, it is significant that he willed his house and property to the Seventh-day Adventist Publishing Association in 1866. For his part, White reciprocated in the mutually sup-portive relationship, donating, wrote the aging Bates, "from his own means to help sustain me in this work."[64]

---

[1] J. White to Sis. Hastings, Aug. 22, 1847.

[2] Ibid.

[3] J. Bates, Opening Heavens, p. 29; J. White, in A Word to the "Little Flock," p. 23.

[4] J. White to [Bro. and Sis. Howland], Nov. 19, 1848.

[5] Ibid.

[6] E. G. White to J. H. Kellogg, Nov. 20, 1903; cf. E. G. White, "Establishing the Foundation of Our Faith," MS 135, Nov. 4, 1903.

[7] Knight, A Search for Identity, pp. 55-89; E. G. White to J. H. Kellogg, Nov. 20, 1903.

[8] J. Litch, An Address to the Public (Boston: Joshua V. Himes, 1841), p. 37; J. Litch, Prophetic Expositions (Boston: Joshua V. Himes, 1842), vol. 1, pp. 49-54.

[9] [E. Jacobs], "The Time," Western Midnight Cry, Nov. 29, 1844, p. 19; A. Hale and J. Turner, "Has not the Savior Come as the Bridegroom," Advent Mirror, Jan. 1845, p. 3.

[10] W. Miller, "Letter From Bro. Miller," Day-Star, Apr. 8, 1845, p. 31.

[11] J. Bates, Second Advent Way Marks and High Heaps, p. 6; J. Bates, Seal of the Living God, p. 39; J. Bates, An Explanation of the Typical and Anti-Typical Sanctuary (New Bedford, Mass.: Benjamin Lindsey, 1850), p. 10.

[12] E. G. White, Early Writings, p. 36; E. G. White, Life Sketches (1915), p. 116.

[13] J. White, "The Day of Judgment," *Advent Review,* Sept. 1850, p. 49; J. White, in *A Word to the "Little Flock,"* p. 24.

[14] J. White, "The Parable, Matthew xxv, 1-12," *Review and Herald,* June 9, 1851, pp. 97-103; J. White, "The Judgment," *Review and Herald,* Jan. 29, 1857, p. 100; E. Everts, "Communication From Bro. Everts," *Review and Herald,* Jan. 1, 1857, p. 72.

[15] R. W. Schwarz, *Light Bearers to the Remnant* (Mountain View, Calif.: Pacific Press Pub. Assn., 1979), p. 54.

[16] J. White, "Letter from Bro. White," *Day-Star,* Oct. 11, 1845, p. 47; J. White and E. G. White, *Life Sketches* (1888), p. 126.

[17] J. White, in *A Word to the "Little Flock,."* p. 22; cf. E. G. White, *Early Writings,* p. 22.

[18] J. Bates, *An Explanation of the Typical and Anti-typical Sanctuary,* p. 10.

[19] E. G. White, "Dear Brethren and Sisters," *Present Truth,* Nov. 1850, pp. 86, 87; E. G. White, "Dear Brethren," *Review and Herald* Extra, July 21, 1851, p. [4].

[20] [J. White], "Our Present Work," *Review and Herald,* Aug. 19, 1851, p. 13.

[21] [J. White], "Oswego Conference," *Review and Herald,* Sept. 16, 1851, p. 32; E. G. White to Bro. and Sis. Howland, Nov. 12, 1851.

[22] H. S. Gurney, "This Generation," *Review and Herald,* Oct. 14, 1858, p. 165; J. Bates, "The Second Advent," *Review and Herald,* May 7, 1867, p. 254.

[23] J. Bates, *The Seventh Day Sabbath* (1846), p. 32.

[24] *Ibid.,* pp. 32, 43.

[25] J. Bates, *Vindication of the Seventh-day Sabbath,* pp. 80, 81; J. Bates, *Seal of the Living God,* p. 38.

[26] J. White, "Time to Commence the Sabbath," *Review and Herald,* Feb. 25, 1868, p. 168.

[27] *Ibid.*

[28] J. White to Bro. [Howland], July 2, 1848.

[29] *Ibid.*

[30] *Ibid.*

[31] J. Bates, "Dear Bro. White," *Review and Herald,* Aug. 5, 1851, p. 6; J. Bates, "Time to Commence the Holy Sabbath," *Review and Herald,* Apr. 21, 1851, p. 71; *ibid.,* reprinted, May 26, 1853, pp. 4, 5; J. N. Andrews, "The Time of the Sabbath," *Review and Herald,* June 2, 1851, pp. 92, 93.

[32] J. White, "Time of the Sabbath," *Review and Herald,* Dec. 4, 1855, p. 78; J. White, "Time to Commence the Sabbath," *Review and Herald,* Feb. 25, 1868, p. 168.

[33] J. White, "Time of the Sabbath," *Review and Herald,* Dec. 4, 1855, p. 78.

[34] J. N. Andrews, "Time for Commencing the Sabbath," *Review and Herald,* Dec. 4, 1855, pp. 76-78.

[35] J. White, "Time to Commence the Sabbath," *Review and Herald,* Feb. 25, 1868, p. 168; [U. Smith], "Not Satisfactory," *Review and Herald,* Aug. 30, 1864, p. 109.

[36] Editors, Appendix, in E. G. White, *Testimonies for the Church,* vol. 1, p. 713; J. White, "Time to Commence the Sabbath," *Review and Herald,* Feb. 25, 1868, p. 168.

[37] [U. Smith], "Not Satisfactory," *Review and Herald,* Aug. 30, 1864, p. 109.

[38] J. White, "Time to Commence the Sabbath," *Review and Herald,* Feb. 25, 1868, p. 168.

[39] J. Bates, "Communication from Bro. Bates," *Review and Herald,* Dec. 27, 1855, p. 104.

[40] Editors note, in Ellen G. White, *The Publishing Ministry* (Washington, D.C.: Review and Herald Pub. Assn., 1983), p. 15; J. Bates, *Seal of the Living* God, p. 26.

[41] J. White to [Bro. and Sis. Howland], Nov. 19, 1848.

[42] E. G. White, *Life Sketches* (1915), p. 125.

[43] [J. White], "Dear Brethren and Sisters," *Present Truth,* July 1849, p. 6.

[44] J. White, "Making Us a Name," *Review and Herald,* Apr. 26, 1860, p. 182.

[45] J. White to Bro. Bowles, Oct. 17, 1849.

[46] J. White to Bro. Hastings, Jan. 10, 1850; J. White to Bro. and Sis. Hastings, Jan. 3, 1850.

[47] J. White to Bro. Hastings, Jan. 10, 1850; J. White to Bro. and Sis. Hastings, Jan. 3, 1850.

[48] J. White to Bro. Hastings, Jan. 10, 1850.

[49] E. G. White quoted in *ibid.;* E. G. White, "Need of Present Truth," MS 2, Jan. 9, 1850.

[50] J. White to Bro. Hastings, Jan. 10, 1850.

[51] A. L. White, *Ellen G. White* (Wash., D.C.: Review and Herald Pub. Assn., 1985), vol. 1, p. 172; E. G. White, "Need for Unity Among Spiritual Shepherds," MS 14, Oct. 1850.

[52] E. G. White, "Need for Unity Among Spiritual Shepherds," MS 14, Oct. 1850.

[53] *Ibid.*

[54] *Ibid.*

[55] E. G. White, untitled, MS 15, Oct. 23, 1850.

[56] E. G. White to the Church in Bro. Hastings' House, Nov. 27, 1850; E. G. White, "Vision at Paris, Maine," MS 11, Dec. 25, 1850.

[57] J. Bates, "Dear. Bro. White," *Review and Herald,* March 1851, p. 55; J. Bates, "Dear Bro. White," *Review and Herald,* Aug. 5, 1851, p. 6; J. Bates, "The Paper," *Review and Herald,* June 10, 1852, p. 24.

[58] E. G. White to Bro. and Sis. Loveland, Apr. 1, 1851; J. White, "A Sketch of the Past," *Review and Herald,* May 6, 1852, p. 5.

[59] J. White to Bro. and Sis. Collins, Sept. 8, 1849.

[60] E. G. White, "Need for Unity Among Spiritual Shepherds," MS 14, Oct. 1850.

[61] E. G. White to Bro. Byington, cir. 1859.

[62] A. L. White, *Ellen G. White,* vol. 1, p. 205; E. G. White to Bro. Ingraham, cir. 1864.

[63] [J. White, editorial note], *Review and Herald,* Mar. 29, 1864, p. 142.

[64] J. Bates to Brn. Andrews, Bell, and Smith, in *Defense of Eld. James White and Wife* (Battle Creek, Mich.: Seventh-day Adventist Publishing Assn., 1870), p. 24, cf. pp. 69, 70; J. Bates, Last Will and Testament, Mar. 23, 1866.

Chapter XI

SABBATARIAN ADVENTISM'S
FIRST MISSIONARY

B ATES was a man of action, a person driven by a mission based upon the logic of his chain-of-events theology flowing out of the messages of the three angels of Revelation 14. He believed the Second Advent was at hand, and that there was no time to lose.

"I have parted with all my company," he wrote in September 1849, "to seek out the scattered sheep further East. . . . God has manifested his power at both the conference[s] in N. Paris and Topsham, healed the sick, cast out Devils, and caused many to tremble at his mighty power. Ellen had a vision at each conference. *The cry from the holy city is speed the messengers, speed the messengers, the work is [al]most done.* Souls are starving. [It's] almost too late, almost too late to save any more. Some souls are dallying, dallying & trembling too long. Their chance is small. O the tremendous hour that's now approaching. The vision says spare neither money nor any thing to do the work now. Soon it will be forever too late. . . . *I am hastening on with all speed.*"[1]

A TRAVELIN' MAN AGAIN

The scattering time of the post-1844 period had ended, and by 1849 what the Sabbatarian leaders thought of as the gathering time had arrived. Connected with that understanding was a transformation of the Sabbatarians from being a shut door people to a movement that proclaimed that it had an open door before it to evangelize everywhere on the basis of the third angel's message.

As James White put it in August 1851, "We have passed through the long dark night of scattering, and the flock has become faint and scattered by a strange diversity of views. And as they are now being gathered to the truth, many will be inclined to hold on to erroneous views received in the

time of scattering. Therefore it should be a very important part of the present work of those who teach the truth to lead the minds of the brethren
from distracting views, and to show them that they must be united in the
third message, as we were in the former ones."[2]

Bates was at the forefront of the new evangelism as Sabbatarian
Adventism went from perhaps 200 believers in 1849 to more than 2,500
in 1851. He reported on August 5, 1851, that Vermont and New
Hampshire had more than four times the number of adherents than two
years before and double the number of a year ago. Two weeks later he rejoiced that it was "encouraging to meet with so many true believers in the
third angel's message where but a few months ago there was no gathering
on God's Holy Day."[3]

Those figures harmonized with those James White published in May
1852. He counted nearly 1,000 believers in New York State, "where there
was but about a score of advent brethren" three years earlier. In addition,
he estimated more in New England than in New York, along with several
hundred in the western states (i.e., Michigan, Wisconsin, and Indiana)
and Canada, where there had been none in 1849.[4]

And why the great increase? In part it resulted from the circulation
of the *Review and Herald* among the ex-Millerites, but even moreso it was
due to the incessant traveling and evangelizing of Bates, who had not
only opened up the Sabbatarian work in the West and Canada, but had
personally stimulated much of the movement's growth in New York and
New England.

Godfrey T. Anderson, his first biographer, estimated that after 1850
Bates spent about 75 percent of his time away from home. In 1851 alone,
Anderson counted some 35 towns, mainly in New York and New
England, in which he did evangelism.[5]

January 1852 found Bates in Canada with Hiram Edson, where "we
have waded through the deep snow from two to forty miles" to meet with
evangelistic prospects. In such a manner, he notes, he had traveled "hundreds of miles" in five weeks. "The first twenty days of our journey," he
reported, "we were much tried with the deep snow, and tedious cold
weather, and with but few exceptions cold and impenetrable hearts."
Fortunately, they soon came across many who were "hungry for the
truth." On February 17 he reported that he and Edson had made a com-

plete circuit around Lake Ontario and "left more than one hundred interested in present truth."[6]

February 1852 found them back in western New York, where they "visited about twenty places, and held meetings with the scattered flock" between February 2 and March 11. Later that year would find Bates itinerating in Michigan, Wisconsin, and other points west. The next year followed the same pattern. Everett Dick traced one tour in which Bates left home on December 1, 1853, and lectured in New Hampshire, Massachusetts, New York, Michigan, Illinois, and Ohio before he returned home on May 22, 1854, after a nearly six-month absence. Often he was only home a few days before setting out on another extended itinerary. It is little wonder that Dick calls him "the great pathbreaker."[7]

Such was Bates' schedule year after year. Dick, in tracing his travels, notes that he arrived home in October 1857 after an absence of apparently 18 months, stayed a few weeks, and was back in Michigan to chair a meeting in early November.[8]

And please remember that Bates' travels did not take place with the sort of comfort we are used to today. But then what was comfort to him if it meant the winning of souls for God's kingdom. During the winter of 1861 the 69-year-old itinerant reports cutting a hole through the ice of a running stream in which "seven were buried with Christ by baptism into death." The next year he reported traveling with "double teams through swamps, over logs, and through a deep mire a good part of the way for six miles" so that he could baptize six.[9] Even as an old man he was unstoppable.

GATHERING IN THE WHO'S WHO
OF SABBATARIAN ADVENTISM

As we noted in chapter 6, Bates was the person who brought the Sabbath to James and Ellen White, Hiram Edson, F. B. Hahn, and O.R.L. Crosier in late 1846. While Hahn and Crosier would eventually give up the seventh-day Sabbath, the other three converts would join Bates in forming a Sabbatarian core group in 1847.

But those three leaders weren't the only prominent people that Bates brought into Sabbatarianism. His list of converts makes up a large section of the who's who of the early Seventh-day Adventist Church.

One of Bates' most successful mission fields was southern Michigan, which he first visited in 1849 in his search for ex-Millerites who would listen to his message. The first city he worked in Michigan was Jackson. In August of 1845 a J. C. Bowles of that community had complained that the few ex-Millerites there who had held onto the belief in God's leading in 1844 were "on the 'flat rock,' and refuse every invitation to leave."[10] It would be Bates who would help them get off of their "flat rock." But Bowles wouldn't be the first man he approached when he arrived in Jackson in the summer of 1849.

Rather, his first convert would be a blacksmith by the name of Dan R. Palmer. Given Bates' forthrightness and the specificity of his mission, one of the first questions he asked after arriving in Jackson was whether there were any Adventists there. Someone directed him to Palmer's blacksmith shop. Palmer, the leader of the Adventist congregation, didn't even stop working as Bates launched into a Bible study on the Sabbath and its place in the flow of the three angels' messages. But busy as he was, the blacksmith soon concluded that Bates had the truth. That resulted in Bates receiving an invitation to speak to the Adventist congregation the next Sunday. All those present accepted the Sabbath. But one important member was not there that morning. As a result, in the afternoon Palmer and Bates visited Cyrenius Smith at his farm. Smith not only joined them in the Sabbath truth, but soon became a leader among the Sabbatarians in Michigan, eventually selling his farm so that he could put the money into God's work. He and Palmer along with J. P. Kellogg and Henry Lyon would be the four men who would in 1855 provide the money for the Sabbatarians to establish their first publishing house in Battle Creek, Michigan.[11]

A few weeks after Bates' visit, Bowles wrote to James White, noting that "the little band here have received the truth on the Sabbath, without an exception. And we thank the Lord for ever inclining Bro. Bates' mind to come to Jackson. O, sound the alarm, and let the message fly! I think it is the last one to the remnant." Tell Bates, he said, that "we are all strong in the Lord, rejoicing in the truth." Bowles had written to request the *Present Truth*. White responded that "the grand reason why you were prepared to receive the truth of the little paper is, Brother Bates had, by the help of God, waked you up to see the truth, and feel the subject of the Sabbath, therefore you were all ready for the little paper."[12] Even at that early date White had a vision of integrating the witness of the living preacher with an ongoing periodical—a vision that Bates, as we saw in chapter 10, had not yet fully grasped.

Bates returned to Jackson in 1852 with equally important results in his public meetings. A young first-day Adventist preacher by the name of Merritt E. Cornell passing through Jackson stopped long enough to hear what Bates was teaching since the branch of Adventism that he belonged to was at that time aggressively fighting against Bates and his Sabbath teaching in the *Advent Harbinger*.[13] Cornell accepted the Sabbath and soon convinced his wife and others on the topic. Subsequently he worked for a time with Bates and eventually became one of the early Sabbatarians most successful evangelists.

After he accepted Sabbatarianism, one of Cornell's earliest contacts was John P. Kellogg, who lived nearby in Hartland, Michigan. Kellogg, who had left a "fallen church" some four years previously, was hungry for truth. "I had honestly supposed for some time," he reported in January 1853, "that the Sabbath was abolished, until July last, when Bro. Cornell came to see me." Cornell had just returned from Jackson where he had accepted the Sabbath. He soon got Kellogg to begin studying the topic. Then, reports Kellogg, "I went to the Conference at Jackson, in August [1852], and heard Bro. Bates; and there, light burst into my mind. I saw clearly that the first and second angels' messages were in the past, and that the third was now being given. And there my soul was filled with joy and peace in believing." Kellogg had established Sabbath services in Hartland with some 15 attending.[14] He and his family would become extremely important in early Adventism. His son John Harvey Kellogg would later become head of the massive Battle Creek Sanitarium, where he started the processed cereal industry—an invention that his brother, W. K. Kellogg, would then exploit.

Meanwhile in March 1853 another of Kellogg's sons, Merritt G., reported that Sabbatarian congregations had formed in several Michigan communities, including Grand Rapids, Bedford, and Tyrone. But it would be the town of Battle Creek that would become central to nineteenth-century Seventh-day Adventist history. Bates first visited Battle Creek in 1852. There was apparently no first-day Adventist congregation there. As a result, according to J. N. Loughborough's recollections, Bates inquired at the post office as to the identity of the most honest man in town. The official referred him to David Hewitt on Van Buren Street. Finding the Hewitts at breakfast, the intrepid evangelist told the head of the family that since people considered David the most honest man in town, Bates had some truth to share with him. Beginning at breakfast and going to evening, he "laid before them the third angel's message and the Sabbath," which they accepted before the sun went down. Bates baptized Hewitt, along with J. P. Kellogg, Cornell, and others in August 1852.[15]

Hewitt's baptism was the beginning of the Sabbatarian congregation in Battle Creek. In 1855 four of Bates' converts—Dan Palmer, J. P. Kellogg, Henry Lyon, and Cyrenius Smith—provided the funds for the Sabbatarians to build a publishing house in that city. Some of those men sold their farms to finance the venture. Battle Creek would become the very center of Adventism for the rest of the century.

The Butler family was another major contribution of Bates' evangelism to the cadre of early Adventist leaders. George I. Butler, who would serve as the Seventh-day Adventist General Conference president from 1871 to 1874 and again from 1880 to 1888, tells us that his parents had been through the 1844 movement but had become "much confused and perplexed" after the October disappointment. "Then," he writes, "came Father Bates, hunting up those who had fallen into discouragement. He was not received very kindly by my father, because he was a no-law Baptist; but mother was a devout Christian, and so he came into the kitchen and hung up his chart and gave her a discourse, and she began to keep the Sabbath." Mrs. Butler observed the Sabbath without her husband or children from 1848 to 1850.[16]

At that point Bates' stubbornness finally broke through to her almost equally stubborn husband, E. P. Butler. "Bro. Butler," Bates exuded in November 1850, "finally yielded to the present truth." Soon after, he reported Butler attending a meeting at which he "drank deeper into the straight truth." Not long after that the Butler's eldest daughter also accepted the Sabbath. Within a month of his conversion, E. P. Butler reported that he had moved the factories he owned from a six-day work week to a five, while paying his workers for six. That witness, he noted, "made no little stir, and I trust has preached to some in that place." Bates' converts were serious about their Sabbath keeping.[17]

E. P. Butler soon became a Sabbatarian preacher who did a good work.

But his son would far outshine him in becoming a major leader of the Seventh-day Adventist Church. George I. Butler reports that he was a skeptic when his parents accepted the Sabbath. He would not join the movement until 1856.[18] Subsequently he became not only a leading minister, but, as noted above, the president of the church for more than a decade.

Another family that Bates' ministry impacted was that of Annie and Uriah Smith, whose parents had gone through the 1844 experience. By 1851 their mother had accepted the Sabbath and had met Bates. The two of them had agreed to pray for her children. Shortly afterward Bates scheduled himself to hold meetings near Annie's residence, which her mother urged her to attend. Annie wasn't much interested but perhaps to please her mother agreed to go.

According to J. N. Loughborough, the night before she attended both Bates and Annie dreamed of seeing each other at the meeting under certain specific circumstances. The next day events matched up with their identical dreams and Annie concluded that God had been leading in her life and that Bates had the truth. Within three weeks she decided to keep the Sabbath. Her experience undoubtedly helped her unsettled brother Uriah to accept the Sabbatarian message in late 1852.[19] James White soon hired both talented siblings to work in Adventist publishing. Annie would make an important contribution, but her life ended prematurely when she died of pulmonary tuberculosis in 1855. Uriah, however, would soon become a dominant force in Adventism, editing the *Review and Herald* for much of the rest of the century, serving as the secretary of the General Conference for nearly 25 years, and becoming the denomination's nineteenth-century expert on prophetic interpretation.

Another leading Sabbatarian whom Bates was instrumental in bringing into the movement was Stephen N. Haskell. By the time Bates met him in 1854 the young first-day Adventist preacher had already encountered the Sabbath but was not yet totally in harmony with the Sabbatarian Adventist understanding of the topic. Someone advised Bates to visit him. The resulting meeting was the deciding factor in Haskell's life. "Brother Bates," he later recalled, "preached to us (there were only two of us) from morning until noon, and from noon until night, and then in the evening until the time we went to bed. He did that for ten successive days, and I have been a Seventh-day Adventist ever since."[20]

Many other early Adventist leaders came under Bates' influence in one way or another as they moved toward joining the Sabbatarian movement, including perhaps John Byington (the first General Conference president) and Roswell F. Cottrell (a former Seventh Day Baptist),[21] but no conversion could have brought more joy to Bates' heart than that of his wife in 1850. For more than five years he had preached the Sabbath, written the Sabbath, and traveled and sacrificed for the Sabbath even though his own wife hadn't accepted his message. One can only imagine the tension that it must have brought into their relationship.

"Sister Bates, the wife of our faithful Bro. Bates," James White penned in November 1850, "is strong in the present truth. The deceptive influence of some who professed to preach the true advent faith, blinded her mind, and prejudiced her against the truth. Bro. Bates persevered, and for years, yes, all through the scattering time, has kept the Holy Sabbath alone. But when the gathering time came, and God began to reach out his arm to recover his precious 'jewels' from beneath the 'rubbish,' sister Bates was led to examine the truth for herself. And now she and her husband are walking in all the commandments and ordinances of the Lord." A year later she herself could write, "I love the Holy Sabbath better and better, and pray that it may be sanctified to all the dear children who are trying to keep it."[22]

NEW ENEMIES FROM OLD FRIENDS

That Bates and the Sabbatarians should come into conflict with other ex-Millerite Adventist groups in the early 1850s is to be expected, given the aggressive tactics used by the Sabbatarians to preach their message. We also need to remember that other Adventist groups were the main target of Sabbatarian outreach in the late 1840s and early 1850s, a period during which Sabbatarian membership went from a couple of hundred in 1849 to about 2,500 two years later.

Bates, of course, was at the forefront of what the other Adventist groups must have thought of as "sheep stealing" activities. He even took the message to William Miller's widow in Low Hampton, New York, in 1852. Speaking of his preaching to the congregation meeting in the Advent Chapel on Miller's farm, Bates noted that "we gave them the third angel's message, and believe the Lord accompanied it by his Spirit."

Several took Sabbatarian literature so that they could study the topic further. "Sister M.," Bates reported, "welcomed us, and listened attentively to our explanation of the last message from the Chart: said she did not know but the Sabbath which we taught was true."[23]

Bates could be just as aggressive in words as he was in action. According to him, Himes and the Albany Adventists had been "SINNING AGAINST GOD EVER SINCE" they had moved away from Miller's understanding of the 2300 days of Daniel 8:14. They were nothing less than "Rebels" since the forming of the Laodicean Church in April 1845 at Albany, New York. He pled with his readers "to flee from all such delusive, treacherous, soul-destroying teaching."[24]

It was only natural that Himes and those associated with him would vigorously respond to Bates. An M. L. Clark wrote to Himes from Canada, reporting that Bates had arrived at his church "professing to be an Advent preacher. . . . We had an interview with him, and found his 'message' was the Sabbath, or seventh day, and shut door; that is except ye keep the seventh day ye cannot be saved. . . . He made several requests for permission to lecture, but we gave him none." Soon after, Bates scheduled a private meeting and made several converts. Clark wanted some advice on how to handle "this delusion, which is dividing and scattering the little wayworn flock of God."[25]

In response, Himes, who had known Bates since their New Bedford days in the 1820s, wrote that "Capt. Bates is an old personal friend of ours, and so far as we know, is better as a man than most of his associates; but we have no confidence in his teaching.—He should not be tolerated for a moment." Isaac Wellcome, an Advent Christian who also knew Bates personally, later reported that he was "an able speaker and writer, who was very useful in the work of Christ until he became a Seventh Day Sabbath advocate." Wellcome's opinion of the Whites was even worse. James, he noted, "ran well for a season" until he went off the track, but Ellen was "a wonderful fanatic and trance medium."[26]

One of the more sustained attacks on the seventh-day Sabbath and Bates' ministry was that of Joseph Marsh's *Harbinger and Advocate,* which fought a running battle with the Sabbatarians for much of the early 1850s. One of the *Harbinger's* foremost anti-Sabbath writers was O.R.L. Crosier, whom, as we noted in chapter 6, had accepted the seventh-day Sabbath from Bates in November 1846. As early as March 1852 we find Marsh apologizing for publishing so much on the Sabbath. "But what we have said," he noted, "has not been in vain, for it has been the means of rescuing *very many* from the errors of the shut-door sabbatarian delusions."[27]

A few months later the *Harbinger* published an extensive letter regarding "Mr. Joseph Bates' Misrepresentations." The authors especially sought to prevent people from being "deceived by the false statements and misrepresentations of Mr. Bates and his associates" and their claim that "those who worship God on the first day of the week, instead of the seventh, are sailing under the black flag of the Papacy—have the mark of the beast—cannot be saved—that they themselves are the 144,000 that are sealed" in their keeping of the seventh day.[28]

Bates and other Sabbatarians regularly responded to the *Harbinger* through the pages of the *Review and Herald*. For example, Bates indicated that the *Harbinger* had misrepresented him rather than the other way around. On the mark of the beast, for example, he wrote that "we do not teach that those who keep the first day of the week have the mark of the beast." Rather, a people had to consciously "reject the commandments of God in which is the true or bible [sic] mark" and then "receive the mark of the beast understandingly" before they could have it. Bates went on to deal with the accusations of the *Harbinger* against him point by point.[29]

James White, as editor of the *Review and Herald*, claimed that he found it "extremely unpleasant to occupy space in the *Review and Herald*, in noticing the unchristian treatment, and abusive language of the conductors of the *Harbinger* toward those who claim the right to teach and keep all the commandments of God."[30] But he seems to have been more than generous in regularly supplying such space in the ongoing dialogue between the Sabbatarians and their detractors.

Both sides found the other equally intractable. One correspondent to the *Harbinger*, for example, wrote that he had "been to visit a band of Sabbath keepers, and found them as impregnable as the rock Gibralter, to truth or reason." On the other hand, at least two first day preachers came over to the seventh day side at the height of the debate—J. B. Frisbie, who had been "bitter in opposition" to the message of the third angel, and M. E. Cornell, who had stood solidly behind Crosier and the *Harbinger* until convicted about the Sabbath after Bates in private discussion demonstrated the "many absurdities" of the *Harbinger* position.[31] Each man would become a successful minister for the Sabbatarians.

The opposition Bates faced did not merely consist of printed material. At times it was also physical. On one occasion in 1853 Bates faced a congregation, who "with stamping and pounding the chairs" on the floor, sought "to convert us to what they believed was the true Sanctuary." Finally one man seized Bates by the collar and shook him "most violently," claiming that it was not him who had done the shaking, but God who wished to divest him of error. At other times Bates faced verbal violence.[32]

One of Bates' most persistent enemies would be Crosier, who never tired of arguing that "God's holy law is abolished." The year 1860 found him dogging Bates' itinerary in an attempt to disrupt his work. James White reports one such occasion in which Crosier sought to speak after the Sabbatarians had closed their meeting. "Having failed in [his] wily attempt at abusing us," White reported. "C. was not so well prepared to speak. His congregation was tired, and he had a hard job before him. He worried himself dealing out light blows against the truth, like one hold[ing] the large end of the maul. Several wagonloads left while he was speaking, and some others scattered, and some engaged in conversation in the tent. And some of his friends stated to our brethren that they were disappointed in the man. And so the fierce boaster slew himself."[33]

On the more positive side of Bates' work among his old acquaintances was his encounter with the well-known abolitionist Gerrit Smith, who was "keeping the seventh-day Sabbath, but not in the message of the third Angel." Smith listened respectfully to Bates and said he would examine the subject further. But nothing seems to have come from their meeting.[34]

BATES' EVANGELISTIC METHOD

Bates and the other early Sabbatarian preachers knew exactly who their primary target audience was—ex-Millerites, preferably those who had accepted both the first and second angels' messages of Revelation 14. For example, Bates took advantage of the fact that the *Harbinger* and other Adventist papers often provided the names and addresses of their subscribers. Using such information, Bates sought to visit them as he passed through their part of the country.[35]

On the other hand, he didn't seem to need an audience that had previous knowledge of Adventism. As occasion permitted he would hang up a prophetic chart in a train station or on the deck of a boat, draw a crowd, and launch into his presentation. J. O. Corliss, who worked in evangelism with Bates for some time, recalled that "he did not wait for an audience in some public building, though he had the power to interest large gatherings. But upon finding a friendly home in some community, as soon as he had settled, he would invite the family to a study from the Bible. Then hanging up his prophetic chart, he would cover the world's history in prophetic outline so tersely and earnestly as to convince his hearers of the truth in a single study." Bates had even no qualms about preaching in a field to a farmer midcourse in his plowing.[36]

According to Ellen White, Bates' special talent was "to talk the Word. None had a gift like his. He could talk to a small company when there were no more than two present, as well as to a large company." The man had a gift "greatly needed in the church."[37]

Probably Bates wasn't what we would call a great preacher, but rather he presented his messages with an utter sincerity and a profound personal conviction that moved his hearers. His central topic was his chain-of-events approach to prophecy that tied the Sabbath and the heavenly sanctuary into an endtime scenario. His sermon style featured a large number of Bible texts held together by personal comments as he presented his study. While his approach may have fallen short in homiletical technique, it was long on conviction. One man reports leaving Bates' meetings not fully settled on the Sabbath. But when he attended a Sunday school celebration that featured a wagon with a Ten Commandments chart on its side, Bates' powerful words came back to him and he decided to start keeping the Sabbath. Another man who had no special interest in either the Sabbath or the Advent went to hear Bates out of curiosity, then left with a desire to unravel the truth about Sabbath and Sunday. Soon he resolved to observe the Sabbath. Joseph Bates had a message whose implications were hard to escape once a person had heard him.[38]

Because of the often rough and tumble communities in which the early Sabbatarians worked it was crucial that a speaker had some control over the audience. The ex-sea-captain was certainly up to that task. In one place he reported that an "unusual howling and groaning, and an attempted exhortation" by one of the females in the congregation had dis-

turbed his meetings. "Timely rebuke in the name of the Lord quieted her during her stay with us." At another location Bates asserted that there wasn't one text in the New Testament that taught that the Sabbath had changed from the seventh day to the first day of the week. "An intelligent gentleman interrupted by saying, 'There are more than twenty.' 'Well,' said Bro. Bates, 'will you please . . . give us one?' The gentleman replied, 'I can give you twenty.' Bro B. urged, 'If you can give twenty, you can certainly give one. We wait for one; only give us one text.' The gentleman was silent; and Bro. B. went on with his subject." The record indicates that Bates was quick on his feet as he faced a variety of detractors in his public meetings.[39]

Not only was Bates a preacher of the Word, he was also a man of prayer. "I had the privilege of laboring with Father Bates," J. O. Corliss recalled. "He taught me how to pray. I had prayed a good deal before that, but I had never learned how to talk with the Lord as I did after I had been with Father Bates." The evangelist "would bow down there in my presence and talk with the Lord just as if he was a friend of his and had hold of his hand." On another occasion Corliss wrote that "when I knelt with him to address the heavenly throne, I was touched with his quiet earnestness and familiar confidence expressed in the power of God to help and save." Bates was a firm advocate of not only reverent kneeling in prayer but also of "lifting up holy hands" while praying.[40]

LIVING ON THE FINANCIAL EDGE

Joseph Bates was totally dedicated to his belief in the Adventist message. He not only gave all his time to preaching it without any regular compensation but by the mid-1840s he had donated the $10,000 that had provided him a comfortable retirement fund in 1828. James White wrote of him in 1849 that "he once stood high in society, and had some eight or ten thousand dollars of the deceitful [i.e., riches]. But he is an 'outcast,' and has spent all his property in the Holy Advent cause. Yet he is rich, yes, glory to God, he is a rich servant of Jesus Christ. But few know of his trials, labors, sufferings in the cause of present truth, in which he devotes his whole time."[41] His wife, who until 1850 didn't even accept the Sabbath message to which Bates was totally devoted, undoubtedly increased those trials.

On another occasion White wrote that he and his wife had met the "old pilgrim" in Brooklyn. He rejoiced that Bates "had been able to leave things comfortable at home, and had two dollars in his pocket." Bates, of course, wasn't alone in his poverty. In April 1848 White was able to write of himself and Ellen that "all we have including clothes, bedding, and household furniture we have with us in a three-foot trunk, and that is but half full. We have nothing else to do but to serve God and go where God opens the way for us."[42]

Travel wasn't always easy in those days, especially if a person was broke. Bates, for example, felt deeply impressed in early 1849 that it was his duty to preach the message in Vermont. Having no money he decided to walk from southern Massachusetts. But he wasn't the only one under conviction regarding that missionary tour. Ellen White's sister Sarah had the impression that she should help him. As a result, she requested advance pay from her employer and worked for $1.25 per week as a hired girl to pay his way.[43]

According to James, the trip to Vermont had amply paid for the sacrifice that had gone into it. Bates, White wrote, "had a hard time, but God was with him and much good was done. He found or left quite a number in the Sabbath."[44]

For those of us living in a more prosperous time, it is difficult to grasp the privations that the early Adventist leaders underwent as they traveled from place to place. "The few that taught the truth," James White later wrote, "traveled on foot, in second-class cars, or on steamboat decks, for want of means." His wife was more graphic. "For want of means," she recalled, "we took the cheapest private conveyance, second-class cars, and lower-deck passage on steamers." Such travel, she added, exposed them to "the smoke of tobacco, besides the swearing and vulgar conversation of the ship hands and the baser portion of the traveling public." At night they often slept on the floor, cargo boxes, or grain sacks with their suitcase for a pillow and overcoat for a covering. In winter they walked the deck to keep warm.[45]

One of Bates' favorite sayings was "the Lord will provide." And He did. In earlier chapters we noted that others supplied funds to cover the cost of publishing his several books, which he then distributed free of charge. The same was true of his travel and other expenses. Remember, he had no salary and there was no church organization to support him and the other early Sabbatarian workers. His letters and reports from time to time offer thanks to individuals or groups of believers who sent him a few dollars. His was a faith mission. One story tells that Bates, who was under conviction that he needed to preach at a certain place, actually took a seat on a train with neither money nor a ticket. He had been seated only a few moments when a perfect stranger came and handed him $5.00 to assist him in his work.[46] Such providences were not out of the ordinary in his ministry.

The Allegan and Monterey, Michigan, congregations seemed to have had a special concern to help Bates. Around 1857 he wrote to them, thanking them for a $12.00 gift for the purchase of a coat. He went on to note that he had a slim financial base, since "I have been laboring mostly in new places . . . where the wants of messengers are not much thought of." "For the last eleven years," he added, "I have tryed [sic] to cheerfully devote all my time (except when resting) to spread the present truth where duty seemed clear, and souls willing to hear. Nor would I change my occupation for any consideration whatever unless in obedience to the Lord. All my poor services and a thousand times more could never pay the purchase of my redemption. I want to remain in his service while I continue in this mortal state."[47]

About that same time, Prudence Bates wrote to Sarah Belden, the woman who had worked for $1.25 per week to pay Bates' way to Vermont, thanking her for the $8.00 she had helped raise for their sustenance. "The brethren," Prudy wrote, "have my thanks for the interest they have taken for my dear husband, that they have helped him 'after a godly sort,' and above all I thank my kind heavenly Father that he has disposed your hearts to sacrifice for his cause."[48]

Ellen White attached a rare personal note to that published letter, urging believers to remember those who had dedicated their lives to God's work. "Let us not," she penned, "forget that they sacrifice their pleasant homes, the society of their families, and travel in the heat and cold for weeks and months together. They often feel weary and sad, and perhaps when you least realize it, are troubled about their families at home. Often they have not means to send to the relief or support of their families. The servants of God need your support and comfort. . . . Look closely, and see if they are comfortably clothed. Don't wait for them to express their wants.

. . . Our dear Bro. and Sr. Bates deserve our prayers, sympathy and support. We will remember them in their self-denial and sacrifice, and see that their wants are well supplied."[49]

Ellen White and her husband practiced what they preached in that matter. Bates, looking back in 1869, reported that James had "most generously donated from his own means to help sustain me in this work," at one time even providing the Bates family a house for 14 months, for which he refused rent.[50]

Even though Bates and his family lived near the financial edge, that did not mean that they were totally destitute. The 1860 federal census shows Bates having real estate valued at $200 and personal property worth $100. Those figures had reached $1000 and $400 respectively in the 1870 census. While they show some increase in value as Bates got older, they were a far cry from his prosperity in money and property in the 1820s and 1830s. In 1868 he wrote to his non-Adventist sister Harriet that the reports that she had received from their cousin that he and his wife were financially destitute were false. But some of his argument may have been a bit of bluster, since their cousin was positioned through a Baptist minister in Bates' hometown to have some knowledge on the topic. It is only natural that a man of some pride would not want "outsiders" to know of any financial problems.[51]

A LOVED MINISTER

Notes of appreciation for Bates and his ministry appear frequently in the pages of the *Review and Herald.* Typical is that of B. B. Brigham, who wrote that "the Lord has greatly blessed the labors of Bro. Bates in this region, and there was much weeping on his departure; but . . . he left, full of faith and the Holy Ghost." Jessie Dorcas reported in the *Review* that "Bro. Bates has been among us with the power and demonstration of the Spirit; and I can say for myself, that I now see clearly the glorious light of the coming day. But I am not able to express my gratitude to God, for sending so efficient and patient a laborer into this part of the harvest, to make known to us the power and coming of the Lord. I left Bro. Bates a few days ago in Richland County declaring the truth, though much opposed by the professing churches."[52]

Ellen White tells the story of a young man on his deathbed who was having a difficult time making himself understood due to the ravages of his disease. But after communicating his confidence in being in the first resurrection, he said, "Tell Bro. Bates that I will meet him then." People felt a special closeness to the man who had brought them a message of hope.[53]

Some people's feelings went beyond love for Bates to almost worship. One woman exclaimed upon being introduced to him, "'Can this be Brother Bates who wrote that hewing [i.e., cutting or to make smooth] book on the Sabbath? And come to see us? I am unworthy to have you come under my roof. But the Lord has sent you to us, for we are all starving for the truth.'"[54]

It appears that Arthur Spalding is correct when he wrote that "'Brother Bates'" was the man that "all loved"—at least all the Sabbatarians.[55]

---

[1] J. Bates to Bro. and Sis. Hastings, Sept. 25, 1849 (italics supplied.)

[2] J. White, "Our Present Work," *Review and Herald,* Aug. 19, 1851, p. 12.

[3] J. Bates, "Dear Bro. White," *Review and Herald,* Aug. 5, 1851, p. 6; J. Bates, "Dear Bro. White," *Review and Herald,* Aug. 19, 1851, p. 14.

[4] J. White, "A Brief Sketch of the Past," *Review and Herald,* May 6, 1852, p. 5.

[5] Anderson, *Outrider of the Apocalypse,* p. 71.

[6] J. Bates, "Dear Bro. White," *Review and Herald,* Jan. 13, 1852, p. 80; J. Bates, "Dear Bro. White," *Review and Herald,* Feb. 17, 1852, p. 95.

[7] J. Bates, "From Bro. Bates," *Review and Herald,* May 6, 1852, p. 6; J. Bates, "Extracts of Letters," *Review and Herald,* July 22, 1852, p. 47; Dick, *Founders of the Message,* pp. 143-145.

[8] Dick, *Founders of the Message,* p. 147.

[9] J. Bates, "Report From Bro. Bates," *Review and Herald,* Mar. 12, 1861, p. 132; J. Bates, "Meetings at Buck Creek, Mich.," *Review and Herald,* Apr. 29, 1862, p. 176.

[10] J. C. Bowles, "Letter From Br. Bowles," *Voice of Truth,* Sept. 24, 1845, p. 464.

[11] A. W. Spalding, personal interviews, in *Origin and History of Seventh-day Adventists,* vol. 1, pp. 251, 263 (notes 13, 14); see also Brian Strayer, "Early Advent Waymarks in Jackson, Michigan: Parts I & II," unpub. ms., Aug. 24, 1985.

[12] J. C. Bowles, "Dear Bro. White," *Present Truth,* Sept. 1849, p. 32; J. White to Bro. Bowles, Nov. 8, 1849.

[13] J. Bates, "Jackson, Mich., Conference," *Review and Herald,* July 8, 1852, p. 40; M. E. Cornell, "From Bro. Cornell," *Review and Herald,* July 16, 1852, p. 79; A.M.A. Cornell, "From Sister Cornell," *Review and Herald,* July 16, 1852, p. 79.

[14] J. P. Kellogg, "From Bro. Kellogg," *Review and Herald,* Jan. 6, 1853, p. 136.

[15] M. G. Kellogg, "Bro. M. G. Kellogg," *Review and Herald,* Mar. 3, 1853, p. 168; "Sabbath Services," 1895 *General Conference Bulletin,* p. 208; J. N. Loughborough, "Second Advent Experience—No. 7," *Review and Herald,* July 26, 1923, p. 5; J. Bates, "Jackson,

Mich., Conference," *Review and Herald,* Sept. 2, 1852, p. 69.

[16] G. I. Butler, in 1909 *General Conference Bulletin,* pp. 4, 120.

[17] J. Bates, [letter] *Present Truth,* Nov. 1850, p. 88; E. P. Butler, [letter], *Review and Herald,* Dec. 1850, p. 20.

[18] G. I. Butler to W. C. White, Dec. 4, 1912; Emmett K. Vande Vere, *Rugged Heart: The Story of George I. Butler* (Nashville, Tenn.: Southern Pub. Assn., 1979), pp. 14-16.

[19] Loughborough, *Great Second Advent Movement,* pp. 313-315; Eugene F. Durand, *Yours in the Blessed Hope, Uriah Smith* (Washington, D.C.: Review and Herald Pub. Assn., 1980), pp. 23, 24.

[20] S. N. Haskell, in *General Conference Bulletin,* p. 92; cf. S. N. Haskell, "How I Accepted the Sabbath," *Review and Herald,* Apr. 7, 1896, p. 217; Ella M. Robinson, *S. N. Haskell: Man of Action* (Washington, D.C.: Review and Herald Pub. Assn., 1967), pp. 22, 23.

[21] Anderson, *Outrider of the Apocalypse,* p. 103; Spicer, *Pioneer Days,* p. 253.

[22] [J. White], "Conferences," *Advent Review,* Nov. 1850, p. 72; P. M. Bates, "Extracts of Letters," *Review and Herald,* Dec. 23, 1851, p. 72.

[23] J. Bates, "From Bro. Bates," *Review and Herald,* Feb. 3, 1853, p. 151; cf. Elon Everts, "From Bro. Everts," *Review and Herald,* Jan. 20, 1853, p. 144.

[24] J. Bates, "Midnight Cry in the Past," *Review and Herald,* Dec. 1850, pp. 23, 24; cf. J. Bates, "New Testament Seventh Day Sabbath," *Review and Herald,* Jan. 1851, pp. 31, 32.

[25] M. L. Clark, "Letter From M. L. Clark," *Advent Herald,* May 4, 1850, pp. 110, 111.

[26] J. Bates, *Autobiography,* p. 250; J. V. Himes, "Note," *Advent Herald,* May 4, 1850, p. 111; Wellcome, *History of the Second Advent Message,* pp. 346, 401, 402; cf. Johnson, *Advent Christian History,* pp. 196-198.

[27] [J. Marsh, editorial note], *Harbinger and Advocate,* Mar. 20, 1852, p. 316.

[28] C. W. Low et al, "Mr. Joseph Bates' Misrepresentations," *Harbinger and Advocate,* July 10, 1852, p. 27; cf. O.R.L. Crosier, "Vain Talkers," *Harbinger and Advocate,* Aug. 28, 1852, p. 85; A. H. Mason, "Seventh Day Sabbath Abolished," *Harbinger and Advocate,* Sept. 11, 1852, p. 104.

[29] J. Bates, "Reply to Wrong Statements Respecting 'Misrepresentations,'" *Review and Herald,* Aug. 5, 1852, p. 56.

[30] [J. White], "The Advent Harbinger," *Review and Herald,* Oct. 14, 1852, p. 92.

[31] W. J. Greenleaf, "Seventh Day Sabbath Abolished," *Harbinger and Advocate,* Jan. 29, 1853, p. 259; J. B. Frisbie, "Letter From Bro. J. B. Frisbie," *Review and Herald,* July 7, 1853, p. 29; M. E. Cornell, "From Bro. Cornell," *Review and Herald,* Sept. 16, 1852, p. 79.

[32] J. Bates, "From Bro. Bates," *Review and Herald,* Mar. 31, 1853, p. 182; Luther Paine, "From Bro. Paine," *Review and Herald,* Mar. 17, 1853, p. 174; J. Bates, "Meetings in Jackson Co., Mich.," *Review and Herald,* June 9, 1859, p. 24.

[33] J. Bates, "Report From Bro. Bates," *Review and Herald,* June 5, 1860, pp. 21, 22; J. White, "Caledonia Conference," *Review and Herald,* July 3, 1860, p. 52.

[34] J. Bates, "Dear Bro. White," *Review and Herald,* Mar. 1851, p. 55.

[35] J. N. Loughborough, "Second Advent Experience—No. 5," *Review and Herald,* July 5, 1923, p. 5.

36 J. O. Corliss, "The Message and Its Friends—No. 2: Joseph Bates as I Knew Him," *Review and Herald,* Aug. 16, 1923, p. 8; J. Bates, "Letter From Bro. Bates," *Review and Herald,* Nov. 20, 1856, p. 24; J. Bates, "Meetings in Mich." *Review and Herald,* May 28, 1857, p. 40.

37 E. G. White, "Need for Unity Among Spiritual Shepherds," MS 14, Oct. 1850.

38 C. L. Palmer, "From Bro. Palmer," *Review and Herald,* July 14, 1863, p. 55; I. N. Pike, "No Weekly Sabbath but the Seventh Day, Taught in the Bible," *Review and Herald,* Mar. 12, 1857, p. 145.

39 J. Bates, "Meetings in Northern, Mich.," *Review and Herald,* July 16, 1861, p. 56; J. White, *Life Incidents,* p. 276.

40 J. O. Corliss, in 1913 *General Conference Bulletin,* p. 5; J. O. Corliss, "The Message and Its Friends—No. 2: Joseph Bates as I Knew Him," *Review and Herald,* Aug. 16, 1823, p. 8; J. Bates, "Attitude in Prayer," *Review and Herald,* Jan. 1851, p. 40.

41 J. White to Bro. Bowles, Oct. 17, 1849.

42 J. White to Bro. and Sis. Hastings, Aug. 26, 1848; J. White to Bro. and Sis. Hastings, Apr. 27, 1848.

43 J. White to Bro. and Sis. [Hastings], Mar. 22, 1849; E. G. White, *Life Sketches* (1915), p. 276; J. White, *Life Incidents,* p. 270; E. G. White to Frank Belden, Oct. 20, 1905.

44 J. White, postscript in E. G. White to Bro. and Sis. Hastings, Apr. 21, 1849.

45 J. White, *Life Incidents,* p. 292; E. G. White, *Testimonies for the Church,* vol. 1, p. 77.

46 M. Ellsworth Olsen, *A History of the Origin and Progress of Seventh-day Adventists* (Washington, D.C.: Review and Herald Pub. Assn., 1925), p. 188.

47 J. Bates to the Church in Monterey and Allegan, cir. 1857.

48 P. Bates, [letter], *Review and Herald,* Feb. 21, 1856, p. 167.

49 E. G. White, [note], *Review and Herald,* Feb. 21, 1856, p. 167.

50 J. Bates to Brn. Andrews, Bell, and Smith, Nov. 1, 1869, in *Defense of Eld. James White and Wife,* pp. 23, 24.

51 Anderson, *Outrider of the Apocalypse,* pp. 99, 114; J. Bates to Sis. Harriet, July 19, 1868.

52 B. B. Brigham, "Jackson, Mich., Conference," *Review and Herald,* Sept. 2, 1852, p. 72; J. Dorcas, "Dear Bro. White," *Review and Herald,* Dec. 5, 1854, p. 126.

53 E. G. White, *Spiritual Gifts,* vol. 2, p. 92.

54 James and Ellen White, *Life Sketches* (1888), p. 251.

55 Spalding, *Origin and History of Seventh-day Adventists,* vol. 1, p. 41.

CHAPTER XII

SENIOR STATESMAN

THROUGHOUT his life on both sea and land Bates had been a travelin' man. He would continue to be so for the rest of his life, but after 1855 he would more and more restrict his travels to Michigan. Part of that was due to the maturing of Sabbatarian Adventism, which was gradually turning into a denomination, and part of it resulted from the fact that Bates was aging. After all, in 1855 he turned 63, a time when men began to look toward retirement. But not Bates. He merely traveled in a more restricted circle.

A MICHIGAN EVANGELIST

Among the changes that took place in his life in the mid-1850s was the beginning of tent evangelism among the Sabbatarians. One student of Bates' life points out that he held tent efforts in some 12 places during the summer of 1855. The novelty of large meeting tents in that time period helped gather a crowd. Beyond that, they solved the problem of where to assemble in a small community with limited facilities. The use of tents was often quite effective. For example, one series of tent meetings that Bates held with M. E. Cornell in Hillsdale, Michigan, led to more than 50 baptisms in a place where no Sabbatarians had previously existed.[1]

In order to be closer to the new center of his work, Bates and Prudy moved to Michigan in 1858. The recently founded Adventist colony in Battle Creek had requested that the couple make their home there in 1856, but they finally decided to settle in Monterey, a small village north of Allegan, Michigan, where they would live for the rest of their lives. In 1863 Prudy made a trip back to New England where she spent a summer with her children and friends, but her husband apparently never once returned to the region where he had lived for more than 60 years, although in 1868 he did express a hope to his sister to see New England "once more before [it is] lain in ruins"—presumably at the Second Advent.[2]

Greater change would come to both Sabbatarian Adventism and to Bates' work in the 1860s. Between 1861 and 1863 the Sabbatarian movement would become the Seventh-day Adventist Church. As a result, by 1866 we find the Michigan Conference being divided into two parts, with Bates receiving responsibility for the eastern Michigan district of churches at the annual meetings of the Michigan Conference in both 1866 and 1867, while John Byington had the western district.[3] That assignment was worlds apart from the free wheeling decisions that Bates made as to where he would go during the forties and fifties.

Of even more interest is the shift in the nature of Bates' work in the sixties. In November 1868, for example, he speaks of "encouraging and strengthening . . . those who love to walk in the way of God's commandments" and of visiting the "scattered members and professed Sabbath-keepers. "On other occasions he writes of working with churches that had undergone trials and affliction.[4]

In short, Bates now had a different function and a different audience. Whereas once he scoured land and sea to bring people to the Sabbath, now he spent more and more of his time pastoring those already Sabbatarians.[5] Gradually Bates' role shifted away from that of itinerant evangelist to that of a pastor with a well defined circuit of churches.

SENIOR STATESMAN—FOR A TIME

We saw in chapter 10 that by 1850 James White had taken over the leadership role of Sabbatarian Adventism from Bates. No doubt existed as to who was directing and shaping the movement in the 1850s. Yet the two men continued to work well together, with James charting the course into the future and Bates chairing the meetings that gave visible, institutional shape to that future. Everett Dick points out that the two men, 29 years different in age, worked like father and son. Bates, Dick suggests, functioned as the first general conference executive in that he chaired the annual general conferences of the Sabbatarians from 1855 up into the early 1860s.[6]

The elderly Bates may have by that time had just the temperament to function as an effective senior statesman. His 60-plus years of experience along with the respect in which all parties of Sabbatarians held him uniquely qualified him for the position. Beyond that, as J. O. Corliss later pointed out,

Bates "knew how to set wrongs right without 'fuss and feathers.'"[7]

Thus it was that we find Bates chairing every general meeting that led to the shaping of the Seventh-day Adventist Church between 1855 and 1862. Probably one of the most difficult sessions for him to head was the 1855 general meeting that voted to change his cherished 6:00 p. m. Sabbath beginning to the sunset time. It says much for the man that he was able, after resisting for a time, to change his view—after he was sure it was the Lord's teaching.[8]

Bates not only chaired the 1855 general meeting but also the crucial 1857 Battle Creek conference that decided to purchase a power printing press and to build a meeting house in Battle Creek adequate enough to seat the large number who convened for general meetings.[9]

Once again Bates was chairman of the 1858 and 1859 general meetings. The 1859 conference was of special importance since the believers accepted the plan of Systematic Benevolence at that time.[10] "Sister Betsy," as some may have called it, was the first program developed by Sabbatarian Adventists for the systematic financial support of the gospel ministry. The tithing plan would not emerge for another 20 years. Systematic Benevolence was significant not only because it provided financial security for the ministry, but because it was a major step in the process of church organization.

The next major move in that direction took place at the 1860 general meeting. With Bates in the chair that conference took three significant steps toward formal organization. The first involved the adoption of a constitution for the legal incorporation of the publishing association. The second was that "individual churches so . . . organize as to hold their church property or church buildings legally." And the third was the selection of a denominational name. After much discussion, David Hewitt, "the most honest man in town" and Bates' first Battle Creek convert, resolved "that we take the name of Seventh-day Adventists." His motion carried, many delegates recognizing that it was "expressive of our faith and [doctrinal] position."[11]

Bates also chaired the all-important October 1861 general meeting. The central item of business was the recommendation "to the churches in the State of Michigan to unite in one Conference, with the name of The Michigan Conference of Seventh-day Adventists." The delegates adopted the recommendation along with a simple structure consisting of a conference chairman, a conference clerk, and a conference committee of three. The session chose Bates as chair for the first year. Thus, in actuality Bates served as the first conference president among Seventh-day Adventists. In that position he also acted as the chairman of the first annual session of the Michigan Conference in October 1862, a meeting that developed the functions of the conference so that it could truly become an effective unit. Bates' tenure as conference chairman ended at that meeting.[12]

Significantly, Bates did *not* chair the May 1863 conference that formed the General Conference of Seventh-day Adventists. Nor from that point forward did he chair the general meetings of the church. His role as senior statesman of the church had come to an end. Structural formality had put an end to his informal leadership. From 1863 we might think of him as honorary senior statesman.[13]

BATES REORGANIZES HIS VIEWS ON ORGANIZATION

While Bates as senior statesman chaired each of the meetings that led to the organization of the Seventh-day Adventist Church, he had not always been in favor of formal church structure. In early 1845, for example, he was quite certain that "organization and a creed" were not "necessary for God's waiting people at this last moment of time." "The next organization for God's people, after leaving Babylon" in 1844 in response to the second angel's message, "will be in the air with our glorious King."[14] In other words, because time was so short there would be no more genuine church organizations before the Second Advent.

In late 1850 he was still teaching that all organized denominations were Babylon ("confusion") and that they came in three types: "Roman, Greek, and Protestant." God's people were not to form a new church but were to be called out of the existing ones to the Sabbatarian Adventist message.[15]

We should note that Bates opposed organized denominations but not the forming of local congregations. "A Christian Church," he wrote in 1847, "is an assembly or congregation of *faithful men.*" That congregationalist mentality reflected his Christian Connexion background and harmonized with the February 1844 teaching of George Storrs that "no church can be organized by man's invention but what it becomes Babylon *the moment it is organized.*" Storrs, Bates, and many other post-Millerite Adventists had not forgotten the Babylonianish characteristics of the de-

nominations in the mid-1840s when they expelled Second Advent believers from their congregations. That "domineering, lordly spirit; a spirit to
suppress a free search after truth, and a free expression of our conviction
of what is truth," according to Storrs, was what Babylon was all about. The
last thing in Bates' mind in the late 1840s and early 1850s was to begin
another denomination.[16]

But time continued longer than Bates or the other early Sabbatarians
expected. And with it came the problems and complexities of living in a
less than perfect world. In an earlier chapter we noted that Bates had disturbed some of the Albany Adventists by showing up at their services and
wanting to preach his Sabbath message. J. V. Himes had responded that
such congregations should "demand that those who come as teachers shall
give evidence of possessing the confidence of those in whom they have
confidence." If, Himes cautioned, they took that precaution, then "these
roaming adventurers, who seek to live by teaching novelties, will find
their occupation gone."[17]

That problem, as we might expect, cut both ways. Not only were the
first-day Adventists being imposed on by the seventh-day variety, but vice
versa. As a result, in order to protect their congregations from "false
brethren," by 1853 James White and Bates had adopted a plan whereby
approved preachers received a card "recommending them to the fellowship of the Lord's people everywhere, simply stating that they were approved in the work of the gospel ministry." The card received by John
Loughborough in January 1853 carried the signatures of James White and
Joseph Bates.[18]

Bates' views on church order took a radical step forward in 1854. On
December 6, 1853, James White in a frustration born of his desire and attempts to get the Sabbatarians to work together, initiated a series of four
articles on "Gospel Order" in the *Review*. The first found him redefining
Babylon. "It is a lamentable fact," he asserted, "that many of our Advent
brethren who made a timely escape from the bondage of the different
churches [Babylon] . . . have since been a more perfect Babylon than ever
before. Gospel order has been too much overlooked by them. . . . Many
in their zeal to come out of Babylon, partook of a rash, disorderly spirit,
and were soon found in a perfect Babylon of confusion. . . . To suppose
that the church of Christ is free from restraint and discipline, is the wildest

fanaticism." Later that month Ellen White produced her first extensive call for structure, noting that "the Lord has shown that gospel order has been too much feared and neglected. . . . There is more real need of order than ever before."[19]

Apparently Bates had reached the same conclusions, probably in collusion with the Whites. It is significant that his home church of Fairhaven selected a deacon in mid-December 1853. According to the congregation, such a move was in harmony with "Gospel Order." Beyond that, 1854 found Bates teaching and implementing Gospel Order on a regular basis as he traveled from church to church.[20]

However, the most significant indication of a change in his thinking on the topic was an extensive article from his pen published in the April 29, 1854, *Review and Herald,* in which he claimed that biblical church order must be restored to God's people before the Second Advent. He argued that during the Middle Ages the "law-breakers" had *"deranged"* such essential elements of Christianity as the Sabbath and biblical church order. God had used the Sabbatarian Adventists to return the seventh-day Sabbath to His church, and it was "perfectly clear" to Bates' mind "that God will employ law-keepers as instruments to restore . . . a 'glorious Church, not having spot or wrinkle.' . . . This unity of the faith, and perfect church order, never has existed since the days of the apostles. It is very clear that it must exist prior to the second advent of Jesus, and be completed by the refreshing from the presence of the Lord, in restoration of all things, & c."[21]

In Bates' thinking in 1854 "church order" still meant "a particular congregation of believers in Christ, united together in the order of the gospel."[22] The next decade, however, would see a radical shift in his position as James White led the Sabbatarians step by step into a unified denomination, with Bates' chairing (as we saw in the previous section) the meetings that put each new step into place.

FAMILY LIFE

Joseph and Prudy had what might be thought of as an interesting relationship. As a travelin' man both at sea and for the Lord, Bates spent extensive amounts of time away from home. But he and his wife had obvious affection for each other as shows through in Bates' early logbook and in their later letters. Having been the daughter of a sea captain, Prudy was undoubtedly conditioned for an absentee husband.

The Bateses both appear to have been strong minded. We have not the slightest doubt on that score regarding Joseph. But it also appears to be true of his wife, who withstood him on the Sabbath for five years. And, given what we know about Bates, that was no small accomplishment.

But after Prudy accepted the Sabbath they seemed to walk in spiritual harmony. A few months after her acceptance she could proclaim that she loved the "Holy Sabbath better and better." She wanted "to be sanctified by obedience to the truth" and "to be more holy."[23]

For all of her love of the Sabbath, however, it appears that Mrs. Bates never had a comfortable religion. Her letters throughout her life reflect a lack of spiritual assurance, even though she always "hoped" she would be saved. "I have felt more sensibly," she penned in 1851, than "ever before, the need of entire consecration to God, and realize, in some degree, how pure and holy we must be to stand before him without a Mediator. O, how I tremble and weep before him, when I think what a poor unworthy creature I am." Then, with a gospel emphasis, she went on to state that she realized that Jesus "is my only hope."[24]

Unfortunately, she never seemed to come to grips with the full depth of the gospel hope in Christ. In 1856 she wrote that "though unworthy, I do hope to be found among" God's people. And the next year she expressed her uncomfortableness by noting that she could not rest satisfied "without an abiding evidence" that her ways pleased God. Given how much of her time she felt that she was wasting, she was experiencing some tension in being "ready for translation at any moment."[25]

Then a few days before her death in 1870 she penned a letter to her husband, claiming that "'I long to have my mind free from care and so many household duties, that I may more exclusively give my mind and time to the all-important subject of getting just right before the Lord.'"[26]

The depth of her lifelong spiritual anxiety may have been related to the legalism of her husband, a position that emphasized salvation based on law keeping. We noted in chapter 5 the gospel emphasis of James White in contrast to Bates' legalistic approach to Adventism. Those contrasting emphases have run parallel in Seventh-day Adventism throughout its history.

While it is impossible to determine the exact nature of the spiritual experience of Joseph and Prudy Bates, history does indicate that none of their five children accepted their beliefs. The first son couldn't, of course, since he died as an infant in 1821. But the second son, Joseph Anson, ran off to sea at age 14 in apparent rebellion the very day before the October 1844 disappointment. He died as a sailor in September 1865 at the age of 35. Their three daughters—Helen, Eliza, and Mary—outlived the parents, Mary and her son Willie residing with the Bateses during the last few years of their lives.[27]

Speaking of her daughters, Prudy wrote in 1868 that "we feel almost discouraged about our children, fearing they will never take the truth." She felt most hopeful about Mary. "Mary is convinced," wrote the distraught mother. "She told us the last time she left us she believed we had the truth. She believed the seventh day was the Sabbath, and that the Lord was soon coming, and she meant *to try to do the best she could.* But she is under such an influence it is almost impossible to rise above it. She often says *she cannot be good* away from her father and mother." After relating more information, Prudy wrote that "I feel more than ever *the necessity of striving to overcome.*"[28]

It is impossible, given the information we have, to be precise about the exact reasons for the Bates children's rejection of their parents' beliefs. But we do know that both parents tended to put the emphasis on behavior, law, and judgment rather than on salvation in Christ. Note, for example, the behavioral emphases in the previous quotation from Prudy's letter and the absence of gospel content. Young people have never found that approach to religion to be overly attractive, especially if they are honest about their own faults and shortcomings.

Joseph Bates doesn't seem to have been any more effective with his siblings than he had been with his children. He had first tried to evangelize his seafaring brother Franklin in 1827. Forty-two years later he was still at it when he sent Franklin a copy of James White's *Life Incidents,* a book emphasizing the Sabbath and the message of the third angel. The year before he had given his brother a copy of his own *Autobiography* and a subscription to the *Review and Herald.* Franklin responded in a letter in which he "talked of going home [dying] but is not yet ready."[29]

Bates also sent a copy of his *Autobiography* to his sister Harriet, noting that "much that I had written of my experience since 1844 is left out for want of room. . . . Still I hope my friends will read carefully what I have written respecting the great Advent movement." He was especially concerned that Harriet "look at the list of [Adventist] books from p. 312" to "see if there is not some that would interest you to see the fulfillment of prophecy." Joseph closed his letter with a sense of evangelistic urgency: "I do really want to help you see the precious truths of the Advent doctrines." [30]

February 25, 1868, was Joseph and Prudy's fiftieth wedding anniversary. They spent the occasion "in trying to get nearer to God by humiliation, fasting, and prayer, mixed with praise for sparing us so long to each other." Some weeks before that we have the only record of Prudy traveling with her husband on one of his itineraries. They were gone some six weeks. "Enjoyed myself very much," she penned. "Had good meetings in all these places. Returned home together and have enjoyed the society of my husband ever since." [31]

They would share two and one half more years of marriage. Prudence Bates passed to her rest after 10 days of illness on Sabbath, August 27, 1870, at the age of 77 years and six months. [32]

SEVENTH-DAY ADVENTISM FINALLY CATCHES UP WITH ITS FIRST HEALTH REFORMER

Prudy wasn't the only Bates who would get sick. Her 68-year-old husband took ill during the fall of 1859. He appears to have been quite surprised, noting that "I had no more strength to speak out the precious truths of the third angel's message." Being on an itinerary, he writes of riding on a freight train for about three hours. Arriving at the station, he reports, I "drank water enough to quench in part, the fire that seemed to be consuming my very vitals." By mid-November he could thankfully report that he was daily gaining strength. [33]

It appears that Bates had what we would today call malaria, a disease not difficult to come by in the swampy parts of Michigan during the mid-nineteenth century. He experienced what may have been a relapse in the year of 1860. That time he was ill for about two months. It caught his wife quite off guard. "Mr. Bates," she wrote a friend, "has been sick again with that Michigan scourge, fever, and ague. His health seems to be failing him. It seems strange indeed to have him sick. He has always enjoyed such perfect health. I cannot for a moment think he will be laid away before the Lord comes."[34]

In contrast to the other Sabbatarian leaders, however, Bates had had an exceptionally healthy life. From the time he left the sea in the late 1820s, he was ill only two times that we know of. Both of those occasions appear in the nearly weekly reports of his activities published in the *Review*. As we have just seen, the first involved his bout with what was presumably malaria in 1859-1860. The second consisted of a recurrence of the same disease in 1866.[35]

Bates attributed his exceptional well-being to the rigorous health regimen he had followed since the 1820s. At that time, as we saw in chapter 3, he had given up alcohol and tobacco in all their forms, along with tea and coffee. In 1843 he deleted flesh foods, butter, grease, cheese, pies, and rich cakes from his diet. In his seventy-ninth year, in front of a health convention at Battle Creek he told of his early health reform experiences and reported on the excellent health that had resulted. "Contrary to my former convictions, that if I was ever permitted to live to my present age, I should be a suffering cripple from my early exposure in following the sea, thanks be to God and our dear Lord and Saviour, whose rich blessing ever follows every personal effort to reform, that I am entirely free from aches and pains, with the gladdening, cheering prospect that if I continue to reform, and forsake every wrong, I shall, with the redeemed followers of the Lamb, 'stand without fault before the throne of God.'" James White, in reporting on Bates' 1871 convention presentation, claimed that he "stood as straight as a monument, and could tread the side-walks as lightly as a fox. He stated that his digestion was perfect, and that he never ate and slept better at any period of his life."[36] In short, White held Bates to be an excellent example of the results of a life of health reform.

What Bates had for long years practiced in relative silence became an important and visible issue in Seventh-day Adventism between 1863 and 1865. On June 5, 1863, Ellen White had her most significant health reform vision. "I saw," she recorded the next day, "that it was a sacred duty to attend to our health, and arouse others to their duty. . . . We have a duty to speak, to come out against intemperance of every kind,—intemperance in working, in eating, in drinking, and in drugging—and then point them to

God's great medicine, water, pure soft water, for diseases, for health, for cleanliness, and for a luxury. . . . I saw that we should not be silent upon the subject of health but should wake up minds to the subject."[37]

A second health reform vision in December 1865 not only led to the establishment of a Seventh-day Adventist health reform institution in Battle Creek, but also tied health reform to the third angel's message. "The health reform," Ellen White wrote, "is a part of the third angel's message and is just as closely connected with it as are the arm and hand with the human body." She claimed that the topic of health would help prepare people for the Second Advent.[38]

Those two visions taken together proved to be one of Ellen White's most significant contributions to the development of Seventh-day Adventism. They would affect the personal lifestyle of the individual members of the church, and they set in motion the creation of a chain of health institutions that would eventually circle the globe.[39]

Her health reform visions also were important to Bates personally. Up into the 1860s, according to both James White and the printed record, he "did not mention his views of proper diet in public . . . , nor in private, unless questioned upon the subject,"[40] in spite of the fact that he was a practicing health reformer. Apparently he did not want to distract from what he saw as the center of the Sabbatarian message. But after 1863 he became increasingly more open with his views on the topic.

The first note from Bates on his public teaching on health reform in the new era appears in the *Review* of June 1865, in which he reports that he had been studying the topic with his home church in Monterey, Michigan. "Our brethren," he wrote, "are entering more deeply into the subject of how to live, and improve our bodily strength and health in this great day of atonement."[41]

Thereafter we find Bates' reports in the *Review* sprinkled with comments of his public teaching of health reform principles. In June 1866, for example, we find him reporting on meetings he held with the Whites and Dr. Horatio S. Lay (soon to be director of the Health Reform Institute in Battle Creek, which would open in September of that year), all speaking on health reform principles. The next month he noted that he had lectured at Centerville, Michigan, and several other churches on the subject of the Health Institute and health reform. "We hope," he urged, "they will continue to learn how to live, and not be behind any of the churches in discharging their whole duty."[42]

The year 1867 was the high point in what Bates published in the *Review* regarding his activities in propagating the health message. Typical is his report of meetings in Detroit. "I have endeavored among other things," he wrote, "to press home the importance of heeding the faithful and true Witness in the Laodicean message, and coming up to the figures [goals] on Systematic Benevolence, and living up to the light on health and dress reform, all of which I think, must be regarded as necessary to qualify those who will be esteemed worthy to carry out the loud cry of the third angel's message. In this I am happy to say that most all who hear are convinced of duty. I am also happy to say that a goodly number are endeavoring to learn how to live and be ready. I hope this good example will be followed by all of God's dear children who love and keep his commandments."[43]

Prudy indicated the views of herself and Joseph in 1868 when she wrote that "we believe the health and dress reforms are a part and parcel of the third angel's message: Calculated to fit up a people for translation." About that same time he wrote to his sister that "our living is hygienic[—]the best grains, fruit and vegetables the land affords. Such as God prepared for man when in his most perfect state. See Gen. 1:29."[44]

Turning 78 in 1870, the elderly reformer continued his usual habits of abstemiousness and hard work while such younger men as James White and J. N. Andrews struggled with chronic health problems. The furthest thing from Bates' mind as he sailed into the new decade was genuine retirement.

---

[1] Anderson, *Outrider of the Apocalypse,* pp. 82, 83; M. E. Cornell and J. Bates, "Tent Meeting at Hillsdale, Mich.," *Review and Herald,* Sept. 11, 1856, p. 149.

[2] M. E. Devereaux to Sis. Below, cir. Nov. 4, 1856; J. Bates, "Meetings in Mich.," *Review and Herald,* Oct. 13, 1863, p. 158; J. Bates to Sis. Harriet, July 19, 1868.

[3] Mich. Conf. Com., "Labor in Mich.," *Review and Herald,* May 29, 1866, p. 204; Mich. Conf. Com., "Labors in Michigan," *Review and Herald,* May 28, 1867, p. 288.

[4] J. Bates, "Report of Meetings in Mich.," *Review and Herald,* Nov. 3, 1868, p. 229.

[5] J. Bates, "Meetings in Michigan," *Review and Herald,* Oct. 2, 1866, p. 142; J. Bates, "Meetings in Mich.," *Review and Herald,* Feb. 21, 1865, p. 106.

[6] Dick, *Founders of the Message,* p. 150.

[7] J. O. Corliss, "The Message and Its Friends—No. 2: Joseph Bates As I Knew Him," *Review and Herald,* Aug. 16, 1923, p. 8.

[8] See chapter 10 above.

[9] J. Bates and U. Smith, "Business Proceedings of the Battle Creek Conference," *Review and Herald,* Apr. 16, 1857, p. 188.

[10] [U. Smith], "The Conference," *Review and Herald,* June 9, 1859, p. 20.

[11] J. Bates and U. Smith, "Business Proceedings of B. C. Conference" *Review and Herald,* Oct. 16, 1860, pp. 169-171; Oct. 23, 1860, pp. 177-179.

[12] J. Bates and U. Smith, "Doings of the Battle Creek Conference, Oct. 5 & 6, 1861," *Review and Herald,* Oct. 8, 1861, p. 148; J. Bates and U. Smith, "Business Proceedings of the Michigan State Conference," *Review and Herald,* Oct. 14, 1862, pp. 156, 157.

[13] J. Byington and U. Smith, "Report of General Conference of Seventh-day Adventists," *Review and Herald,* May 26, 1863, pp. 204-206; for an overview of the history of Seventh-day Adventist organizational formation, see Knight, *Organizing to Beat the Devil.*

[14] J. Bates, "Letter From Bro. Joseph Bates," *Jubilee Standard,* May 29, 1845, p. 90.

[15] J. Bates, "Third Waymark, The Fall of Babylon," *Advent Review,* Nov. 1850, p. 67.

[16] *Ibid.;* J. Bates, *Second Advent Way Marks and High Heaps,* pp. 24, 25; Knight, *Organizing to Beat the Devil,* pp. 15-23; Geo. Storrs, "Come Out of Her My People," *Midnight Cry,* Feb. 15, 1844, pp. 237, 238.

[17] J. V. Himes, "Note," *Advent Herald,* May 4, 1850, p. 111.

[18] J. N. Loughborough, *The Church: Its Organization, Order and Discipline* (Washington, D. C. : Review and Herald Pub. Assn., [1906], p. 101.

[19] [J. White], "Gospel Order," *Review and Herald,* Dec. 6, 1853, p. 173; E. G. White, *Early Writings,* p. 97.

[20] H. S. Gurney, "From Bro. Gurney," *Review and Herald,* Dec. 27, 1853, p. 199; J. Bates, "From Bro. Bates," *Review and Herald,* Aug. 15, 1854, p. 6; J. Bates, "From Bro. Bates," *Review and Herald,* Dec. 5, 1854, p. 126.

[21] J. Bates, "Church Order," *Review and Herald,* Aug. 29, 1854, pp. 22, 23.

[22] *Ibid.,* p. 22.

[23] P. Bates, "Extracts of Letters," *Review and Herald,* Dec. 23, 1851, p. 72.

[24] *Ibid.*

[25] P. Bates, "Extracts of Letters," *Review and Herald,* Jan. 24, 1856, p. 135; P. Bates, "From Sister Bates," *Review and Herald,* Aug. 6, 1857, p. 111.

[26] P. Bates, quoted in J. Bates, [Obituary], *Review and Herald,* Sept. 6, 1870, p. 95.

[27] J. Bates, [Obituary], *Review and Herald,* Dec. 5, 1865, p. 7; Anderson, *Outrider of the Apocalypse,* p. 41.

[28] P. Bates to Sis. Below, Feb. 25, 1868 (italics supplied).

[29] J. Bates to Dear Brother, Sept. 26, 1827; J. Bates, Logbook, Sept. 30, 1827; J. Bates, Diary, Dec. 22, 1869; J. Bates to Sis. Harriet, July 19, 1868.

[30] J. Bates to Sis. Harriet, July 19, 1868.

[31] P. Bates to Sis. Below, Feb. 25, 1868.

[32] J. Bates, [Obituary], *Review and Herald,* Sept. 6, 1870, p. 95.

[33] J. Bates, "Meetings in Ionia and Livingston Counties," *Review and Herald,* Nov. 3, 1859, p. 188; J. Bates, "Note From Bro. Bates," Dec. 1, 1859, p. 16.

[34] P. Bates to Sis. Below, Aug. 12, 1860; J. Bates, "Reply," *Review and Herald,* Sept. 4, 1860, p. 128.

[35] J. Bates, "Report From Bro. Bates," *Review and Herald,* Sept. 11, 1866, p. 119.

[36] J. Bates, "Experience in Health Reform," *Health Reformer,* July 1871, p. 21; J. White, *Bible Hygiene,* p. 255.

[37] E. G. White, "Testimony Regarding James and Ellen White," MS 1, [June 6, 1863].

[38] E. G. White, *Testimonies for the Church,* vol. 1, p. 486.

[39] For treatments of the development of the Seventh-day Adventist health system, see Dores Eugene Robinson, *The Story of Our Health Message* (Nashville, Tenn. : Southern Pub. Assn., 1955); George W. Reid, *A Sound of Trumpets: Americans, Adventists, and Health Reform* (Washington, D. C. : Review and Herald Pub. Assn., 1982).

[40] J. White, *Bible Hygiene,* p. 252.

[41] J. Bates, "Note From Bro. Bates," *Review and Herald,* June 20, 1865, p. 24.

[42] J. Bates, "The Allegan Monthly Meetings," *Review and Herald,* June 19, 1866, p. 24; J. Bates, "Report From Bro. Bates," *Review and Herald,* July 24, 1866, p. 61.

[43] J. Bates, "District Labor in Mich.," *Review and Herald,* Mar. 26, 1867, p. 183.

[44] P. Bates to Sis. Below, Feb. 25, 1868; J. Bates to Sis. Harriet, July 19, 1868.

CHAPTER XIII

AND WHAT IS RETIREMENT?

IF Bates' life ever did slow down at any time, the year 1868 is a good candidate. A careful reading of his reports suggests that at 76 his activities were not quite as vigorous as they had been earlier, even though his pace was still faster than that of many younger men.

The year 1868 is also the year he published his *Autobiography,* a book, James White noted, largely written "from memory, without the help of any sort of memorandum." "Having been a rigid vegetarian for more than twenty years," White added, "he lives to bless the world at his advanced age with a book showing the mental vigor of youth." Any profits from the book were to "go for the benefit of this pioneer of the cause, whom we all love."[1] Those "royalties" may be regarded as part of Bates' "retirement pay."

AND WHAT ABOUT RETIREMENT?

Whereas some people look forward to retirement, Bates wasn't one of them. In the next to the final sentence in his *Autobiography,* he commented that "it is my earnest desire to spend the remainder of my days in the service of God, and for the advancement of his truth, that I may have a place in his soon-coming kingdom."[2]

In October 1859, about the time of Bates' serious bout with malaria, James White may have been hinting at his fellow leader's need to retire when he wrote that "there would appear the greatest propriety in [Bro. Bates] enjoying the fruits of his former labors, in his advanced years." But James knew that the older man had no intention of following that path. Rather, "he is continually breaking new ground, laboring incessantly, preaching from five to ten times a week, and receiving a limited support."[3]

There came a time, however, when more open suggestions were appropriate. When, very late in his life, "his younger and most intimate fellow-laborers [that definitely included James White, the author of this account] told him that his age should excuse him from the fatigue of itinerant life and public speaking, he laid his armor off as a captured officer would surrender his sword on the field of battle."[4]

But even that reluctant capitulation hardly meant that he was ready to quit. One of his fellow ministers at that time wrote that Bates had told his younger colleague that "'I want to still go along beside you, [even] if I can't do a great deal.' He said that his position reminded him of what happened when he was a boy. He said that a farmer had a horse that was so old it was left in the stable when the others were taken out to plow. The men heard a tremendous noise at the stable. They went to see what the matter was, and found the horse kicking to get out. So they put a collar on the horse, and hitched him by the side of the others, and he would walk around beside the others, perfectly contented. So with Brother Bates. He could not work, and he said, 'Brethren, if I can not do any more, let me have a collar on, and walk by the side of the rest.'"[5]

AND WHEN IS A RETIREE RETIRED?

It is difficult to determine just when Bates "surrendered his sword." In March 1869, for example, he reports his intention of doing missionary work among the six or seven hundred convicts of the Michigan state prison in his spare time, of working with an ex-Methodist preacher who in his earlier days had also shipped out of New Bedford, of seeking to evangelize his former Christian Connexion pastor, and of trying to convert those he met on railroads and while walking the plank roads of southern Michigan's swampy areas. All those activities, of course, were outside of his schedule of public meetings.[6]

His wife's death in August 1870 affected Bates deeply, but hardly slowed him down. A. W. Spalding concluded that after her death "he halted not at all, it would appear from his reports, only occasionally resting at his home, as before." And Godfrey Anderson counted more than 100 meetings held in his 11 months of itinerant travel in 1871. And, it should be noted, those meetings were in addition to the ones he attended or spoke at in camp meetings, conferences, and his local church. And meetings were only the tip of the iceberg in terms of the effort he continued to put forth. The week of March 14-21, for example, found him visiting from house to house the members of a church "struggling to hold themselves in the message." They had to be contacted in their scattered homes because the "deep muddy roads" made a meeting unfeasible.[7] It appears that the man who in his sixties could wade through miles of snow could in his late seventies plow through deep mud. He was a motivated person to the very end of his life.

In the spring of 1871 Bates made a speech of "remarkable interest" to a health reform convention in Battle Creek, Michigan, in which he "incorporated some items of his personal history and experience." According to White, the aged man "electrified the audience" with both his presentation and his evident vigor.[8]

In February of that year Bates attended one of his last General Conference sessions. "The annual meeting," he exuberantly reported, "was one of deep, stirring interest to the cause. It was encouraging to hear what had been accomplished the past year, and to learn of the wide openings for missionary work, and the urgent and pressing calls for ministerial labor throughout the wide harvest field, and in what order the work of God should move forward the ensuing year. How cheering to be associated with brethren and sisters all deeply interested for the salvation of souls." He closed his report of his last General Conference session in December 1871 with a prayer: "O Lord, in Jesus' dear name, help us, with this dear people, to fulfill our sacred promise, and may all thy remnant, waiting people also enter into covenant with thee."[9]

Bates reported his last work with James and Ellen White in a February 19, 1872, letter. He noted that since the middle of January he had been in "one continued protracted meeting [i.e., evangelistic series]" and that the Whites had spent the weekend of January 13 and 14 with him and W. H. Littlejohn (the main speaker).[10] It would be his final account in the *Review*, the end of a faithful reporting that had been almost weekly since he had healed his breach with White over the paper in 1850.

Joseph's last recorded contact with Ellen White took place in February 1872. On the second of the month she wrote a forceful letter to him saying that someone had notified her that he was only eating one meal a day. She went on to say that such a course of action was wrong on his part, that he was "in danger of being too abstemious," and that he did not have the strength for such "severe discipline." She claimed also that he had "erred in fasting two days." "God did not require it of you," she penned. "I beg of you to be cautious and eat freely good, wholesome food twice a day."[11]

Beyond dietary issues, Mrs. White told Bates that he should "not carry the burden of leading the church in meetings," that younger people should take that responsibility. She went on to say that she had advised Charles Jones "not to encourage or allow" him to go to different churches to work. "You," she wrote Bates, "are not in a condition of body and mind to labor. You must stop and rest and be happy, and not worry your mind about the responsibilities of the work and cause of God. Be peaceful, calm, and happy, and trust yourself in the work and cause of God, feeling that you are now to soften, sweeten, ripen up for heaven. God loves you. But, with your advanced age and your strong peculiarities, you will certainly mar the work of God more than you can help it. You have simply to rest in the hands of God and feel that your work to preach the truth is done. . . . God has released you."[12]

Those were strong words for a man with extremist tendencies who didn't want to retire. Although he may have grown old, the fire in him hadn't yet gone out. On February 14 he penned a lively response to Ellen White, writing that "I learn from report that I am starving." He went on with a sprightly defense of his health reform past and provided her with an inventory of the food he had in his house. "I think," he concluded, that "I am now well supplied with good, nutritious food. And if there is any lack, I have some good, faithful brethren who seem to be waiting to do all the needful." At the end of his letter he signed himself as Joseph Bates, "Now on retired pay."[13]

Bates went into his "final earthly retirement" one month and five days after his letter to Ellen White. On March 19, 1872, he passed to his rest at the Adventist's Health Reform Institute in Battle Creek, dying of "diabetes and putrid erysipelas" in his eightieth year. "His last hours," W. H. Littlejohn reported, "though characterized by pain such as few men have been called upon to pass through, afforded a marked evidence of the superiority of a faith in Christ over the bodily suffering and the prospect of certain and rapidly approaching death." He was buried next to Prudy in the Poplar Hill Cemetery in Monterey, Michigan.[14]

AND WHAT ABOUT THE MAN?

On September 5, 1872, the Michigan Conference in its first session after Bates' death passed the following resolution: "That as a tribute of respect, we recognize in the decease of our beloved Bro. Joseph Bates the loss of a great and good man; eminent for piety and Christian virtue; a pioneer in the third angel's message, always at his post of duty. We miss him in our assemblies, at our Conference, in our churches, at our fireside homes; and while we deeply mourn our loss, we will remember his counsels, imitate his virtues, and endeavor to meet him in the kingdom of God." The March 1873 General Conference session passed a similar resolution.[15]

On a more personal level are the evaluations of the Whites, the two individuals who with Bates founded the Seventh-day Adventist Church. Ellen White was quite parsimonious in her remembrances. Some months after Bates' death she wrote to her son Edson that she had met a German physician who was keeping the Sabbath. "He is a smart, intelligent man above sixty years old. He is active, straight, and gentlemanly. He reminds me of Brother Bates." Some years later she compared him to a sea captain she had met who was "intelligent" and "noble in appearance."[16]

James was a little more effusive. Soon after meeting the older man he wrote that "from my first acquaintance with him I have loved him much. And the more I see of his devotedness to the holy advent cause, his caution, his holy life, his unfeigned love for the saints; the more I love and esteem him."[17]

In spite of their occasional differences, White's evaluation of Bates remained constant across time. In 1868 in introducing Bates' *Autobiography* to the public, White portrayed the author as possessing an "independent mind, a noble and courageous soul, and a heart imbued with love to God, and to his fellow men." And after his death White described Bates as "a man of great natural firmness and independence." Bates, White claimed, was a person who "held a large place in the hearts of his people. Those who knew him longest and best, esteemed him most highly."[18]

And Bates was all of those things. But from another perspective he could be stubborn, opinionated, legalistic, and a bit fanatical at times. Those more negative traits could have made it difficult for those who had to work with him. Yet in the long run it was the positive side that showed through most of the time. The positive allowed him to make the massive contribu-

tion that he did to the founding of the Seventh-day Adventist Church
Then again, even some of the negative may have contributed to his success.
After all, a bit of stubbornness and opinionatedness are probably essential
personality characteristics for anyone who must swim against the current in
establishing a religious orientation and movement.

AND WHAT ABOUT HIS ACCOMPLISHMENTS?

The short answer to the question of Bates' accomplishments and contributions is the fact of the Seventh-day Adventist Church. That is, without Bates there would be no Seventh-day Adventist Church. In my
Foreword to Gerald Wheeler's *James White* I noted that "without White
there would be no Seventh-day Adventism."[19] That is true, but Bates' position in the flow of Adventist history is even more fundamental. Without
his theological and missionary outreach there would have been no
Sabbatarian Adventism for White to build upon. Bates not only developed
the theology that became the basis for the Sabbatarian movement, but he
also introduced a rather reluctant White to the Sabbath and its place in
prophetic history. It is therefore safe to say that the *real* founder of
Seventh-day Adventism was Joseph Bates. James White would by 1850
become more prominent than the older man and would be the architect
of the developmental movement from Sabbatarian Adventism to Seventh-
day Adventism, but he was expanding upon the foundation already laid
by Bates.

Among Bates' more specific contributions to Seventh-day Adventism,
none stands more prominently than the fact that he was the denomination's first theologian. By early 1847 he had formulated an apocalyptic
theology. In that understanding he was far in advance of the majority of
his Adventist successors in the twenty-first century, who tend to see the
27 items in their 1980 Statement of Fundamental Beliefs as 27 more or
less separate doctrines.[20] But Bates, for all of his shortcomings, managed
to develop a truly theological perspective that united the second apartment ministry of Christ in the heavenly sanctuary to the Sabbath and both
of them to the Second Advent, all within the framework of Revelation 10
through 14.

Closely tied to Bates' contribution as Sabbatarian Adventism's first
theologian is the fact that he was also the movement's first historian. But

for Bates theology and history were never disconnected. Rather, they were two sides of the same coin. He saw history in its prophetic aspect and collated Adventism's history with the flow of the book of Revelation's central chapters, especially in his understanding of the progressive nature of the three angels of Revelation 14 and the crucial role of verse 12 ("Here is the patience of the saints: here are they that keep the commandments of God, and the faith of Jesus") as history moved toward its climax at the Second Advent in verses 14-20. His uniting of his apocalyptic theology within the framework of eschatological history led him to the formulation of what has come to be known as great controversy theology out of the passage running from Revelation 12:17 up through the end of chapter 14. Bates' unique combining of theology, history, and prophecy also made him in essence Seventh-day Adventism's first mission theorist. The missiological platform that he constructed would eventually inspire the denomination to sponsor outreach in every corner of the world.

That mission theory would motivate Bates himself in his role as Sabbatarian Adventism's first missionary and make him a catalyst for a movement. He not only became, with James and Ellen White, one of the co-founders of Seventh-day Adventism, but he brought the other two founders to the doctrinal/historical knowledge that made it possible for them to participate. Beyond that, his nearly constant travels not only spread Adventism across the face of the map from Michigan to northern New England and Canada, but it brought into Sabbatarian Adventism a significant number of those who would become the leaders of the movement's second generation.

A fifth contribution that Bates made in the development of Seventh-day Adventism had to do with health reform. Interestingly enough, however, even though Bates was by far in the chronological forefront of the other leaders in this area, he turned out to be a follower rather than leader in Adventist health reform. Believing that other issues were more central, and not wanting to create dissension in the thin ranks of Sabbatarian Adventism during its early years, he remained a silent witness on that topic until he believed it to be an important part of the Adventist message in the mid-1860s. Subsequently, he became a more active advocate of health reform and related lifestyle reforms.

A final contribution to the development of Adventism was Bates' role as its first senior statesman. The passing years had not only given him a bit of wisdom, but they had also tended to make him less impetuous. Combined with a natural ability in leadership that he first demonstrated as a seafaring captain, those traits made him the obvious choice as a chairman to guide the budding denomination through its organizational development in the late 1850s and early 1860s. It was a role that James White could not effectively perform due to his obvious vested interest. Bates, who by that stage of his life knew how to guide things without too much "fuss or feathers,"[21] was just the man for the job.

But his contributions to the development of Adventism were not all positive. His legalistic tendencies, his confusion between behavior and religion, and his living in the fear of judgment perspective did not have a healthy influence on later Seventh-day Adventism. Still those negative aspects were potentially correctable, as the struggle over righteousness by faith at the 1888 General Conference[22] began to demonstrate. Thus, while Bates' negative contributions were serious, the positive framework he established for the development of Adventist understandings far overshadowed them. Others would not only build upon his positive contributions but eventually move away from those of his ideas that were less than helpful.

In conclusion, we can honestly say that without Joseph Bates there would be no Seventh-day Adventism. He was the source of a great deal that was true and helpful. Although not without faults, he was one of great stature in early Adventism. In 1871, after Bates made an impressive speech on health reform, J. N. Andrews was called upon for a bit of teaching. Upon rising his first words were, " 'What shall the man do who comes after the king?' " Bates' contributions to Adventism have cast a long shadow in which all Seventh-day Adventists still exist. One Bible verse written on his burial monument is quite significant: " 'He being dead, yet speaketh.' "[23] No passage could have been more appropriate for Joseph Bates, the real founder of the Seventh-day Adventist Church.

---

[1] J. White, "The Autobiography," *Review and Herald,* Nov. 17, 1868, p. 248.

[2] J. Bates, *Autobiography,* p. 306.

[3] J. White, "New Fields," *Review and Herald,* Oct. 6, 1859, p. 156.

[4] J. White, ed., *Early Life and Later Experience and Labors of Elder Joseph Bates,* p. 316.

[5] J. N. Loughborough, 1901 *General Conference Bulletin,* p. 460.

[6] J. Bates, "Miscellaneous," *Review and Herald*, Apr. 13, 1869, p. 125; cf. J. Bates, "Meetings in Michigan," *Review and Herald*, Mar. 1, 1870, p. 86.

[7] Arthur Whitefield Spalding, *Footprints of the Pioneers* (Washington, D. C. : Review and Herald Pub. Assn., 1947), p. 168. Anderson, *Outrider of the Apocalypse*, p. 115; J. Bates, "Meetings in Michigan," Apr. 18, 1871, p. 142.

[8] J. White, *Bible Hygiene*, p. 253; J. White, ed., *Early Life and Later Experience and Labors of Elder Joseph Bates*, p. 316.

[9] J. Bates, "Michigan," *Review and Herald*, Mar. 7, 1871, p. 94; J. Bates, "Meetings in Michigan," *Review and Herald*, Jan. 23, 1872, p. 46.

[10] J. Bates, "Michigan," *Review and Herald*, Mar. 5, 1872, p. 95; J. White, "Meetings at Monterey," *Review and Herald*, Jan. 23, 1872, p. 48; W. H. Littlejohn, "The Effort in Monterey, Mich.," *Review and Herald*, Feb. 20, 1872, p. 78.

[11] E. G. White to Bro. Bates, Feb. 2, 1872.

[12] *Ibid.*

[13] J. Bates to E. G. White, Feb. 14, 1872, p. 143.

[14] W. H. Littlejohn, [Obituary], *Review and Herald*, Apr. 16, 1872, p. 143.

[15] U. Smith and J. R. Trembley, "Michigan Conference of S. D. Adventists," *Review and Herald*, Sept. 10, 1872, p. 102; Geo. I. Butler and U. Smith, "Proceeding of the Eleventh Annual Meeting of the General Conference of S. D. Adventists," *Review and Herald*, Mar. 25, 1873, p. 116.

[16] E. G. White to Edson and Emma, Aug. 18, 1872; E. G. White to U. Smith, Sept. 24, 1886.

[17] J. White to Sis. Hastings, Aug. 22, 1847.

[18] J. White, "The Autobiography," *Review and Herald*, Nov. 17, 1868, p. 248; J. White, *Bible Hygiene*, pp. 253, 255.

[19] Wheeler, *James White*, p. xi.

[20] The 27 Fundamental Beliefs appear in the Seventh-day Adventist *Church Manual* and in the denomination's annual *Yearbook*. For a discussion on the need to adequately conceptualize Adventist theology, see G. R. Knight, "Twenty-Seven Fundamentals in Search of a Theology," *Ministry*, Feb. 2001, pp. 5-7.

[21] J. O. Corliss, "The Message and Its Friends—No. 2: Joseph Bates as I Knew Him," *Review and Herald*, Aug. 16, 1923, p. 8.

[22] For a treatment of the 1888 General Conference session, see George R. Knight, *A User-Friendly Guide to the 1888 Message* (Hagerstown, Md. : Review and Herald Pub. Assn., 1998).

[23] J. O. Corliss, "The Message and Its Friends—No. 2: Joseph Bates as I Knew Him," *Review and Herald*, Aug. 16, 1923, p. 8; Bert Van Horn, "Early History of the Church at Monterey, Mich.," *Review and Herald*, Jan. 23, 1919, p. 24.

INDEX